BATTLEFIELDS

To

BOARDROOMS

NAVIGATING THE SHIFT FROM MILITARY PRECISION TO CORPORATE VISION

William E. Burgess III

Dedication

To my mom you taught me some of life's most important lessons: the value of hard work, determination, and standing up for what's right. Your guidance has profoundly shaped who I am today. Though you were taken from me during a pivotal time in my life, your strength and wisdom have continued to guide me. The values you instilled in me have been a constant source of strength throughout my journey.

To my family, your unwavering support has been the foundation of my success. To Emma, my granddaughter, whose curiosity and wonder remind me of the importance of lifelong learning and openness to new ideas. You all inspire me to keep growing. Without your love and encouragement, none of this would have been possible.

A Note to Future Leaders!

As you step into corporate security, remember that true leadership goes far beyond managing risks. It's about embracing change, leading with integrity, and continuously pushing the boundaries of innovation. The security landscape is always evolving, and it demands leaders ready to challenge the status quo and adapt to new challenges as they emerge.

You are the future of this industry, and your choices today will shape tomorrow's security landscape. Stay curious, stay committed, and never stop learning. Your leadership will protect people and assets and build the trust and resilience businesses need to thrive in an ever-changing world.

Acknowledgment

I would like to express my deepest gratitude to the colleagues, mentors, and friends who have played an instrumental role in my security journey.

To Ken Powers and Greg Anderson, thank you for seeing my potential beyond formal qualifications and giving me the chance to prove myself. Your trust and encouragement were crucial in helping me pursue my degree, a milestone that has significantly shaped my career and my life.

To Tom Lebrun, your invaluable mentorship and our many insightful discussions on all aspects of security have been a constant source of inspiration. Your belief in my story gave me the courage to take on the challenge of writing this book.

To the incredible teams I've had the privilege of working with your passion and dedication to security have inspired me every single day.

And to the readers and fellow security professionals, thank you for your continued commitment to advancing this vital field. Your innovation and leadership will shape the future of corporate security.

About the Author

William E. Burgess III is a seasoned expert in corporate security with over 30 years of experience across military, law enforcement, and corporate roles. He holds a degree in Justice Studies, specializing in Terrorism and Homeland Security. His career began in the military and law enforcement, where he developed strong skills in crisis management, strategic planning, and leadership.

William transitioned to corporate security, taking on pivotal roles at Valero Energy Corporation, where he progressed from Security Superintendent to Security Manager and Facility Security Officer (FSO). At the Valero Port Arthur Refinery, he managed extensive security operations and regulatory compliance. He played a key role in designing, executing, and training for the Emergency Operations Center (EOC) and led one of Southeast Texas's largest active shooter exercises, coordinating efforts among 12 agencies and 300 participants.

William later served as the Security Director for Volvo Group North America, overseeing security operations across the Northeast and Canada. Currently, he is the Senior Director of Security Operations at Tanger, where he leads physical and technical security, CSOC operations, and executive protection for the company's leadership. His tenure at Tanger has seen the integration of advanced security technologies, including AI, drones, and robotics, to enhance safety across its properties.

William is also a sought-after speaker at industry events, where he shares his expertise on risk management, crisis leadership, and the evolving role of security in modern businesses. His approach emphasizes continuous learning and innovation to stay ahead of emerging threats.

William wrote this book with the hope of guiding readers on the right path and equipping them with the knowledge and foundation needed to transition into the corporate world. Initially aimed at those with military or law enforcement backgrounds, this book offers valuable insights for anyone navigating their corporate journey from new employees starting their careers to CEOs seeking a deeper understanding of security's role in their organizations. It embodies William's commitment to helping others succeed in corporate security by sharing lessons from his extensive experience.

Contents

Chapter 1:
Understanding the Military and Law Enforcement Mindset

Understanding the military and law enforcement mindset is crucial to appreciating how these experiences shape individuals' lives, both personally and professionally. This mindset, forged through rigorous training and real-world challenges, cultivates traits like discipline, attention to detail, and rapid decision-making under stress. These skills not only transform individuals into effective leaders but also prepare them to excel in various civilian roles. The unique work culture, defined by a clear chain of command, mission-first mentality, and strong sense of camaraderie, leaves a lasting impact. By exploring these elements, we gain insights into how such a background can be both an asset and a challenge, profoundly influencing career transitions and personal growth.

The same thing happened to me too!!!!!

On the morning of June 21, 1993, I woke up feeling an urgent need for a significant change in my life. The early sunlight filtered through my bedroom window in small-town New Hampshire, casting a warm glow. Restlessness gnawed at me; I knew my life wasn't heading where I wanted it to go. After getting dressed, I drove into town with a clear resolve: I needed to join the US Marines full-time active duty. Walking into the recruiting station, I felt a mix of anxiety and determination. In high school, my graduating class in Canaan, New Hampshire, was just 92 students. Sports were my sanctuary, where I could excel and find focus, unlike academics, which were always a struggle. I played basketball, soccer, and baseball, always pushing myself and my teammates to win. The thrill of victory was intoxicating, and any loss only fueled my drive to improve.

Despite my love for sports, I craved more discipline in my life. I wasn't ready to commit to the military full-time yet, as I also wanted to experience college life. By the time I graduated in 1991, I decided to join the Army Reserves and reported to Fort Knox, Kentucky, home of the Cavalry and Armor. Completing my training and getting assigned to a unit in Fort Devens, Massachusetts, allowed me to gain the discipline I needed while still pursuing my college education.

Balancing the roles of a citizen soldier, working, and attending school soon became overwhelming. My reserve unit was nearly 2.5 hours away, and the challenges of traveling there were becoming too much. To ease the burden, I transferred to the Army National Guard and joined Charlie Company, 3rd Battalion, 172nd Infantry Regiment (Mountain), out of Lebanon, NH, much closer to home. Yet, my life still felt scattered and unfulfilled. Unlike sports, where effort leads to clear successes, my current situation left me feeling adrift. That June morning in 1993, joining the US Marines full-time seemed like the clear solution. I explained to the recruiter how I was a high school jock who enjoyed good times and kept just enough of a GPA to stay eligible for sports. I needed discipline and a fresh start. I wanted to leave small-town New Hampshire, see the world, and experience different cultures.

Before long, I received my orders to report to Marine Corps Boot Camp at Parris Island, SC. Knowing I had some military experience, I felt somewhat relieved. I knew it would be a challenging three months, but I was familiar with weapons, drill and ceremony, and the chain of command. I told myself to endure the training, and soon, I would be in the fleet. Upon graduation, I had my standard 10-day leave and returned home to visit family and friends. Everyone was amazed by my physical and mental transformation. I had graduated boot camp at 163 pounds, 36 pounds lighter than when I entered.

After my leave, I headed to Camp Pendleton in Oceanside, California, where I was assigned to Tango Battery, 5th Battalion, 11th Marines. As the new guy, or "BOOT," I quickly adjusted to life as a United States Marine. The deployments and West Pacs were some of the greatest experiences of my life. I built lifelong friendships with people I remain in contact with to this day.

Even in the afterlife, I believe we will reconnect and continue where we left off. During my military service, I learned to do more with less and that teamwork is essential. Most importantly, I learned that failure is not an option. This lesson became a core part of my mindset, a mindset employers should recognize in veterans. We don't know failure; we don't stop working until the job is done. When my enlistment ended in June 1997, I pursued a childhood dream of joining law enforcement. I quickly found myself working for the Sheriff's Office in Florida, with my first assignment as a Drill Instructor at the sheriff's Juvenile Boot Camp. This was an eye-opening and rewarding experience, perfectly suited to my transition from the Marines. Within a year, I sought a lateral transfer back to my home state of New Hampshire. Soon, I joined the Police Academy, completing the law portion of the training and earning my NH Law Enforcement certification.

After Several years of Law enforcement, I met Michael Smith one day while working out at a local gym. We hit it off instantly, quickly finding common ground in many areas, such as fitness, security, and law enforcement. Michael started sharing intriguing stories about protecting celebrities and high-profile clients. I was captivated by his experiences and wanted that life When I asked if I could do something similar, his answer was yes. He explained that my military and law enforcement training had provided me with transferable skills for executive protection. For several years, Michael took me under his wing, tutoring, mentoring, and recommending various trainings and studies. After working various jobs with Michael over the years, I sought something more stable and consistent. I applied for a Security Superintendent position at Valero Energy Corporation at an inland oil refinery in Sunray, Texas. My first interview was with George Perel, a Marine and current Sr. Regional Security Manager with Valero. The Marine Brotherhood we shared created an instant connection. He knew my military and law enforcement background would translate to a strong work ethic and a team-oriented approach. I was offered the position and relocated to Dumas, TX, in 2012.

After relocating to the Panhandle of Texas (Dumas), I was quickly identified as an outsider. Now, I can safely assume it was a strong New England accent with a touch of Boston. I was met with great challenges, mostly because it was a small, tight community where generations of families worked at the refinery, which didn't welcome any outsiders and would question any motive or change. After considerable pushback from the very beginning, I started remembering my conversations with George Perel and Robert Lawson (Director of Valero Corporate Security), who was also a former State Trooper and attorney. I was advised that I would be challenged in every way, but someone from the outside (not from the area) needed to come in and identify the problems, address the issues, and execute the mission.

It was only a few months into my new position that I started to rethink my decision. However, it was not about the job or company but the location. There just wasn't a lot to do in my free time or even a place to visit within a reasonable distance. I believe this was something George and Robert did realize. Of course, this was not something I was going to let them know; it just wasn't in my character. I looked at this as a stepping stone, even a "hardship tour," like in the military. I knew after I completed my mission to get the refinery up to speed and where it needed to be (security-wise) that opportunities would present themselves.

In 2014, that opportunity came. I was asked if I would be interested in a manager position in Port Arthur, TX. I, without hesitation, said yes, finally a way out of the Panhandle and back to civilization. George and Robert both offered me the new position 2.5 years later, stating success and a job well done. This was something I truly thought of as a "Hardship Tour," but without the pushups.

To me, it would have never been something I would have succeeded at if it wasn't for the commitment and determination to succeed that was instilled in me in the military and law enforcement. If it wasn't for my background, I clearly would have given up and sought something easier.

However, there was a catch. George said this would be a lateral move for you. I did not understand; it was Valero's flagship coastal refinery with much greater responsibility; how was I not going to get the title and pay? I was quickly reminded how well I did in the panhandle, and there was no doubt I could handle this much greater responsibility, but to get the title and pay, I needed a 4-year degree. I was stunned, maybe even in disbelief at this time. My gratitude and relief of being relocated outweighed the news of it being just a lateral move. I also took it as just another exercise. So, with a new motivation and end goal in sight, with a title and a pay increase, I enrolled in college, aiming for a BS in Justice Studies with a major in Terrorism and Homeland Security. This time, my performance was different— Out of the gate, I made the dean's list, thanks to the discipline instilled in me by the military and law enforcement. The promise of an immediate promotion upon graduation motivated me further. It was very clear at this moment that to climb the corporate ladder, I needed a piece of paper. Strange enough, it could have been in underwater basket weaving. A degree was the only requirement, which in itself I thought was strange.

The military and law enforcement experiences shaped my mindset by instilling discipline, attention to detail, and resilience under pressure. These traits transformed my approach to challenges, fostering a strong work ethic and an unwavering commitment to achieving goals, both in my professional and personal life.

Key Traits and Skills Developed in Military and Law Enforcement Professions

Key traits and skills developed in military and law enforcement professions, such as discipline, attention to detail, and rapid decision-making under stress, are essential for both personal and professional success. These skills not only shape individuals into effective leaders but also equip them with the tools necessary to excel in various civilian careers, particularly in corporate security roles.

Discipline is a foundational trait cultivated extensively in the military and law enforcement. According to a study published by the Journal of Applied Psychology, individuals with a military background often exhibit higher levels of self-discipline compared to their civilian counterparts. This is due to the rigorous training and strict protocols they follow, which instill a strong sense of duty and responsibility. In the military, every action is guided by protocols and regulations, ensuring that service members maintain high standards of behavior and performance. This ingrained discipline translates seamlessly into corporate environments, where adhering to company policies and maintaining consistency in performance is crucial.

Attention to detail is another critical skill honed through military and law enforcement training. In these fields, even the smallest oversight can have significant consequences. For instance, a 2020 report by the RAND Corporation highlighted that meticulous attention to detail is crucial in combat scenarios, where overlooking a minor detail could result in mission failure or loss of life. This skill is equally vital in corporate security, where professionals must assess risks, develop comprehensive security plans, and ensure the protection of assets and personnel. The ability to notice and address small details can prevent larger issues from arising, making attention to detail an invaluable asset in any professional setting.

Rapid decision-making under stress is a hallmark of both military and law enforcement training. In high-pressure situations, these professionals must quickly assess the situation, consider potential outcomes, and make decisions that could have life-or-death consequences. A study by the American Psychological Association found that veterans and law enforcement officers often excel in high-stress environments due to their extensive training in crisis management and decision-making. This ability to remain calm and make sound decisions under pressure is highly transferable to the corporate world, especially in roles that require crisis management and quick problem-solving.

Incorporating these skills into a corporate security career offers numerous benefits. Discipline ensures that security protocols are consistently followed, reducing the risk of breaches and ensuring a safe work environment. Attention to detail allows for thorough risk assessments and the identification of potential threats before they escalate. Rapid decision-making under stress ensures that security professionals can effectively handle emergencies, minimizing damage and ensuring the safety of all stakeholders.

Moreover, the **leadership skills** developed in the military and law enforcement are invaluable in corporate settings. According to a survey conducted by the Society for Human

Resource Management (SHRM), 68% of employers reported that veterans often display higher levels of leadership and teamwork skills compared to their civilian peers. These skills are crucial in corporate security, where leading a team and coordinating efforts are essential for effective security management.

The transition from military and law enforcement to corporate security is not without its challenges. However, the structured nature of these professions and the skills acquired through rigorous training provide a solid foundation for success. Employers increasingly recognize the value of hiring veterans and former law enforcement officers, understanding that their unique skill sets contribute significantly to organizational resilience and security.

Military and Law Enforcement Work Culture

Now, we will delve into the unique work culture of the military and law enforcement, exploring essential concepts such as the chain of command, the mission-first mentality, and the profound sense of camaraderie that binds individuals in these professions. Understanding these cultural elements is crucial for appreciating how they shape behaviors, attitudes, and professional relationships, both in the field and in subsequent civilian careers.

Chain of command is a fundamental aspect of military and law enforcement culture. It establishes a clear hierarchy and delineates roles, responsibilities, and reporting structures. This hierarchy ensures that orders are followed efficiently and that accountability is maintained at every level. In the corporate world, understanding and respecting the chain of command can lead to more streamlined operations and effective management. It helps create a structured environment where tasks are delegated appropriately, and everyone knows their role and to whom they report.

The mission-first mentality is another cornerstone of military and law enforcement work culture. This mentality prioritizes the completion of the mission above all else, often requiring individuals to go above and beyond their limits. According to a study by the RAND Corporation, this focus on mission success fosters a sense of purpose and determination, driving individuals to overcome obstacles and achieve their objectives. In corporate security, adopting a mission-first mentality ensures that security teams remain focused on protecting assets, personnel, and information, often under challenging circumstances. It instills a proactive approach to problem-solving and a relentless pursuit of excellence.

Camaraderie in the military and law enforcement is unparalleled, forged through shared experiences, challenges, and sacrifices. This deep sense of brotherhood and sisterhood creates a supportive network that individuals can rely on both during and after their service. A survey conducted by the Pew Research Center found that 84% of veterans felt a strong sense of camaraderie with their fellow service members, a bond that often extends into their civilian lives. In a corporate setting, fostering a similar sense of camaraderie can enhance team cohesion, improve morale, and increase productivity. It encourages collaboration, mutual support, and a collective commitment to the organization's goals.

The unique work culture of the military and law enforcement is also characterized by a strong emphasis on discipline and respect. Respect for authority and adherence to protocols are ingrained from the earliest stages of training. This disciplined approach ensures that operations run smoothly and that everyone works toward the same objectives. In the corporate world, these values translate into a professional environment where respect for colleagues and adherence to company policies are paramount. It creates a culture of accountability and reliability, where employees are motivated to perform their duties to the best of their abilities.

Transitioning from military and law enforcement to civilian careers, individuals often bring with them these cultural traits, which can be highly beneficial in various professional contexts. A study by the Institute for Veterans and Military Families (IVMF) at Syracuse University found that veterans often excel in leadership, teamwork, and problem-solving roles due to their unique cultural backgrounds. Employers increasingly recognize the value of these traits, with many actively seeking to hire veterans and former law enforcement officers for their ability to enhance organizational culture and performance.

Moreover, the strong sense of ethics and integrity ingrained in military and law enforcement personnel is highly valued in the corporate world. These professions demand the highest standards of ethical behavior and integrity, as individuals are often entrusted with significant responsibilities and must make decisions that can have profound consequences. This ethical foundation is critical in corporate security roles, where trust and reliability are essential for safeguarding assets and ensuring organizational resilience.

Adapting Military and Law Enforcement Mindset in Corporate Security

This concluding section will highlight how the military and law enforcement mindset can serve as both an asset and a challenge during the transition to corporate security. This duality will be explored through specific scenarios where this thinking is advantageous and situations where adaptation might be necessary.

Advantages in Corporate Security:

➢ **Crisis Management:** Military and law enforcement professionals excel in high-pressure situations due to their training in rapid decision-making under stress. In corporate security, this translates to effective crisis management. For instance, during an emergency such as a security breach or natural disaster, their ability to remain calm, assess the situation quickly, and implement a response plan is invaluable. Their experience in handling crises ensures they can efficiently protect assets and personnel.

➢ **Leadership and Teamwork**: The leadership skills and teamwork ethos developed in the military and law enforcement are critical assets in corporate environments. These professionals are adept at leading teams, delegating tasks, and maintaining morale even in challenging circumstances. A study by the Center for Creative Leadership found that veterans are often more effective leaders in corporate settings due to their experience in managing diverse teams and complex operations. This ability to inspire and guide a team is crucial for maintaining a cohesive and motivated security force.

➢ **Discipline and Reliability:** Discipline and reliability are core traits of military and law enforcement personnel. In corporate security, these traits ensure that protocols are followed meticulously and tasks are completed reliably. Their structured approach to work, coupled with a strong sense of duty, guarantees that security measures are consistently enforced, reducing the risk of breaches and ensuring a safe environment.

Challenges and Need for Adaptation:

➢ **Hierarchical Rigidness:** The rigid hierarchical structure in the military and law enforcement can sometimes be a hindrance in the more flexible corporate environment. In scenarios where a collaborative or flat organizational structure is preferred, former military and law enforcement professionals might struggle with the lack of a clear chain of command. Adapting to a more fluid decision-making process and being open to input from various levels can be challenging but necessary.

➢ **Mission-First Mentality:** While the mission-first mentality is beneficial for achieving objectives, it can lead to a workaholic approach that may not always align with corporate culture. In corporate settings, work-life balance is often emphasized, and a relentless focus on mission completion can lead to burnout. Learning to balance dedication to the mission with personal well-being and team morale is crucial for long-term success in the corporate world.

➢ **Communication Styles:** The direct and sometimes authoritative communication style prevalent in military and law enforcement can be perceived as too blunt or rigid in corporate environments. Effective communication in corporate settings often requires a more nuanced and collaborative approach. Adapting to this style, understanding corporate communication norms, and developing soft skills can help in building better relationships with colleagues and stakeholders.

Specific Scenarios:

➢ **Advantageous Scenario:** During a cybersecurity threat, the rapid decision-making and crisis management skills of former military personnel can lead to swift containment and mitigation of the threat, minimizing damage and ensuring business continuity.

➢ **Adaptation Scenario:** In a corporate project team setting where innovation and brainstorming are encouraged, the hierarchical and mission-first mindset might need to be adapted to foster a more inclusive and creative environment. Encouraging open dialogue and valuing diverse perspectives can enhance team collaboration and innovation.

In conclusion, the military and law enforcement mindset offers numerous advantages in corporate security, including superior crisis management, strong leadership, and disciplined reliability. However, transitioning to the corporate world also requires adapting to different organizational cultures and communication styles. Recognizing when to leverage these strengths and when to adapt can help former military and law enforcement professionals succeed and thrive in their new careers.

Chapter 2: The Corporate Security Landscape

In today's dynamic world, corporate security is a high-stakes game of chess where cyber and physical threats intertwine. Companies must forge robust alliances between traditional and digital security teams, crafting a seamless defense strategy. As technology evolves, so too must our approach—leveraging cutting-edge tools and data-driven insights to stay one step ahead. The future of corporate security demands agility, innovation, and an unyielding commitment to protecting assets. By embracing emerging trends and fostering interdisciplinary collaboration, businesses can fortify their defenses and navigate the complexities of an ever-shifting security terrain with confidence.

Let's delve deeper!!!!!!

Defining the Corporate Security Environment

The corporate security environment refers to the measures and practices that organizations use to protect their assets, information, and people. Traditionally, corporate security focused mainly on physical security. This included guards, locks, surveillance cameras, and other tools to protect buildings and physical assets. However, the corporate security environment has evolved significantly over the years. Today, it encompasses a much broader range of responsibilities and disciplines.

Traditional Physical Security

Physical Security Measures:

Physical security still plays a critical role in the corporate security environment. This includes securing the physical premises of an organization to prevent unauthorized access, theft, vandalism, and other threats. Traditional physical security measures include:

- ➢ **Surveillance Systems:** Closed-circuit television (CCTV) cameras and other monitoring systems to keep an eye on physical spaces.

- ➢ **Access Control:** Systems like key cards, biometric scanners, and security personnel to control who can enter and exit facilities.

- ➢ **Guards and Patrols:** Security personnel who monitor and protect physical spaces.

- ➢ **Alarms and Sensors:** Devices that detect unauthorized entry or unusual activity and alert security personnel.

Shift to a Holistic Security Approach

In recent years, the corporate security environment has shifted from focusing solely on physical security to a more holistic approach. According to a report by Gartner, Worldwide end-user spending on security and risk management is projected to total $215 billion in 2024, an increase of 14.3% from 2023, according to a new forecast from Gartner, Inc. In 2023, global security and risk management end-user spending was estimated to reach $188.1 billion. This shift is driven by the increasing complexity of threats and the interconnected nature of modern businesses. Organizations now recognize the need to integrate various aspects of security, including cybersecurity, risk management, and business continuity.

Cybersecurity

Importance of Cybersecurity

Cybersecurity has become a critical component of the corporate security environment. As businesses rely more on digital technologies, the risk of cyber threats has increased. Cybersecurity involves protecting an organization's information systems, networks, and data from cyber-attacks such as hacking, malware, phishing, and ransomware.

Key Cybersecurity Measures

> ➤ **Firewalls and Antivirus Software:** Tools to protect networks and computers from unauthorized access and malicious software.

> ➤ **Encryption:** Techniques to protect sensitive data by converting it into a secure format that can only be read by authorized users.

> **Employee Training:** Educate employees about cybersecurity best practices, such as recognizing phishing emails and using strong passwords.

> **Incident Response Plans:** Strategies for responding to and recovering from cyber-attacks.

Risk Management

Understanding Risk Management

Risk management involves identifying, assessing, and mitigating risks that could impact an organization. This process helps organizations prepare for and respond to various threats, whether they are physical, cyber, or operational.

Steps in Risk Management

> **Risk Identification:** Recognizing potential threats, such as natural disasters, cyber-attacks, supply chain disruptions, and employee misconduct.

> **Risk Assessment:** Evaluating the likelihood and impact of identified risks.

> **Risk Mitigation:** Implementing measures to reduce the likelihood and impact of risks. This may include physical security upgrades, cybersecurity enhancements, and employee training.

➢ **Risk Monitoring:** Continuously monitoring the risk landscape to identify new threats and assess the effectiveness of mitigation measures.

Business Continuity

What is Business Continuity?

Business continuity involves planning and preparing to ensure that an organization can continue to operate during and after a disruption. This includes maintaining essential functions, services, and processes, even in the face of significant challenges. For example, During Hurricane Katrina, Tulane University Medical Center maintained essential healthcare services by implementing its business continuity plan. They established temporary facilities to continue patient care, managed their supply chain to ensure medical supplies were available, and maintained clear communication with staff and external agencies to coordinate emergency response efforts effectively. This proactive approach helped them mitigate the impact of the disaster and ensure continuity of operations during a challenging time.

Key Components of Business Continuity

➢ **Business Continuity Plans (BCPs):** Detailed plans that outline how an organization will continue to operate during a disruption. These plans typically include procedures for maintaining critical functions, communication strategies, and recovery plans.

➢ **Disaster Recovery Plans (DRPs):** Specific plans for recovering IT systems and data after a disaster, such as a cyber-attack or natural disaster.

➢ **Testing and Exercises:** Regularly testing and practicing business continuity and disaster recovery plans to ensure they are effective and up to date.

➢ **Backup Systems:** Ensuring that critical data and systems are backed up and can be quickly restored in the event of a disruption.

Integration of Security Disciplines

The modern corporate security environment involves integrating physical security, cybersecurity, risk management, and business continuity into a cohesive strategy. This holistic approach ensures that organizations are better prepared to handle a wide range of threats and disruptions.

Building a Holistic Security Strategy

Collaboration and Communication

A successful holistic security strategy requires collaboration and communication across different departments and functions within an organization. This includes security personnel, IT staff, risk managers, and business continuity planners working together to identify and address potential threats.

Leadership and Governance

Effective security governance involves establishing clear leadership and accountability for security initiatives. This includes appointing a Chief Security Officer (CSO) or Chief Information Security Officer (CISO) to oversee security efforts and ensure that security policies and procedures are implemented and followed.

Technology and Innovation

Leveraging advanced technologies and innovative solutions is essential for a holistic security strategy. This includes using artificial intelligence (AI) and machine learning to detect and respond to threats, implementing advanced surveillance and access control systems, and continuously updating and improving cybersecurity measures.

Training and Awareness

Educating employees about security risks and best practices is a critical component of a holistic security strategy. Regular training and awareness programs help ensure that employees understand their role in protecting the organization and can recognize and respond to potential threats.

Challenges in the Corporate Security Environment

Evolving Threat Landscape

The threat landscape is constantly evolving, with new and more sophisticated threats emerging regularly. This requires organizations to stay vigilant and continuously update their security measures to address new risks.

Balancing Security and Business Operations

Implementing robust security measures can sometimes impact business operations. Organizations must find a balance between ensuring security and maintaining efficient and effective operations.

Resource Constraints

Developing and maintaining a comprehensive security strategy can be resource-intensive. Organizations must allocate sufficient resources, including budget, personnel, and technology, to ensure their security measures are effective.

The corporate security environment has evolved from a focus on traditional physical security to a more holistic approach that includes cybersecurity, risk management, and business continuity. This shift reflects the increasing complexity and interconnectedness of modern businesses and the need to address a wide range of threats and disruptions. By integrating these various aspects of security into a cohesive strategy, organizations can better protect their assets, information, and people in an ever-changing threat landscape.

The Future of Corporate Security

Looking forward, the blending of cyber and physical security risks highlights the critical need for integrated collaboration and advanced technology among security professionals. Chief Security Officers (CSOs) must foster deliberate partnerships with their cybersecurity colleagues to effectively address and mitigate threats to their organizations. Investments in cutting-edge digital security tools and strategies are essential for boosting organizational resilience against ever-evolving threats.

As the security landscape continues to transform, organizations must stay agile and proactive by adopting intelligence-driven methods for corporate security risk management. By embracing new trends and encouraging cross-functional teamwork, businesses can strengthen their defenses and ensure a secure and resilient future amidst constant change.

Key Differences Between Military and Law Enforcement and Corporate Security

First, I'll share my experience!

In 2012, I transitioned from a military and law enforcement career to a corporate role, joining Valero Energy Corporation as the security superintendent for the McKee Refinery. This shift allowed me to leverage my skills in a new environment. Seven years later, I joined Volvo Group North America as the Security Director for the North Region, including all of Canada. This move enhanced my skill set over a much larger territory, encompassing many locations, including manufacturing plants, central distribution centers, customer experience sites, and office spaces.

In 2022, I applied for a Senior Director Corporate Security role at Tanger. Despite concerns about my lack of retail experience, I emphasized how my positions and military and law enforcement background brought fresh perspectives and innovative security solutions, such as robots and drones. Today, as the Senior Director of Corporate Security at Tanger, I manage executive protection, the Corporate Security Operations Center (CSOC), and both physical and technical security, applying my disciplined, strategic approach from my previous career to enhance corporate security.

Now, we will explore key differences between military and law enforcement and corporate security, focusing on aspects like stakeholder management, profit-driven decision-making, and the balance between security and business facilitation.

One of the primary differences between military and law enforcement and corporate security is the nature of stakeholder management. In the military and law enforcement, the primary stakeholders are often the government, the public, and the internal chain of command. Decisions and actions are typically driven by mission objectives, public safety, and adherence to strict protocols. There is a clear hierarchy, and orders are expected to be followed without question to maintain discipline and effectiveness.

In contrast, corporate security involves a broader range of stakeholders, including employees, customers, shareholders, regulatory bodies, and the public. The priorities and interests of these stakeholders can vary significantly, and corporate security professionals must navigate these complexities. They need to balance security needs with the expectations and concerns of different groups, often requiring negotiation, persuasion, and diplomacy. Effective communication and stakeholder engagement are crucial in the corporate environment to ensure that security measures are understood, accepted, and supported.

Another key difference lies in profit-driven decision-making. Military and law enforcement operations are primarily focused on achieving strategic objectives, maintaining order, and ensuring public safety. While budget considerations are important, the primary focus is not on profit but on fulfilling a mission. Resources are allocated based on the need to achieve objectives and respond to threats, often with significant public funding. The article *"Private and/or Corporate Security: Are There Conceptual Similarities and Differences?"* explores the distinctions between military and law enforcement and corporate security. It highlights key differences in their operational focuses and organizational structures. Military and law enforcement entities are typically driven by public safety mandates, adhering to strict protocols and a hierarchical command structure. Their roles often involve a broader scope of authority, including enforcing laws and responding to emergencies.

In contrast, corporate security operates within a more defined, private context, emphasizing risk management, loss prevention, and safeguarding corporate assets.

Corporate security professionals work under a more flexible framework, often adapting to business objectives and organizational policies. The study underscores that while both fields share common goals of protection and safety, their approaches and operational environments differ significantly, reflecting their distinct objectives and structures.

In the corporate world, decisions are heavily influenced by the bottom line. Security measures must be justified not only in terms of risk mitigation but also in terms of cost-effectiveness and return on investment.

Corporate security professionals must demonstrate how security investments contribute to the overall business objectives, such as protecting assets, ensuring business continuity, and maintaining customer trust. They need to align security initiatives with the company's financial goals and priorities, often requiring innovative solutions to deliver effective security within budget constraints. Balancing security and business facilitation is another critical aspect where military law enforcement and corporate security diverge. In military and law enforcement, security is often the primary concern, with a clear mandate to protect and defend, even if it means imposing strict measures and controls.

Operational success is measured by the ability to prevent, respond to, and mitigate threats, sometimes with minimal regard for convenience or business impact. In the corporate environment, security must coexist with business operations. Security measures should be protected without hindering productivity, efficiency, and customer satisfaction.

Corporate security professionals must design and implement security protocols that are robust yet unobtrusive, allowing the business to operate smoothly. They need to work closely with other departments, such as IT, operations, and human resources, to ensure that security measures integrate seamlessly into the business processes and enhance rather than obstruct business objectives.

Furthermore, the approach to risk differs significantly between the two domains. In military and law enforcement, risk tolerance can be lower, with a focus on eliminating or minimizing threats to the greatest extent possible. The consequences of failure can be severe, including loss of life, significant property damage, or national security breaches. In corporate security, risk management often involves assessing and balancing risks with business benefits. Some level of risk may be acceptable if the cost of mitigation outweighs the potential impact. Corporate security professionals must evaluate risks in the context of business priorities and develop strategies that provide adequate protection while supporting the company's goals and operations. This often involves a more nuanced approach, using risk assessments, cost-benefit analyses, and strategic planning to make informed decisions.

I have always believed that military and law enforcement cultures are characterized by a strong sense of duty, discipline, and adherence to protocols. There is a clear chain of command, and decisions are often made at higher levels, with strict enforcement of rules and procedures.

Corporate culture, on the other hand, can be more flexible and collaborative. Decision-making processes may involve input from various levels within the organization, and there is often a greater emphasis on innovation, adaptability, and employee engagement.

Corporate security professionals must adapt to these cultural differences, learning to work within a more dynamic and sometimes less hierarchical environment. They need to build relationships across departments, foster a culture of security awareness, and encourage proactive involvement from employees at all levels.

Evolution of Threats and Challenges in the Corporate World

"As cyber threats evolve, we need to evolve as well."
Christopher A. Wray –
Director of The Federal Bureau of Investigation

The corporate world today faces a rapidly evolving landscape of threats and challenges that can significantly impact business operations, profitability, and reputation.

As organizations become more interconnected and reliant on digital technologies, they must navigate a complex array of risks. This section will discuss some of the most pressing threats and challenges, including insider threats, intellectual property protection, and the impact of geopolitical events on multinational corporations.

Insider Threats

Insider threats pose a significant risk to organizations because they involve individuals within the company who have access to sensitive information and systems. These insiders can be employees, contractors, or business partners who misuse their access, intentionally or unintentionally, to harm the organization.

Types of Insider Threats

> **Malicious Insiders:** These are individuals who deliberately misuse their access to cause harm, steal data,

or disrupt operations. Their motivations can range from financial gain to espionage, sabotage, or personal grievances.

➤ **Negligent Insiders:** These individuals do not intend to cause harm but may do so through carelessness or lack of awareness. This can include poor cybersecurity practices, such as weak passwords, falling for phishing attacks, or mishandling sensitive information.

➤ **Compromised Insiders:** These insiders have their credentials or access compromised by external attackers. Cybercriminals can exploit compromised accounts to infiltrate the organization and carry out malicious activities.

Mitigating Insider Threats

To mitigate insider threats, organizations must implement a comprehensive approach that includes both technical and non-technical measures:

➤ **Access Controls:** Implementing strict access controls ensures that employees only have access to the information and systems necessary for their roles. Regularly reviewing and updating access permissions is crucial.

➤ **Monitoring and Auditing:** Continuous monitoring of user activities can help detect unusual behavior that may indicate insider threats. Auditing access logs and system activities can provide insights into potential issues.

➢ **Employee Training:** Educating employees about security policies, recognizing phishing attempts, and safe handling of sensitive information is essential. Regular training sessions can reinforce good practices.

➢ **Incident Response Plan:** Having a well-defined incident response plan helps organizations quickly identify and respond to insider threats. This plan should include procedures for investigating, containing, and mitigating incidents.

Intellectual Property Protection

Intellectual property (IP) is a critical asset for many organizations, encompassing patents, trademarks, copyrights, trade secrets, and proprietary technologies. Protecting IP is vital for maintaining a competitive edge, fostering innovation, and ensuring business success.

Threats to Intellectual Property

➢ **Cyber Espionage:** Cybercriminals and state-sponsored actors may target organizations to steal valuable IP. This can involve hacking into systems, deploying malware, or using social engineering techniques to gain access.

> **Employee Theft:** Employees with access to sensitive information may steal IP for personal gain, to start a competing business, or to sell to competitors or foreign entities.

> **Counterfeiting and Piracy:** Counterfeiters may produce and sell fake versions of products, undermining the original brand and causing financial losses. Piracy involves unauthorized copying and distribution of copyrighted materials.

Strategies for Protecting Intellectual Property

> **Legal Protections:** Registering patents, trademarks, and copyrights provides legal protection and enables organizations to take legal action against infringers. Non-disclosure agreements (NDAs) and employment contracts with IP clauses can help protect trade secrets.

> **Technical Safeguards:** Implementing robust cybersecurity measures, such as encryption, firewalls, and intrusion detection systems, helps protect digital IP from cyber threats. Data loss prevention (DLP) tools can monitor and control the flow of sensitive information.

> **Physical Security:** Securing physical access to areas where sensitive information is stored or developed is important. This includes using access controls, surveillance cameras, and security personnel.

> ➢ **Employee Training and Policies:** Educating employees about the importance of IP protection and establishing clear policies for handling sensitive information can reduce the risk of internal threats. Encouraging a culture of confidentiality and respect for IP is also crucial.

Geopolitical Events and Multinational Corporations

Geopolitical events can have profound impacts on multinational corporations (MNCs), affecting their operations, supply chains, market access, and overall stability. These events include political instability, trade wars, regulatory changes, and international conflicts.

A notable incident involving geopolitical events and multinational corporations is the 2014 crisis in Ukraine and its impact on multinational companies operating in the region. When Russia annexed Crimea in 2014, the geopolitical turmoil created significant challenges for multinational corporations with business interests in Ukraine and Russia.

Many companies faced operational disruptions and had to reassess their strategies in response to sanctions imposed by Western nations against Russia. For example, companies like PepsiCo, which had substantial investments in both Ukraine and Russia, had to navigate the complex political landscape, adapting their operations to comply with sanctions while trying to maintain their market presence.

The crisis illustrated how geopolitical events can profoundly impact multinational corporations, forcing them to reevaluate their risk management strategies and operational plans in response to shifting political and economic conditions.

Impact of Geopolitical Events

➢ **Supply Chain Disruptions:** Political instability, natural disasters, or trade restrictions in one country can disrupt the global supply chain, leading to delays, increased costs, and shortages of critical materials or components.

➢ **Regulatory Changes:** Changes in laws and regulations in different countries can create challenges for MNCs, requiring them to adapt their operations, compliance practices, and strategies to meet new requirements.

➢ **Market Access:** Geopolitical tensions, such as trade wars or sanctions, can limit or block access to key markets. This can result in lost revenue and the need to find alternative markets or suppliers.

➢ **Reputational Risks:** MNCs may face reputational risks if they are perceived as complicit in political or ethical issues in the countries where they operate. This can lead to consumer boycotts, loss of trust, and negative publicity.

Strategies for Managing Geopolitical Risks

> **Risk Assessment and Planning:** Conducting thorough risk assessments to identify potential geopolitical risks and their impact on the business is crucial. Developing contingency plans and diversifying supply chains can help mitigate these risks.

> **Stakeholder Engagement:** Engaging with local stakeholders, including governments, communities, and business partners, helps build positive relationships and navigate regulatory and political challenges.

> **Compliance and Adaptation:** Staying informed about regulatory changes and adapting operations to meet new requirements is essential. This includes compliance with local laws, trade regulations, and international standards.

> **Reputation Management:** Proactively managing the company's reputation by maintaining high ethical standards, practicing corporate social responsibility, and transparently addressing any concerns can help mitigate reputational risks.

The Intersection of Cybersecurity and Geopolitics

The intersection of cybersecurity and geopolitics is an area of growing concern for multinational corporations. Cyber-attacks by state-sponsored actors, politically motivated hackers, or cybercriminals can disrupt operations, steal sensitive information, and damage reputations.

State-Sponsored Cyber Attacks

State-sponsored cyber-attacks often target MNCs for espionage, intellectual property theft, or to disrupt operations. These attacks can be sophisticated and well-coordinated, posing significant challenges for organizations.

Politically Motivated Hacktivism

Hacktivist groups may target corporations to promote political agendas, protest policies, or draw attention to social issues. These attacks can involve defacing websites, leaking sensitive information, or disrupting services.

Cybersecurity Measures

To protect against these threats, MNCs must implement robust cybersecurity measures, including:

> ➢ **Threat Intelligence:** Monitoring and analyzing threat intelligence to stay informed about emerging threats and vulnerabilities.

> ➤ **Incident Response:** Developing and regularly testing incident response plans to detect, contain, and mitigate cyber-attacks quickly.

> ➤ **Collaboration:** Collaborating with industry peers, government agencies, and cybersecurity experts to share information and best practices.

> ➤ **Advanced Technologies:** Utilizing advanced cybersecurity technologies like artificial intelligence (AI) and machine learning to detect and respond to threats in real time.

The Role of Corporate Security Leadership

Effective corporate security leadership is crucial in navigating the complex threat landscape. Security leaders must possess a deep understanding of both traditional and emerging threats, as well as the ability to communicate the importance of security to other business leaders and stakeholders.

Building a Security-First Culture

Creating a security-first culture within the organization involves:

> ➤ **Leadership Commitment:** Security leaders must demonstrate a strong commitment to security and lead by example. This includes prioritizing security initiatives and ensuring adequate resources are allocated.

➤ **Employee Engagement:** Engaging employees at all levels to foster a sense of responsibility and awareness about security. The key components are regular training, communication, and recognition of good security practices.

➤ **Cross-Department Collaboration:** Encouraging collaboration between security teams and other departments, such as IT, operations, and legal, to ensure a holistic approach to security.

Adapting to Changing Threats

Corporate security leaders must stay agile and adaptable in the face of evolving threats. This involves:

➤ **Continuous Learning:** Staying informed about the latest trends, technologies, and threats in the security landscape. Participating in industry forums, conferences, and training programs is essential.

➤ **Innovation:** Embracing new technologies and innovative approaches to enhance security measures. This can include adopting AI-powered threat detection, blockchain for secure transactions, and cloud-based security solutions.

➤ **Proactive Risk Management:** Implementing proactive risk management practices to identify and address potential threats before they materialize. This includes regular risk assessments, scenario planning, and stress testing.

Skills Valued in Corporate Security

The corporate security environment requires a unique set of skills to effectively navigate the diverse and dynamic range of threats and challenges. As organizations increasingly recognize the importance of a holistic security approach, the demand for professionals with a blend of strategic thinking, business acumen, and effective communication skills has grown. This chapter will conclude with an overview of these essential skills.

Strategic Thinking

Strategic thinking is paramount in corporate security. Security professionals must be able to anticipate potential threats, understand their implications, and develop comprehensive strategies to mitigate risks. This involves a deep understanding of the organization's operations, goals, and the broader threat landscape. Strategic thinkers can see the bigger picture and align security initiatives with business objectives, ensuring that security measures support the organization's long-term success.

Effective strategic thinking includes:

> ➤ **Threat Assessment and Risk Management:** Continuously evaluating the risk environment to identify emerging threats and vulnerabilities. This requires staying informed about the latest trends, technologies, and geopolitical developments that could impact the organization.

> ➤ **Proactive Planning:** Developing proactive strategies to address potential threats before they materialize. This includes scenario planning, stress testing, and creating robust incident response plans.

> ➤ **Resource Allocation:** Prioritizing security investments and initiatives based on their potential impact and alignment with business goals. This ensures that resources are used efficiently and effectively.

Business Acumen

Corporate security professionals must possess strong business acumen to understand the organization's operations, financial goals, and strategic priorities. This skill enables them to make informed decisions that balance security needs with business objectives, ensuring that security measures do not hinder productivity or profitability.

Key aspects of business acumen include:

> **Understanding Business Operations:** Gaining a deep understanding of how the organization functions, including its supply chain, customer base, and key business processes. This knowledge helps security professionals develop tailored security strategies that protect critical assets and support business continuity.

> **Financial Literacy:** Being able to read and interpret financial statements, budgets, and cost-benefit analyses. This skill is essential for justifying security investments and demonstrating their value to the organization.

> **Strategic Alignment:** Ensuring that security initiatives align with the organization's strategic goals. This involves working closely with other business leaders to integrate security into broader business strategies and initiatives.

Effective Communication

Effective communication is crucial for corporate security professionals. They must be able to articulate security concepts, risks, and strategies to non-security professionals, including executives, employees, and other stakeholders. Clear and persuasive communication helps build support for security initiatives and fosters a security-first culture within the organization.

Important communication skills include:

➢ **Simplifying Complex Concepts:** Translating technical security jargon into simple, understandable language. This ensures that all stakeholders, regardless of their technical expertise, can grasp the importance of security measures.

➢ **Persuasion and Influence:** Building a compelling case for security investments and initiatives. This involves presenting data, case studies, and real-world examples to demonstrate the potential impact of security threats and the value of proactive measures.

➢ **Active Listening:** Engaging with stakeholders to understand their concerns, priorities, and perspectives. Active listening helps security professionals address specific needs and build stronger relationships across the organization.

➢ **Crisis Communication:** Effectively communicating during security incidents or crises. This includes providing clear, concise, and timely information to stakeholders, managing expectations, and maintaining trust and transparency.

In conclusion, the skills most valued in corporate security encompass strategic thinking, business acumen, and effective communication. Strategic thinking allows security professionals to anticipate and mitigate risks, aligning security initiatives with organizational goals. Business acumen ensures that security measures support business operations and financial objectives, while effective communication helps build support for security initiatives and fosters a security-first culture. By cultivating these skills, corporate security professionals can navigate the complex threat landscape, protect their organizations, and contribute to long-term success.

Chapter 3: Recognizing Transferable Skills

"The future belongs to those who learn more skills and combine them in creative ways."
- Robert Greene - An American Author

Transitioning from military or law enforcement to corporate security can be both challenging and rewarding. The core skills honed in these high-stakes fields, such as threat assessment, crisis management, and leadership, are highly transferable and valuable in a corporate setting. This chapter explores how these skills seamlessly apply to corporate security roles, offering insights into translating experiences into civilian terms. By effectively understanding and showcasing these abilities, individuals can leverage their unique backgrounds to enhance organizational safety and operations.

Transferrable Skills from Military and Law Enforcement to Corporate Security

The core skills developed in military and law enforcement careers are highly valuable for corporate security roles for several key reasons. By leveraging the core skills developed in military and law enforcement careers, corporate security professionals can enhance their ability to proactively address security challenges, respond effectively to incidents, and maintain the overall safety and integrity of the organization. Let's discuss some of them.

Threat Assessment

Threat assessment is a critical skill honed in the military and law enforcement, where the ability to identify, evaluate, and prioritize potential threats can mean the difference between success and failure or even life and death. This skill translates seamlessly into the corporate security realm, where the primary objective is to safeguard an organization's assets, including personnel, information, and physical property.

In a corporate setting, threat assessment involves evaluating potential risks to the company's operations and assets. This could range from identifying vulnerabilities in the IT infrastructure to assessing the physical security of corporate offices. For example, a former military professional might be adept at conducting comprehensive risk assessments for a company's physical locations. They can identify potential security breaches, such as unsecured entry points or insufficient surveillance coverage, and recommend measures to mitigate these risks, such as installing additional cameras or enhancing access controls.

Additionally, those with law enforcement backgrounds bring a keen understanding of criminal behavior and tactics, which is invaluable in preempting and mitigating security threats. They can analyze crime patterns and advise on proactive measures to prevent incidents, such as coordinating with local law enforcement to stay informed about crime trends in the area surrounding corporate facilities.

Crisis Management

Crisis management is another essential skill developed in the high-pressure environments of the military and law enforcement. Personnel in these fields are trained to remain calm under pressure, make rapid decisions, and coordinate responses to emergencies efficiently. These abilities are crucial in corporate security, where crises can range from natural disasters and cyberattacks to workplace violence and executive protection scenarios.

For instance, a former military professional might be responsible for developing and implementing a comprehensive crisis management plan for a corporation. This plan would outline procedures for various emergency scenarios, detailing specific roles and responsibilities, communication protocols, and evacuation procedures. This experience in handling real-life crises enables them to anticipate potential complications and ensure that the plan is both practical and effective. In the event of an actual crisis, the ability to stay calm and make quick, informed decisions is invaluable. They can coordinate the company's response, ensuring that all employees are accounted for and safe, liaising with emergency services, and providing clear and concise communication to all stakeholders. Their leadership and experience can help minimize the impact of the crisis on the company's operations and reputation.

Leadership

Leadership is a cornerstone of both military and law enforcement careers. Personnel in these fields are often placed in positions where they must lead teams, manage resources, and make critical decisions under pressure. This leadership experience is highly beneficial in corporate security roles, where effective team management and strategic decision-making are essential.

A former military leader, for example, might be tasked with overseeing a corporate security team. Their experience in leading diverse groups of individuals, often in challenging and high-stress environments, equips them with the skills needed to manage a security team effectively. They can foster a culture of discipline, accountability, and continuous improvement, ensuring that the team operates at peak efficiency.

Moreover, military and law enforcement leaders are trained to think strategically, considering both immediate and long-term objectives. In a corporate setting, this strategic thinking enables them to develop and implement security policies and procedures that not only address current threats but also anticipate future challenges. They can guide the organization in allocating resources effectively, prioritizing security initiatives that provide the greatest benefit to the company's overall safety and resilience.

Surveillance and Intelligence Gathering

Surveillance and intelligence gathering are fundamental aspects of both military and law enforcement work. These skills involve the systematic collection and analysis of information to identify potential threats and inform strategic decisions. In the corporate world, these abilities are essential for protecting the company's assets and staying ahead of potential security challenges.

For example, a former law enforcement officer might be responsible for implementing a surveillance program within a corporate setting. They can design and deploy advanced surveillance systems, ensuring comprehensive coverage of critical areas and integrating modern technologies such as facial recognition and motion detection. Their expertise in monitoring and analyzing surveillance footage enables them to identify suspicious activities and respond promptly to potential threats.

Additionally, their experience in intelligence gathering allows them to develop effective information-sharing networks, both within the company and with external partners such as local law enforcement and industry peers.

This collaborative approach ensures that the company stays informed about emerging threats and can proactively address potential risks before they escalate.

Investigative Skills

Investigative skills are another area where military and law enforcement personnel excel. These skills involve the ability to gather and analyze evidence, conduct interviews, and draw conclusions based on the available information. In a corporate security context, these abilities are crucial for conducting internal investigations into incidents such as fraud, theft, or policy violations.

For instance, a former detective might be brought in to investigate a case of suspected corporate espionage. They can apply their investigative techniques to gather evidence, interview suspects and witnesses, and compile a comprehensive report detailing their findings. Their methodical approach ensures that all relevant information is considered, and their experience in handling sensitive information helps to maintain confidentiality and protect the company's reputation.

Physical Security

Physical security is a core component of both military and law enforcement training. This involves the protection of physical assets through measures such as access control, perimeter security, and the use of security personnel. In a corporate environment, these skills are essential for ensuring the safety and security of company facilities and personnel.

A former military professional might be responsible for designing and implementing a physical security plan for a corporate headquarters. This plan would include measures such as installing barriers and fencing, deploying security personnel, and establishing access control protocols to restrict entry to authorized individuals. Their experience in securing military installations enables them to identify potential vulnerabilities and implement effective countermeasures.

Moreover, their ability to coordinate with local law enforcement and emergency services ensures a comprehensive approach to physical security, integrating internal and external resources to effectively protect the company's assets.

Cybersecurity Awareness

While not traditionally a focus in military and law enforcement training, cybersecurity has become an increasingly important aspect of corporate security. Personnel from these backgrounds often possess a strong understanding of security principles and protocols, which can be adapted to address cyber threats.

For example, a former military professional might take on the role of a cybersecurity manager within a corporation. Their disciplined approach to security enables them to develop and enforce robust cybersecurity policies, ensuring that all employees follow best practices for protecting sensitive information. They can also coordinate with IT professionals to implement advanced security measures, such as encryption and multi-factor authentication, to safeguard the company's digital assets.

Additionally, their experience in threat assessment and crisis management enables them to respond effectively to cyber incidents, such as data breaches or ransomware attacks. They can lead the company's response, coordinating with internal and external stakeholders to contain the threat and minimize its impact on the organization.

Communication Skills

Effective communication is a vital skill in both military and law enforcement roles. Personnel in these fields are trained to convey information clearly and concisely, both in written reports and verbal briefings. This ability is crucial in corporate security, where clear communication ensures that all stakeholders are informed and aligned in their efforts to protect the company's assets.

For instance, a former law enforcement officer might be responsible for providing security briefings to senior management. Their experience in delivering concise and informative reports enables them to present complex information in an easily understandable manner, ensuring that executives are fully aware of the company's security posture and any potential risks.

Their ability to communicate effectively also extends to training and educating employees on security protocols, ensuring that everyone within the organization understands their role in maintaining a secure environment.

By practicing these abilities, individuals with military or law enforcement backgrounds can significantly enhance an organization's security posture, ensuring the protection of its assets and the safety of its personnel. The ongoing integration of these skills into the corporate environment not only provides a solid foundation for effective security strategies but also contributes to the overall resilience and success of the company.

Translating Military and Law Enforcement Experience for the Civilian Workplace

Translating military and law enforcement experience for the civilian workplace involves highlighting leadership, problem-solving, adaptability, and teamwork skills to showcase their applicability in non-military settings.

We all must have heard about Jocko Willink. He is a retired Navy SEAL officer who successfully transitioned into a corporate leadership consultant by translating his military experience into business language. For example, his role as a SEAL Team Commander, where he led highly skilled individuals in high-pressure situations, translates directly to managing corporate teams, fostering collaboration, and driving performance to meet organizational objectives. Additionally, his experience in mission planning and execution, which required detailed strategic planning and the ability to adapt to rapidly changing circumstances, is comparable to developing and implementing strategic business plans to achieve company goals. Here are some key aspects of translating military and law enforcement experience for the civilian workplace:

Understanding the Need for Translation

Transitioning from a military or law enforcement career to a corporate environment involves more than just changing job roles; it also requires learning to communicate your skills and experiences in a language that civilian employers understand and value.

Many veterans and former law enforcement officers find it challenging to convey their extensive training and achievements in a way that resonates with corporate recruiters and hiring managers.

This section provides a "translation guide" for common military and law enforcement terms and concepts, helping readers reframe their experiences for civilian employers.

From Tactical to Strategic

In the military and law enforcement, much of the language revolves around tactics and operations. In the corporate world, however, the focus is often on strategy and business impact.

For example, a veteran's experience in "mission planning" can be translated into "strategic planning" in a corporate context. Similarly, "operational command" can be reframed as "operational management" or "project management."

Consider a military officer who led a team on a complex mission. In corporate terms, this experience can be described as managing a project with tight deadlines, coordinating cross-functional teams, and achieving critical objectives under pressure. This reframing highlights the strategic and managerial skills that are highly valued in the corporate sector.

Leadership and Team Management

Leadership in the military and law enforcement is often about command and control, while in the corporate world, it's about collaboration and influence. For instance, a sergeant who led a platoon can translate this experience into managing a team, fostering collaboration, and driving performance. Emphasizing skills like team building, conflict resolution, and mentorship can help civilian employers see the value of military and law enforcement leadership experience.

A former law enforcement officer who supervised a precinct or section can describe their role as overseeing a diverse team, managing personnel issues, and ensuring operational efficiency. This highlights their ability to handle complex human resources challenges and maintain high standards of performance, which are critical skills in any corporate leadership position.

Crisis Management to Risk Management

Crisis management is a vital skill in both military and law enforcement roles, but in the corporate world, it's often referred to as risk management or emergency response planning. A military professional who handled crises can present this experience as managing risk, developing contingency plans, and leading emergency response efforts.

For example, a veteran who coordinated a response to a natural disaster can describe their experience as leading a large-scale emergency response operation, developing and implementing crisis management plans, and coordinating with various stakeholders to ensure a swift and effective response. This demonstrates their ability to handle high-pressure situations and make critical decisions, which are essential for corporate risk management roles.

Surveillance and Intelligence Gathering to Data Analysis

Surveillance and intelligence gathering in military and law enforcement roles involve collecting and analyzing information to make informed decisions. In the corporate world, these skills are often framed as data analysis or business intelligence. A former intelligence officer can describe their experience as gathering and analyzing data to identify trends, provide insights, and support strategic decision-making. For instance, an intelligence officer who tracked enemy movements can translate this experience into analyzing market trends, monitoring competitor activities, and providing actionable insights to support business strategies. This highlights their analytical skills and ability to turn data into valuable information for decision-makers.

Physical Security to Asset Protection

Physical security in the military and law enforcement is about protecting people and facilities. In the corporate world, this is often referred to as asset protection or facilities management. A veteran responsible for base security can describe their role as managing security operations, implementing access control measures, and protecting valuable assets.

For example, a former military officer who secured a base can translate this experience into managing corporate security, overseeing access control systems, and ensuring the safety of employees and assets. This demonstrates their expertise in protecting physical assets and creating a secure working environment, which is crucial for any organization.

Cybersecurity Awareness to Information Security

While cybersecurity is a growing concern in both military and corporate settings, the language used to describe it can differ. Military and law enforcement personnel often refer to cybersecurity in terms of defense and protection, while in the corporate world, it's about information security and data protection. A former military cybersecurity expert can describe their experience as managing information security, protecting sensitive data, and ensuring compliance with security protocols.

For instance, a cybersecurity specialist in the military who protects classified information can translate this experience into managing corporate information security, implementing data protection measures, and ensuring compliance with industry regulations. This highlights their expertise in safeguarding sensitive information and mitigating cyber risks.

Communication Skills to Stakeholder Engagement

Effective communication is essential in both military and law enforcement roles, but in the corporate world, it's often referred to as stakeholder engagement or corporate communications. A former military SNCO or officer who briefed senior leaders can describe their experience as delivering presentations, providing strategic insights, and engaging with stakeholders to support decision-making. For example, a military officer who communicated mission plans can translate this experience into developing and delivering strategic presentations, providing insights to senior management, and engaging with stakeholders to ensure alignment and support for business initiatives. This demonstrates their ability to communicate effectively with diverse audiences and build consensus.

Training and Development to Learning and Development

Training and development in the military and law enforcement involve preparing personnel for various roles and responsibilities.

In the corporate world, this is often referred to as learning and development or employee training. A former training officer can describe their experience as designing and delivering training programs, developing curriculum, and assessing training effectiveness.

For instance, a military training officer or NCO who developed combat training programs can translate this experience into designing corporate training programs, developing instructional materials, and assessing the effectiveness of training initiatives. This highlights their ability to enhance employee skills and support organizational growth through effective training and development. By translating military and law enforcement experience into corporate language, veterans and former law enforcement officers can effectively communicate their skills and achievements to civilian employers.

Adaptability and Continuous Learning in the Corporate World

"Adaptability is about the powerful difference between adapting to cope and adapting to win."
– Max Mckeown - An English Writer

Personal Experience

When I began my tenure at Valero Energy Corporation in early 2012 as the Security Superintendent, I felt like I was stepping into a new frontier. My background in the military and law enforcement had equipped me with leadership and crisis management skills, but I quickly realized that succeeding in the corporate world required more than what I already knew—it demanded adaptability and a commitment to continuous learning.

In 2014, I was presented with a significant opportunity to work at Valero's flagship refinery in Port Arthur, TX. However, this role required a degree, which I didn't yet have. This moment highlighted a gap in my qualifications, and I knew I needed to address it if I wanted to advance within the company. Determined not to let this opportunity slip away, I enrolled in college, pursuing a Bachelor of Science in Justice Studies with a concentration in Terrorism and Homeland Security. Returning to academics was different this time. The discipline and dedication I had cultivated through years of military service and law enforcement drove me to excel. In my first couple of semesters, I made the dean's list, a testament to the determination that had carried me through rigorous training and challenging missions. Yet, life was far from straightforward during this period.

My mother was battling cancer, and balancing a demanding 24/7 on-call job with full-time school and the emotional strain of her illness was one of the most challenging experiences of my life.

One day, I received a call that would change everything—the news that if I wanted to see my mother before she passed, I needed to return to New Hampshire immediately. I dropped everything and went home, spending four unforgettable days with her. We relived memories, shared laughter, and said our goodbyes. As I left to return to Texas, I knew it would be the last time I saw her alive.

Returning to work was difficult. The loss of my mother left a deep void, and while I eventually regained my footing professionally, my academic progress stalled. Nearly a year later, I woke up with a renewed sense of purpose, driven by the realization that I had an unfinished mission. I re-enrolled in school as a full-time student, determined to complete my degree. Around this time, I had a dream in which my mother appeared to me, urging me to finish what I had started. Her words were clear and firm, echoing the voice of a Drill Instructor: "What are you doing? This is not you; this is not the man you have become. You don't leave things unfinished."

With renewed determination, I juggled an incredibly stressful schedule, managing my responsibilities at work while pursuing my degree. In May 2018, I finally completed my degree. The sense of accomplishment was overwhelming—I was thrilled to have finished the mission, yet heartbroken that my mother wasn't there to share in the moment.

In 2019, another opportunity presented itself—a chance to be closer to my family in New Hampshire. I joined Volvo Group North America as the Security Director for the North Region, overseeing all of Canada.

This move was both a personal and professional milestone, allowing me to be near my family while stepping into a director-level position. Later that year, I applied for a senior leadership role with Tanger, headquartered in Greensboro, NC. Although I lacked a retail background, I emphasized that my diverse experience in the military, law enforcement, executive protection, and corporate security would bring fresh perspectives to the role. My background enabled me to introduce innovative solutions, such as utilizing robots and drones to enhance security. Today,

I serve as the Senior Director of Corporate Security Operations for Tanger. My responsibilities include executive protection, overseeing the Corporate Security Operations Center (CSOC), and managing both physical and technical security. Reflecting on my journey, I realize that adaptability and continuous learning have been the cornerstones of my career. These qualities enabled me to navigate complex challenges and seize new opportunities.

My journey from Valero Energy Corporation to my current role at Tanger demonstrates the vital importance of these qualities. When faced with the need for further education to advance, I embraced the challenge, pursuing a degree that not only enhanced my qualifications but also opened doors to new career opportunities. I learned that adaptability isn't just about coping with change—it's about embracing it, evolving your skillset, and continuously seeking new knowledge to stay relevant in an ever-changing world.

This mindset has been essential in allowing me to bring innovative solutions to the roles I've taken on, ensuring that I remain a valuable asset to the organizations I serve. For anyone transitioning from military or law enforcement to a corporate role, the ability to adapt and commit to lifelong learning is crucial. These qualities not only help you meet the immediate demands of a new job but also position you for long-term success in your career.

The Importance of Adaptability and Continuous Learning

Embracing Change

Adaptability and continuous learning are crucial in today's fast-paced and ever-changing corporate environment.

My journey from military and law enforcement to corporate security highlights the importance of being flexible and open to new challenges. When I transitioned to Valero's flagship refinery in Port Arthur, TX, I quickly realized the necessity of further education to advance my career. This shift required me to adapt my mindset and embrace the challenge of balancing work, school, and personal life.

Evolving Skillsets

Adapting to new roles often involves evolving one's skillset to meet the demands of different environments. In my case, obtaining a degree in Justice Studies with a concentration in Terrorism and Homeland Security was a strategic decision to enhance my qualifications and align them with corporate requirements. The discipline and resilience developed in the military and law enforcement were pivotal in successfully managing my academic and professional responsibilities.

Continuous Learning

Continuous learning is not just about acquiring new knowledge; it's about staying relevant in a competitive job market. The decision to go back to school and complete my degree, even amid personal challenges, underscores the importance of lifelong learning.

This commitment to education not only prepared me for career advancement but also demonstrated to potential employers my dedication to personal and professional growth.

Navigating Personal Challenges

Balancing personal challenges while pursuing professional goals is a reality many face. My experience of juggling a demanding job, full-time school and the emotional burden of my mother's illness taught me the value of resilience and the importance of a strong support network. The ability to navigate these challenges without losing sight of long-term goals is a testament to the power of adaptability and continuous learning.

Leveraging Experience

Translating military and law enforcement experience into corporate language is an essential skill for veterans transitioning into civilian roles. When I joined Tanger, I leveraged my background in executive protection and corporate security to introduce innovative solutions. My diverse experience allowed me to bring fresh perspectives that elevated the security program in ways not commonly seen in the retail environment.

The Role of Support Networks

Having a strong support network is crucial for overcoming challenges and achieving success. During the most challenging periods of my career and personal life, the support of friends and colleagues was invaluable. They provided the encouragement and assistance needed to stay focused on my goals and complete my degree. This network played a significant role in helping me navigate the complexities of balancing work, school, and personal responsibilities.

Applying Military Discipline

The discipline and structure learned in the military are highly transferable to the corporate world. These attributes were instrumental in my ability to manage a demanding schedule and complete my degree. The military teaches you to prioritize tasks, work under pressure, and maintain a high level of performance—all skills that are equally valuable in a corporate setting.

Innovating with New Perspectives

Bringing new perspectives to a corporate role can drive innovation and improvement. My experience in military and law enforcement enabled me to introduce unconventional solutions at Tanger, such as utilizing robots and drones for security purposes. This innovative approach not only enhanced the security program but also demonstrated the value of diverse experiences in driving organizational success.

Lifelong Commitment to Growth

Adapting and evolving in one's career is an ongoing process. My journey from Valero to Volvo Group North America and then to Tanger reflects a lifelong commitment to growth and learning. Each transition required me to develop new skills, embrace new challenges, and continuously seek opportunities for improvement. This mindset is essential for anyone looking to succeed in today's dynamic corporate environment.

Practical Exercises for Identifying Transferable Skills

➤ **Skill Inventory Exercise:** Start by listing all skills acquired through professional and personal experiences, categorizing them into technical, soft, and leadership skills. Reflect on specific instances where these skills were demonstrated and consider their application in different contexts. For example, leadership skills from managing a military team can translate to corporate team management.

➤ **SWOT Analysis**: Conduct a SWOT analysis to evaluate your Strengths, Weaknesses, Opportunities, and Threats.

Identify your strengths and areas for improvement, and consider external opportunities and threats in your career. This will help you understand where your skills excel and where you might need development.

➤ **Value Identification Worksheet**: List the values most important to you in a work environment, such as teamwork, innovation, or continuous improvement. Understanding your core values can help align your skills with potential career paths and organizations.

➤ **360-Degree Feedback:** Request feedback from a range of peers, supervisors, and subordinates to get a comprehensive view of how others perceive your skills and abilities. This holistic feedback can reveal strengths and areas for improvement you might not have noticed.

➤ **Skill-Specific Feedback Sessions:** Organize feedback sessions focusing on specific skills. For example, seek feedback on your leadership skills by asking for examples of both strong performance and areas for improvement. This targeted feedback offers deeper insights into particular aspects of your skillset.

➤ **Mentorship Feedback**: Find a mentor who has successfully transitioned from a similar background. Their feedback and guidance can provide valuable insights on navigating your transition and identifying crucial skills for success.

➤ **Developing an Action Plan:** Create an action plan based on the self-assessment and peer feedback. Set specific, measurable goals for acquiring or enhancing skills. For example, if a weakness in public speaking is identified, set a goal to join a public speaking group or take a course.

➤ **Documenting Your Skills:** Summarize your findings from the self-assessment tools and peer feedback in a document. Include key transferable skills, examples of demonstrations, and alignment with your career goals. This document can be useful for updating your resume and preparing for job interviews.

➤ **Regular Review and Adjustment:** Treat these exercises as ongoing processes. Regularly review and adjust your action plan based on new experiences and feedback to stay aligned with your evolving career path and goals.

By engaging in these practical exercises, readers can gain a clearer understanding of their transferable skills, how to articulate them, and how to apply them effectively in new career contexts.

In conclusion, successfully adapting military or law enforcement skills to corporate security roles requires strategic communication and continuous learning. By identifying and translating these transferable skills, professionals can demonstrate their value in new contexts. Embracing adaptability and ongoing development ensures that their expertise remains relevant and impactful, ultimately leading to a fulfilling and successful transition into the corporate world.

Chapter 4: Navigating Corporate Culture

"When your values are clear to you, making decisions becomes easier."
– Roy. E Disney

Entering the corporate world felt like stepping into a foreign land, where the rules, language, and unspoken codes of conduct were entirely different from what I had known. Coming from a background in military and law enforcement, I was used to a structured environment with clear commands and decisive actions. However, in the corporate setting, I quickly learned that success required more than just discipline and determination. It demanded an understanding of subtle nuances, a keen sense of emotional intelligence, and the ability to navigate complex social dynamics. This journey was not just about adapting to a new role but transforming how I approached leadership and collaboration.

Transitioning from Law Enforcement to the Corporate World

Stepping into the corporate world felt like entering a different universe. As someone who had spent years in the structured environments of the military and law enforcement, I know that the transition to a corporate setting was not only a career shift but also a significant cultural adjustment. The change was more profound than I had anticipated, touching every aspect of my work life—from communication styles to decision-making processes, team dynamics, and even my approach to work-life balance. In my first few months as a senior leader in corporate security, I experienced several moments of culture shock that highlighted just how different these two worlds were. The military and law enforcement are environments where clarity, precision, and hierarchy are paramount. Orders are given and followed without question, and the chain of command is respected without hesitation. In contrast, the corporate world values collaboration, inclusivity, and a more nuanced approach to leadership.

One of my earliest experiences of culture shock occurred during a routine meeting where I noticed some inefficiencies in our existing procedures. Drawing on my background, I addressed the issue directly. In the military, direct communication is valued—it's clear, concise, and leaves no room for ambiguity. I was accustomed to issuing commands that were meant to be executed immediately. So, I said to one of my team members, *"These procedures are outdated and ineffective. We need to change them immediately. James, I want you to draft a new protocol by the end of the day."*

To my surprise, the reaction in the room was not what I expected. The atmosphere shifted, and I could sense unease among my colleagues. Later, I received feedback from my manager that my approach had been perceived as abrupt and intimidating. It was clear that I hadn't taken the time to involve the team in the decision-making process or explain the reasons behind the changes. This was a stark contrast to the environments

I had previously worked in, where such directness would have been seen as efficient and necessary. In the corporate world, communication isn't just about giving orders—it's about fostering collaboration and ensuring that everyone feels included in the process. I learned that it's important to invite input and encourage dialogue, even when the task at hand is urgent. If I had approached the situation differently, perhaps by saying, *"I've noticed that some of our current procedures might not be as effective as they could be. I'd like us to take a closer look and consider potential improvements. James, could you work on drafting some suggestions for us to review together by the end of the day?"*—the outcome might have been more positive. This experience taught me the importance of adapting my communication style to fit the collaborative culture of the corporate world.

Another significant difference I encountered was in the decision-making process. In law enforcement, decisions are often made quickly and executed with precision. There's a sense of urgency, and the expectation is that once a decision is made, it's implemented without delay. However, in the corporate world, I found that decision-making is a much more complex and collaborative process.

I remember being tasked with implementing a new security system across multiple company locations. I assumed that once the decision was made, we would move swiftly to deployment, just as we would have in law enforcement. However, I quickly realized that this was not the case. Instead of a straightforward rollout, the process involved numerous meetings with different departments—IT, finance, operations, and HR—all of whom had their perspectives and concerns.

Each department needed to weigh in on various aspects of the implementation. IT wanted to ensure system compatibility, finance was concerned about the budget, operations needed to assess the impact on daily activities, and HR focused on how the changes would affect employees. What I thought would be a simple decision turned out to be a lengthy, multi-faceted process that required careful consideration of numerous factors.

This experience highlighted the importance of collaboration and cross-departmental input in the corporate world. While this approach can be frustrating for someone used to rapid decision-making, it ultimately leads to better outcomes. By taking the time to gather input and build consensus, we were able to identify potential issues early on, avoid costly mistakes, and ensure that the implementation was smooth and successful. It was a valuable lesson in the importance of patience and thoroughness—qualities that are essential in the corporate environment.

Team dynamics also proved to be different in ways I hadn't anticipated. In the military, the team is everything. There's an unspoken understanding that your success—and sometimes your survival—depends on the unity, cohesion, and unwavering support of your team members. This sense of mutual reliance is ingrained in every mission and operation.

When I entered the corporate world, I expected to find a similar level of friendship and mutual support within my new team. However, I quickly realized that the dynamics were different. While teamwork is certainly valued in the corporate environment, there's a stronger emphasis on individual achievement and recognition. Team members were often more focused on their own goals, performance metrics, and career advancement than on the collective success of the team. This was a stark contrast to the unconditional support and shared mission focus that I was accustomed to.

I had to learn to navigate and foster a team culture that valued both collaboration and individual contributions. I worked to create an environment where team members felt supported in their individual goals while remaining committed to the success of the team as a whole. This involved encouraging open communication, regular feedback, and aligning team objectives with individual aspirations. It was a balancing act—one that required me to adapt my leadership style to ensure that both the team and its members could thrive.

Another area where I had to adjust was the use of formalities. In the military, formalities are not just a matter of tradition; they are crucial for maintaining order, discipline, and respect. Addressing others by rank or title, saluting, and adhering to strict protocols were second nature to me. When I first entered the corporate world, I expected a similar level of formality. I continued to use formal titles when addressing my colleagues and maintained a formal demeanor in meetings and interactions. However, it didn't take long for me to realize that this approach was out of place. The corporate environment was far more casual. Regardless of rank or position, colleagues addressed each other by first name. The atmosphere was more relaxed, and there was a clear emphasis on approachability and open communication. I began to notice that my use of formal titles and my rigid demeanor sometimes made others feel uncomfortable or created a sense of distance that wasn't conducive to the collaborative culture I was now part of.

This experience taught me an important lesson about the cultural shift between the military and corporate environments. While respect is still a cornerstone of professional interactions, in the corporate world, it's often expressed through more casual and informal means. I learned that being approachable and building rapport with my colleagues was key to effective leadership and collaboration.

Workplace hierarchy was another area where I had to make significant adjustments. In law enforcement, the hierarchy is rigid and well-defined. There's a clear chain of command, and respecting authority is non-negotiable. Orders from superiors are expected to be followed without question, and this structure ensures discipline and efficiency in high-stakes situations. When I first entered the corporate world, I anticipated a similar hierarchical structure. I took a top-down approach to leadership, expecting my team members to execute instructions with minimal discussion, just as I had done in my previous roles. However, I quickly discovered that the corporate environment operated very differently.

In the corporate world, the hierarchy is often flatter, and employees at all levels are encouraged to provide input, challenge ideas, and contribute to decision-making processes. My initial top-down approach was met with hesitation and even pushback from some team members, who felt that their perspectives weren't being valued. What I had intended as clear leadership was perceived as too authoritarian, and it became evident that a different approach was needed.

I began to involve my team in decision-making processes, actively seeking their input and encouraging open discussions before finalizing any decisions. I shifted from a purely directive leadership style to one that emphasizes mentorship, coaching, and empowering others to take ownership of their work. This approach not only improved team morale but also led to better outcomes, as diverse perspectives were considered in every decision. It was a significant adjustment, but one that ultimately made me a more effective leader. Finally, one of the most significant adjustments I had to make was in learning to navigate the concept of work-life balance. In the military, the demands are relentless. Long hours and a high level of commitment are often the norm, with personal time and family life frequently taking a back seat to duty. I carried this mindset into my new corporate role, believing that the same level of sacrifice was required to succeed. When I first entered the corporate world, I maintained a rigorous work schedule, often prioritizing work over my personal life. I believed that putting in long hours was the key to making a strong impression and achieving success. However, it didn't take long for me to notice a stark difference in the corporate culture.

I observed that my colleagues placed a much higher value on work-life balance. Many of them were diligent about using their vacation days, making time for family, and pursuing personal interests outside of work. This was a foreign concept to me, coming from an environment where personal sacrifices were often seen as part of the job.

The real shift in my perspective came when I noticed that even my superiors encouraged maintaining a healthy work-life balance. They emphasized that long-term success wasn't just about working hard; it was also about ensuring you had the energy and well-being to sustain that effort over time. I realized that taking time for myself and my family wasn't just permissible—it was necessary for maintaining productivity, creativity, and overall job satisfaction. This was a valuable lesson that took time to fully integrate into my life. Gradually, I learned to set boundaries, delegate tasks, and take time off when needed. Embracing work-life balance not only improved my well-being but also made me more effective in my role. It was a reminder that success isn't just about how much you work—it's about how well you work and how you sustain that effort over the long term. Reflecting on these experiences, I've come to appreciate the profound differences between the military law enforcement and corporate worlds. Each environment has its own set of values, norms, and expectations, and navigating these differences has been a journey of growth and adaptation. While the transition wasn't always easy, it has taught me valuable lessons about leadership, communication, and the importance of flexibility.

The skills and experiences I brought from my previous roles have been invaluable, but so, too, have the new perspectives I've gained in the corporate world. It's a reminder that no matter where you find yourself, the ability to adapt and grow is key to success.

Mastering Emotional Intelligence in the Corporate Environment

Emotional intelligence (EI) plays a crucial role in navigating the corporate environment, where success is often determined not only by technical skills but also by the ability to understand and manage emotions—both one's own and those of others. In the corporate world, where teamwork, collaboration, and communication are paramount, EI becomes an essential asset for any professional aiming to excel.

One of the most important aspects of emotional intelligence is the ability to read social cues. In a corporate setting, interactions are often nuanced, with unspoken expectations and subtle signals that can significantly impact relationships and outcomes. For instance, understanding body language, tone of voice, and facial expressions can provide valuable insights into a colleague's or superior's true feelings, even when their words suggest otherwise. This awareness allows for more effective communication and helps in avoiding potential conflicts or misunderstandings. To improve your ability to read social cues, developing a habit of active observation is essential. Pay attention not only to what people say but also to how they say it. Are they maintaining eye contact, or do they seem distracted? Is their tone of voice consistent with their message, or is there an underlying tension? By honing your ability to pick up on these subtleties, you can respond more appropriately to the emotional undercurrents in your workplace.

Managing relationships is another critical component of emotional intelligence in the corporate environment. Building and maintaining positive relationships with colleagues, superiors, and subordinates is key to fostering a supportive and productive work atmosphere. Effective relationship management requires a combination of empathy, active listening, and clear communication.

Empathy, or the ability to understand and share the feelings of others, is particularly important. In the corporate world, where diverse teams often work together, understanding different perspectives and responding with empathy can help bridge gaps and build trust. For example, if a team member is struggling with a project, showing empathy by offering support and understanding rather than criticism can strengthen your relationship and encourage a collaborative approach to problem-solving. Active listening is equally important in managing relationships. In a busy corporate environment, it's easy to fall into the trap of half-listening while thinking about your response or the next task on your to-do list.

However, truly listening to others—focusing on their words, asking clarifying questions, and acknowledging their feelings—can make a significant difference in how you are perceived. It shows that you value their input and are genuinely interested in their perspective, which can enhance your credibility and influence within the organization.

Navigating office politics is another area where emotional intelligence is invaluable. Office politics can be complex and sometimes uncomfortable, but they are an inevitable part of corporate life. Understanding the dynamics of power, influence, and alliances within your organization is crucial for advancing your career while maintaining your integrity. To navigate office politics effectively, it's important to remain aware of the informal networks and relationships that exist within your company. Identify key influencers and decision-makers and observe how they interact with others. Building alliances with these individuals can be beneficial, but it's equally important to maintain a reputation for fairness and integrity. Avoid becoming entangled in gossip or negative behavior, as this can damage your credibility and relationships.

Another strategy for navigating office politics is to maintain a level of emotional detachment. While it's important to be empathetic and build strong relationships, it's also crucial not to take things too personally. Office politics can be unpredictable, and decisions or actions may sometimes seem unfair or biased. By keeping a level-headed and objective perspective, you can better manage your emotions and make more rational decisions that align with your long-term goals.

Strategies for Adapting to and Thriving in Corporate Culture

Adapting to and thriving in corporate culture is a skill that requires both self-awareness and social acumen. As corporate environments become increasingly global and diverse, the ability to navigate and succeed within these spaces hinges not just on technical proficiency but also on cultural sensitivity, rapport-building, and an understanding of the often-unwritten rules of corporate etiquette.

Building Rapport with Colleagues from Diverse Backgrounds

One of the most important strategies for thriving in corporate culture is building strong rapport with colleagues, particularly those from diverse backgrounds. As companies become more globalized, teams are often composed of individuals from various cultural, linguistic, and social backgrounds. This diversity is a strength, bringing a wide range of perspectives and ideas, but it also requires a nuanced approach to communication and relationship-building.

To build rapport with colleagues from diverse backgrounds, it's essential to start with genuine curiosity and respect for their experiences and perspectives. This involves being open-minded and willing to learn about different cultures, traditions, and communication styles. For example, some cultures may value direct communication, while others may prefer a more indirect approach. Understanding these differences can help you communicate more effectively and avoid potential misunderstandings.

Active listening is another key component of building rapport. When interacting with colleagues from different backgrounds, make an effort to listen more than you speak. This not only shows respect for their opinions but also gives you a better understanding of their viewpoints. Additionally, being an active listener involves paying attention to non-verbal cues, such as body language and tone of voice, which can vary significantly across cultures.

Another important aspect of building rapport is finding common ground. Despite cultural differences, there are often shared values or interests that can serve as a foundation for stronger relationships. Whether it's a shared passion for a particular hobby, a common professional goal, or a mutual commitment to the company's mission, identifying these commonalities can help bridge cultural gaps and foster a sense of camaraderie.

Empathy is also crucial in cross-cultural interactions. Understanding the challenges and barriers that colleagues from different backgrounds may face, such as language difficulties or cultural adjustments, can help you offer support and create an inclusive environment. Empathy also helps recognize the value of different perspectives, which can lead to more innovative and effective problem-solving.

Interpreting the Unwritten Rules of Corporate Etiquette

In addition to building rapport, thriving in corporate culture also requires an understanding of the unwritten rules of corporate etiquette. These unspoken norms and expectations can vary widely from one organization to another, and learning to navigate them effectively can make a significant difference in your career success.

One of the first steps in interpreting these unwritten rules is observation. Pay close attention to how people in your organization behave, particularly those who are well-respected and successful. Notice how they communicate, how they dress, how they handle conflicts, and how they interact with others in meetings and social settings. These behaviors often provide valuable clues about the corporate culture and the expectations that come with it. For example, some companies may have a more formal culture where professional attire and hierarchical communication are the norms. In contrast, others may have a more casual and collaborative environment where open communication and flexible dress codes are encouraged. Understanding these nuances helps you align your behavior with the company's expectations, which can enhance your professional image and credibility.

Another important aspect of corporate etiquette is understanding the balance between self-promotion and humility. While it's important to advocate for your achievements and contributions, doing so in a way that is perceived as boastful or overly aggressive can backfire. In many corporate cultures, subtlety and tact are valued, so finding the right balance is key. One approach is to focus on highlighting the impact of your work on the team or organization rather than solely on your achievements. Time management and punctuality are also critical components of corporate etiquette. Respecting deadlines, arriving on time for meetings, and being mindful of others' time all demonstrate professionalism and reliability. In some corporate cultures, lateness or missed deadlines can be interpreted as a lack of respect or commitment, so it's important to be aware of these expectations and adhere to them consistently.

Another unwritten rule of corporate etiquette is the importance of building and maintaining a professional network. In many organizations, networking is not just about who you know but how you cultivate and manage those relationships.

This involves staying in regular contact with key colleagues, offering help and support when needed, and being a resource to others. Networking is not just an external activity; it's also about building internal alliances and being seen as a team player. Lastly, interpreting corporate etiquette involves understanding the company's approach to feedback and criticism. In some organizations, direct feedback is encouraged and seen as a way to foster growth and improvement. In others, feedback may be delivered more cautiously, and criticism may be implied rather than stated outright. Understanding how your company handles feedback can help you respond appropriately and use it to your advantage.

Thriving in Corporate Culture

Thriving in corporate culture requires a combination of social intelligence, adaptability, and strategic thinking. By building rapport with colleagues from diverse backgrounds, you create a foundation of trust and mutual respect that enhances teamwork and collaboration. At the same time, by interpreting and adhering to the unwritten rules of corporate etiquette, you align yourself with the organization's values and expectations, positioning yourself for success.

Ultimately, thriving in a corporate environment is about finding the balance between being true to yourself and adapting to the norms and expectations of the organization. It's about being aware of the impact your behavior has on others and making thoughtful decisions that contribute to both your success and the success of your team. By mastering these strategies, you can not only navigate the complexities of corporate culture but also excel in it, turning challenges into opportunities for growth and development.

In conclusion, reflecting on my journey through the corporate landscape, I realize that the most valuable lessons weren't found in any handbook or training manual. They came from the experiences, the challenges, and the moments of growth that shaped my understanding of what it truly means to lead and succeed in this environment. The transition wasn't easy, but it was necessary—a process of unlearning and relearning, of embracing vulnerability, and of finding strength in empathy. As I continue to navigate this world, I carry with me the wisdom that success is not just about what you achieve but how you achieve it and the relationships you build along the way.

Chapter 5: Building a New Professional Identity

Knowing others is intelligence.

Knowing yourself is true wisdom.

Mastering others is strength.

Mastering yourself is true power.
Lao Tzu - Ancient Chinese Philosopher

Redefining your professional identity is a crucial step when transitioning from military or law enforcement roles to the corporate world.

This shift not only involves adapting to a new environment but also grappling with the psychological challenges of leaving behind a well-established identity. Understanding these challenges and how to navigate them effectively is essential for a smooth transition.

In this chapter, we'll explore the importance of rebuilding your professional persona, leveraging past experiences, and crafting a new narrative that aligns with corporate expectations. Through practical exercises and strategic insights, you'll learn how to make this transition successfully.

Transitioning Identities: From Military and Law Enforcement to Corporate Persona

Redefining one's professional identity can be a profound and challenging process, particularly for those transitioning from a career in military or law enforcement to the corporate world. The shift involves not only adapting to new environments but also navigating complex psychological challenges associated with leaving behind a well-established identity. Understanding these challenges is crucial for a successful transition and for maintaining personal and professional well-being.

For individuals accustomed to military or law enforcement roles, their professional identity is deeply intertwined with their daily functions, values, and perceptions of themselves. This identity is often characterized by a clear sense of purpose, discipline, and adherence to a structured hierarchy. These roles come with defined expectations, rigorous routines, and a strong sense of camaraderie. The transition to the corporate world, where the culture and expectations can be vastly different, necessitates a significant shift in mindset and self-perception.

One of the primary psychological challenges in this transition is the feeling of loss. The familiar environment of military or law enforcement work, with its defined roles and responsibilities, is replaced by a new set of expectations and norms. This can lead to a sense of displacement and uncertainty about one's new role and contributions. The structured, mission-oriented mindset of the military or law enforcement may clash with the often more fluid and collaborative nature of corporate settings. Another challenge is the potential loss of status and authority. In the military or law enforcement, one's rank or position often commands respect and authority. In the corporate world, authority is less about formal rank and more about influence and expertise. This shift can be disorienting and may affect self-esteem and confidence. It is essential to recognize that while the sources of respect and authority may change, they can still be earned through demonstrating competence, building relationships, and contributing effectively in the new role.

According to the study *"Human Resources Challenges of Military to Civilian Employment Transitions"* (2020), veterans face significant challenges when moving to civilian roles. Key findings include:

> **Identity Shift:** Approximately 68% of veterans reported difficulty adjusting their professional identity from military to civilian contexts, often experiencing a sense of loss regarding their previous status and rank.

> **Employment Outcomes**: 45% encountered issues aligning their military skills with civilian job requirements, leading to job dissatisfaction and lower retention rates.

> **Adaptation Strategies**: Veterans who utilized career counseling and professional development resources reported better job satisfaction and career advancement. Additionally, emotional and psychological support was crucial for successful adaptation, with those accessing

such resources experiencing higher satisfaction and resilience.

The adjustment to new interpersonal dynamics is also a significant factor. In military or law enforcement environments, interactions are often governed by strict protocols and established hierarchies. The corporate world, however, tends to emphasize collaborative teamwork and informal communication styles. This requires adapting to new ways of interacting with colleagues and superiors, which can be challenging for those used to a more formal or hierarchical structure. Developing new communication skills and understanding the subtleties of corporate culture are crucial for building positive professional relationships.

Furthermore, the sense of mission and purpose that is often central to military or law enforcement careers may be less apparent in corporate roles. In these professions, the focus is typically on achieving specific objectives and contributing to a larger goal. The corporate world, while still having goals and targets, may not always offer the same sense of immediate, tangible outcomes.

This can lead to feelings of frustration or lack of fulfillment. Finding new ways to connect personal values and career goals with the corporate mission is essential for maintaining motivation and job satisfaction. Adapting to a new professional identity also involves recalibrating personal expectations. The skills and experiences gained in military or law enforcement careers are valuable but may need to be reinterpreted to fit the corporate context. It is important to recognize that not all skills transfer directly and that there may be a learning curve in acquiring new competencies relevant to the corporate environment. This can be a humbling experience but is a necessary part of the transition.

Developing a new professional identity involves a process of self-discovery and growth. It requires acknowledging and leveraging the strengths gained from previous experiences while being open to new learning opportunities and perspectives. Engaging in professional development, seeking mentorship, and actively participating in networking opportunities can facilitate this process. Building a new identity in the corporate world is about integrating past experiences with new skills and adapting to the evolving demands of the new role.

Integrating Military and Law Enforcement Achievements into Corporate Success

Leveraging past experiences while embracing new roles involves a strategic approach to integrating achievements from military or law enforcement backgrounds into a corporate narrative. This process is crucial for veterans and professionals transitioning from these fields, as it allows them to highlight their strengths and adapt their skills to new environments. Understanding how to effectively present these experiences can significantly impact career success in the corporate world.

Military and law enforcement professionals bring a wealth of valuable experience to the corporate sector. Skills such as leadership, problem-solving, and crisis management are highly transferable and can be applied to a variety of corporate roles.

According to a report by the U.S. Chamber of Commerce Foundation, 80% of employers believe that military veterans possess strong leadership skills, while 77% recognize their ability to work well under pressure (U.S. Chamber of Commerce Foundation, 2018). These attributes are essential in corporate settings, where decision-making and effective management are crucial.

Framework for Integrating Achievements into a Corporate Narrative

Identify Transferable Skills: The first step in leveraging military or law enforcement experience is to identify skills that are transferable to the corporate world. These include strategic planning, team management, risk assessment, and operational efficiency. For example, a military officer's experience in strategic planning and mission execution can be translated into project management and strategic development roles in a corporate setting. According to a study by the Institute for Veterans and Military Families, 85% of veterans believe their military experience has prepared them well for civilian jobs, particularly in leadership and problem-solving (Institute for Veterans and Military Families, 2019).

Translate Achievements into Business Terms: Once transferable skills are identified, it's important to translate achievements into business language. This means framing military or law enforcement accomplishments in terms that resonate with corporate employers. For instance, instead of describing a role as a "Platoon Leader," it could be framed as "Managed a team of 30 personnel, overseeing operations and ensuring mission success under high-pressure conditions." This approach helps highlight relevant experience in a manner that aligns with corporate expectations.

Develop a Strong Professional Brand: Crafting a compelling professional brand is crucial in establishing a new identity in the corporate world. This involves creating a narrative that integrates past experiences with future career goals. For example, a former law enforcement officer might focus on their expertise in risk management and security, positioning themselves as a valuable asset in roles related to corporate security, compliance, or crisis management. According to LinkedIn's Veteran Hiring Report, 60% of veterans who effectively communicated their military skills and achievements in their resumes and LinkedIn profiles secured interviews within three months (LinkedIn, 2020).

Utilize Networking and Mentorship: Building a professional network and seeking mentorship are essential strategies for integrating into the corporate world. Networking can provide valuable connections, insights, and opportunities, while mentorship offers guidance and support during the transition. The National Veterans Transition Services, Inc. reports that veterans who engage in mentorship programs are 50% more likely to find meaningful employment compared to those who do not (National Veterans Transition Services, Inc., 2021). Engaging with industry-specific networks and veteran support organizations can also facilitate a smoother transition.

Showcase Adaptability and Continuous Learning: Demonstrating adaptability and a commitment to continuous learning is important for successfully integrating into a new role. Employers value candidates who are willing to learn and adapt to new environments. For example, a veteran who undertakes additional training or certifications relevant to their new industry shows a proactive approach to career development. According to a report by the Veterans Employment and Training Service, veterans who pursue additional education and professional development opportunities are 30% more likely to achieve career advancement within the first year of employment (Veterans Employment and Training Service, 2019).

Highlight Achievements with Quantifiable Results: When presenting achievements, it's beneficial to highlight results with quantifiable metrics. This could include improvements in operational efficiency, cost savings, or successful project completions. For example, a former military logistics officer might detail how they managed supply chains with a 20% reduction in costs and a 15% increase in delivery efficiency. Such metrics provide concrete evidence of one's capabilities and contributions.

Address Gaps and Overcome Challenges: It is also important to address any perceived gaps or challenges that may arise during the transition. This could involve addressing concerns about industry-specific knowledge or experience. By proactively discussing how past experiences can be adapted to meet the needs of the new role and by showcasing a willingness to bridge any gaps through additional training or collaboration, professionals can overcome potential obstacles.

Craft a Tailored Resume and Cover Letter: A tailored resume and cover letter that effectively communicates how military or law enforcement experiences align with corporate roles can significantly impact job search success. Tailoring these documents to reflect the skills and achievements relevant to the desired position helps make a strong case for potential employers. A study by the Military Transition Network found that veterans who customized their resumes to align with job descriptions were 40% more likely to receive interview invitations (Military Transition Network, 2020).

Integrating military or law enforcement achievements into a corporate narrative involves identifying transferable skills, translating accomplishments into business terms, developing a strong professional brand, and utilizing networking and mentorship. By highlighting adaptability, continuous learning, and quantifiable results, veterans can effectively position themselves for success in the corporate world. Addressing gaps and crafting tailored application materials further enhances their chances of securing a rewarding career.

Personal Branding in the Corporate World

Personal branding is a crucial element of career development in the corporate world. It involves creating a professional identity that effectively communicates one's skills, values, and unique qualities. A strong personal brand can significantly impact job prospects, professional relationships, and career advancement. To build a compelling personal brand, one must focus on several key areas: developing an engaging LinkedIn profile, crafting an impactful elevator pitch, and maintaining a consistent professional image.

Developing a Compelling LinkedIn Profile

LinkedIn has become a fundamental platform for professional networking and job searching. A well-crafted LinkedIn profile can be a powerful tool for establishing and promoting your brand. Here are key elements to focus on:

➢ **Profile Photo and Headline:** Your profile photo is often the first impression you make on potential employers or networking contacts. Choose a high-quality, professional photo that presents you in a positive light. It should be clear, with good lighting, and feature you dressed in business attire. Alongside your photo, your headline should succinctly capture your professional identity. Instead of just listing your job title, consider using a headline that highlights your key skills and value proposition. For instance, "Experienced Marketing Strategist | Specializing in Digital Campaigns and Brand Development" provides a clearer picture of your expertise.

➢ **Summary Section:** The summary section of your LinkedIn profile is your opportunity to tell your professional story. Start with a strong opening statement that captures your core strengths and career goals. Use this space to highlight your achievements, skills, and what makes you unique. Incorporate keywords relevant to your industry and the roles you are targeting. This approach not only helps in making your profile stand out but also improves its visibility in search results. According to LinkedIn data, profiles with detailed summaries receive 10 times more profile views than those without (LinkedIn, 2021).

➢ **Experience and Achievements:** In the experience section, detail your professional history with a focus on accomplishments rather than just job duties. Use bullet points to outline your key achievements, quantifying results where possible. For instance, rather than stating "Managed marketing campaigns," specify "Led marketing campaigns that increased brand engagement by 30% and boosted sales by 15%." Including metrics provides concrete evidence of your contributions and effectiveness.

➢ **Skills and Endorsements:** List skills that are pertinent to your industry and career goals. LinkedIn allows connections to endorse these skills, which can lend credibility to your expertise. Actively seek endorsements from colleagues, supervisors, and clients to strengthen this aspect of your profile. Studies show that profiles with endorsed skills receive 13 times more profile views than those without (LinkedIn, 2020).

➢ **Recommendations:** Recommendations from former employers, clients, or colleagues can add significant weight to your LinkedIn profile. Request recommendations from individuals who can speak to your work ethic, skills, and achievements. A strong recommendation provides third-party validation of your professional capabilities and can enhance your credibility.

Crafting an Impactful Elevator Pitch

An elevator pitch is a brief, persuasive speech that you can use to spark interest in what you do. It should be concise, engaging, and tailored to your audience. Here's how to craft an effective elevator pitch:

➢ **Start with a Hook:** Begin your pitch with a compelling hook that grabs attention. This could be a unique aspect of your background, a notable achievement, or a problem you solve. For example, "I help companies streamline their operations to reduce costs and improve efficiency, using innovative technology solutions."

➤ **Highlight Your Value Proposition:** Clearly articulate what makes you unique and how you add value. Focus on the skills and experiences that differentiate you from others in your field. For instance, "With over a decade of experience in data analysis and a track record of turning complex data into actionable insights, I help businesses make informed decisions that drive growth."

➤ **Include a Personal Touch:** Adding a personal element to your pitch can make it more memorable. Share a brief story or personal insight that illustrates your passion and dedication. For example, "After working on a high-stakes project that saved my previous company $500,000, I realized how much I enjoy tackling challenging problems and delivering tangible results."

➤ **End with a Call to Action:** Conclude your pitch with a clear call to action, such as requesting a follow-up meeting or offering to provide more information. This helps direct the conversation toward the next steps. For example, "I'd love to discuss how my expertise can benefit your organization. Can we schedule a time to chat further?"

Building a Consistent Professional Image

Maintaining a consistent professional image is vital for reinforcing your brand. Your professional image encompasses your appearance, behavior, and online presence. Here's how to ensure consistency across these areas:

➢ **Professional Appearance:** Your appearance should align with the expectations of your industry. Invest in high-quality, appropriate attire that reflects a professional image. Consistency in your dress code, whether it's business formal or business casual, helps create a coherent professional persona.

➢ **Behavior and Communication:** Your behavior and communication style should reflect the values and standards of your profession. This includes being punctual, respectful, and effective in both verbal and written communication. Demonstrating professionalism in every interaction helps build a positive reputation and reinforces your brand.

➢ **Online Presence:** Ensure that your online presence, including social media profiles and professional websites, aligns with your brand. Regularly update your profiles to reflect your current role, achievements, and career goals. Maintain a professional tone in your online interactions, and be mindful of the content you share.

➢ **Networking and Engagement:** Actively participate in industry-related events, both online and offline. Engaging with professional communities and contributing valuable insights helps build your reputation as a thought leader. Consistent involvement in relevant discussions and forums reinforces your professional image and expands your network.

Regularly seek feedback from peers, mentors, and industry professionals to refine your brand. Constructive feedback helps identify areas for improvement and ensures that your branding efforts are effective. Additionally, staying updated on industry trends and continuously enhancing your skills contribute to maintaining a strong, relevant personal brand.

By focusing on these areas, you can develop a compelling personal brand that enhances your professional presence and supports your career goals.

Let's end the chapter with practical exercises that can help you actively engage in crafting your new professional narrative. These exercises focus on storytelling techniques and developing a personal mission statement, essential tools for creating a compelling and authentic professional identity. Here are some structured exercises to guide readers in this process:

Exercise 1: Crafting Your Personal Story

Identify Key Experiences: Begin by listing significant experiences in your career that have shaped your professional journey. Consider achievements, challenges, and pivotal moments. For example, think about a major project you led, a difficult problem you solved, or an impactful role you held.

Highlight Core Values and Skills: For each key experience, identify the core values and skills you demonstrated. Reflect on what these experiences reveal about your strengths and professional ethos. For instance, if you successfully managed a team through a crisis, the skills you showcased might include leadership, resilience, and strategic thinking.

Create a Narrative Arc: Construct a narrative that weaves these experiences into a cohesive story. Start with an engaging introduction that sets the stage, describes the main events or challenges, and concludes with the outcomes and lessons learned. Ensure your story reflects your unique journey and highlights how your experiences have prepared you for future roles.

Refine and Practice: Write your narrative in a concise, engaging format. Practice delivering it in different contexts, such as during networking events, interviews, or introductions. Adjust your story based on feedback and your comfort level to ensure it effectively communicates your professional identity.

Exercise 2: Developing Your Mission Statement

Reflect on Your Core Values: Take time to reflect on what matters most to you in your professional life. Consider values like integrity, innovation, or collaboration. Write down your top three core values and think about how they influence your career decisions and goals.

Identify Your Unique Strengths and Skills: List the strengths and skills that set you apart in your field. This might include technical skills, leadership abilities, or specialized knowledge. Reflect on how these strengths contribute to your professional success and align with your values.

Define Your Professional Goals: Outline your long-term career goals and aspirations. Think about the impact you want to make in your industry or the achievements you hope to reach. Ensure your goals are specific, measurable, achievable, relevant, and time-bound (SMART).

Combine Values, Strengths, and Goals: Craft a mission statement that integrates your core values, unique strengths, and professional goals. A strong mission statement should be clear, concise, and reflective of your brand. For example: "My mission is to leverage my expertise in data analysis and passion for problem-solving to drive innovation and support data-driven decision-making while fostering a collaborative and inclusive work environment."

Review and Revise: Review your mission statement regularly and revise it as needed to reflect changes in your career goals or personal values. Ensure it remains aligned with your professional journey and serves as a guiding principle in your career development.

Exercise 3: Storytelling Techniques for Professional Narratives

Practice the "STAR" Method: Use the STAR (Situation, Task, Action, Result) method to structure your professional stories. This technique helps in clearly articulating your contributions and outcomes. For each key experience, describe the situation you faced, the task you were responsible for, the actions you took, and the results you achieved.

Incorporate Emotional Appeal: Effective storytelling often involves emotional appeal. Share stories that highlight not only your achievements but also your passion and commitment. For instance, describe a project that was particularly meaningful to you and explain why it mattered.

Use Concrete Examples: Provide specific examples to illustrate your points. Instead of general statements, use concrete data, anecdotes, or testimonials to back up your claims. For example, "I led a team to implement a new CRM system, resulting in a 25% increase in sales and a 30% improvement in customer satisfaction."

Maintain Authenticity: Authenticity is key to impactful storytelling. Be honest and genuine in your narratives, focusing on real experiences and true reflections of your professional journey. Authentic stories build trust and credibility with your audience.

Tailor Your Stories to Your Audience: Adapt your stories to fit the context and audience you are addressing. Consider what aspects of your experience will resonate most with your listeners, whether they are potential employers, clients, or colleagues.

Exercise 4: Personal Branding Feedback

Seek External Feedback: Share your personal narrative and mission statement with trusted colleagues, mentors, or career coaches. Request constructive feedback on how well these elements represent your professional identity and whether they effectively communicate your value.

Conduct Self-Assessment: Regularly assess your brand by reviewing your LinkedIn profile, elevator pitch, and professional interactions. Ensure they align with your desired professional image, and make adjustments as necessary.

Set Development Goals: Based on the feedback and self-assessment, set specific goals for further developing your brand.

This might include refining your narrative, expanding your professional network, or enhancing your skills.

By engaging in these exercises, readers can develop a strong personal brand that reflects their professional journey, values, and goals. Crafting a compelling narrative and personal mission statement not only enhances career opportunities but also provides a clear and authentic representation of one's professional identity.

In conclusion, successfully navigating the transition to a new professional identity requires more than just adapting to a different job environment; it involves a deep rethinking of how you present and perceive yourself. By leveraging your past experiences, embracing new roles, and continuously developing your brand, you can build a compelling corporate identity. Remember, this journey is about integrating your unique strengths into a new narrative that aligns with your career goals. With the tools and strategies outlined in this chapter, you are well-equipped to make a meaningful and impactful transition into the corporate world.

Chapter 6: Networking and Relationship Building

"Your network is your net worth."

— **Porter Gale**

In the corporate world, networking and relationship-building are pivotal skills that differ markedly from the built-in connections of military and law enforcement. Unlike the hierarchical and mission-focused networks of these fields, corporate networking demands a proactive and strategic approach.

Building and maintaining professional relationships is essential for career advancement, opening doors to opportunities, mentorship, and insights into company dynamics. This chapter explores the importance of these skills, offering strategies for effective networking, leveraging existing connections, and nurturing long-term professional relationships in the corporate environment.

Networking in the Corporate World vs. Military and Law Enforcement Networks

Transitioning from a structured military environment, where ranks and roles are well-defined, to the more fluid corporate world can feel like stepping into unfamiliar territory. Early on, I recognized that building relationships in the corporate sphere wasn't just about knowing the right people—it was about forming genuine connections and offering value to others. I recall one of my first corporate networking events, where I felt completely out of my element. Accustomed to mission-focused interactions, I was more of an observer than an active participant. However, when I found a group discussing a topic I was familiar with—risk management strategies in security—I decided to contribute insights from my military experience. This shift from observing to engaging was pivotal. My unique perspective, shaped by my background, resonated with others, and the initial discomfort of the event quickly faded.

From this experience, I learned the importance of consistency in relationship-building. I made it a habit to regularly check in with my connections, not just when I needed something but to offer assistance, share interesting articles, or simply catch up. This approach of reaching out without a hidden agenda helped me cultivate a strong, supportive network over time.

In transitioning from military and law enforcement to the corporate world, networking and relationship-building become essential skills. While these practices might seem unfamiliar or secondary to someone from a highly structured environment like the military, they are crucial for long-term career success in a corporate setting.

Networking in the corporate world differs significantly from the built-in networks found in military and law enforcement. In the military, relationships are often formed naturally through shared experiences and the strong bonds forged during training and missions. The hierarchical structure ensures that communication and relationships flow clearly and directly. However, in the corporate world, networking requires a more proactive approach. The structure is less rigid, and success often depends on the ability to build and maintain a wide range of professional relationships.

The importance of networking cannot be overstated in a corporate environment, unlike the military, where rank and experience largely determine career progression. In the corporate world, who you know can be just as important as what you know. Networking opens doors to opportunities that might not be available through formal channels. It allows individuals to connect with mentors, discover new career paths, and gain insights into the company's culture and dynamics.

Building these relationships requires skills different from those cultivated in the military. It involves active listening, empathy, and the ability to engage in conversations that might seem unstructured or informal. For someone accustomed to the direct and mission-focused communication style of the military, this can be challenging. However, developing these skills is essential for career growth in the corporate world. One key aspect of networking is understanding the importance of reciprocity. In the corporate world, relationships are often based on mutual benefit. Unlike the military, where the chain of command dictates interactions, corporate relationships are more fluid and require a give-and-take approach. Offering assistance, sharing knowledge, or providing support to colleagues can help build strong professional relationships. Over time, these relationships can lead to new opportunities, collaborations, and advancements.

Mentorship is another crucial component of networking in the corporate world. In the military, mentorship often happens organically through the chain of command. In contrast, in the corporate environment, seeking out and establishing a mentor-mentee relationship is often up to the individual. A mentor can provide guidance, offer insights into the corporate culture, and help navigate the complexities of the organization. They can also introduce the mentee to other key individuals within the company, further expanding their network.

Navigating office politics is another area where networking plays a critical role. In the military, decisions are made based on rank and protocol. In the corporate world, however, office politics often influence decision-making processes. Building relationships with key stakeholders, understanding the informal power structures, and being aware of the dynamics at play can help individuals navigate these complexities. Strong networks provide the support and information needed to make informed decisions and avoid potential pitfalls.

Networking also extends beyond the immediate workplace. In the corporate world, industry events, conferences, and professional associations offer opportunities to build relationships outside of the company. These external networks can be invaluable, providing access to new ideas, industry trends, and potential career opportunities. Engaging with professionals from other companies or industries can broaden one's perspective and open doors to new possibilities.

For someone transitioning from a military or law enforcement background, understanding the importance of relationship-building in the corporate world is crucial. It requires a shift in mindset from a focus on tasks and missions to a focus on people and relationships. While this might feel unfamiliar at first, it is an essential component of career success in the corporate environment.

Developing Professional Relationships: Strategies and Techniques

Building meaningful professional relationships in the corporate world involves more than just meeting people; it requires a deliberate approach to establishing and maintaining mutually beneficial connections. One of the key elements in this process is mastering the art of small talk, which serves as the foundation for deeper conversations and lasting relationships.

Small talk is often underestimated, yet it plays a crucial role in relationship-building. Engaging in small talk allows individuals to break the ice, establish rapport, and create a comfortable atmosphere for more meaningful interactions.

In the corporate setting, small talk often revolves around topics like current events, industry trends, or shared interests. To make small talk effective, it's important to be genuinely interested in the other person and to ask open-ended questions that encourage dialogue. For example, rather than asking, *"Did you enjoy the conference?"* a more engaging question might be, "What were your key takeaways from the conference?" This not only invites the other person to share their thoughts but also opens the door to a more substantial conversation.

An important aspect of small talk is active listening. According to a study by Weger, Castle, and Minei (2014), *"The Relative Effectiveness of Active Listening in Initial Interactions,"* active listening significantly enhances interpersonal relationships by improving mutual understanding and reducing conversational misunderstandings.

Active listening involves giving the speaker your full attention, nodding in agreement, and asking follow-up questions that show you're engaged in the conversation. This technique helps to build trust and shows the other person that you value their perspective, which is essential in laying the groundwork for a lasting professional relationship.

Following up after initial meetings is another critical strategy for building meaningful professional relationships. After meeting someone, whether at a conference, networking event or even a casual encounter, following up within 24 to 48 hours is advisable. This can be done through a brief email or a message on a professional networking platform like LinkedIn. The follow-up should be personalized, referencing something specific from your conversation to remind the person of who you are and to reinforce the connection.

For instance, you might say, *"It was great discussing [specific topic] with you at the event yesterday. I found your insights on [subject] particularly valuable and would love to continue the conversation."*

Effective follow-up also involves expressing a desire to keep in touch or suggesting a specific action, such as setting up a meeting or sharing an article related to your discussion. This demonstrates initiative and keeps the momentum of the relationship going. It's important to strike a balance between being proactive and respectful of the other person's time; being too aggressive in follow-ups can be off-putting, while too little follow-up can cause the connection to fade.

Nurturing long-term professional connections requires ongoing effort and engagement. One of the most effective ways to do this is by providing value to the other person. This could be in the form of sharing relevant information, introducing them to potential contacts, or offering support on projects.

The principle of reciprocity is key here—by helping others, you create goodwill that often leads to opportunities down the line. For example, if you come across an article that aligns with a colleague's interests or challenges, sending it with a note like,

"Thought you might find this interesting based on our recent conversation about [topic]," shows that you are thinking of them and are invested in their success. Consistency is another important factor in nurturing long-term professional relationships. Regular check-ins, whether through a quick email, a comment on social media posts, or a coffee meeting, help maintain the relationship and ensure that it doesn't fade over time.

These interactions don't always have to be work-related; sometimes, simply catching up on personal interests or life events can strengthen the bond. The goal is to stay on the other person's radar positively so that when opportunities arise, you are at the top of their mind.

In addition to providing value and maintaining consistent contact, it's important to celebrate others' successes. Recognizing and acknowledging milestones, such as promotions, awards, or successful projects, reinforces the connection and shows that you care about their achievements.

A congratulatory note or a public acknowledgment on social media can go a long way in strengthening the relationship. Another strategy for nurturing professional relationships is to engage in collaborative projects or initiatives.

Working together on a project not only deepens the relationship but also provides an opportunity to showcase your skills and reliability. Collaboration fosters a sense of partnership and mutual respect, which are crucial components of a strong professional relationship. This might involve co-authoring a paper, organizing an event together, or simply offering to assist with a task or project. Finally, it's essential to approach relationship-building with authenticity and sincerity. People are more likely to engage with and support those they perceive as genuine and trustworthy. This means being honest about your intentions, being yourself in interactions, and being mindful of the other person's needs and interests. Authenticity helps to build deeper connections and fosters a sense of loyalty and trust, which are the bedrock of long-lasting professional relationships.

A research study, *"Strategic Authenticity: Signaling Authenticity Without Undermining Professional Image in Workplace Interactions,"* conducted by Pillemer (2024), highlights the importance of balancing competence with warmth in professional relationships. The study found that people are more likely to form trusting relationships with individuals who display both competence and warmth rather than just competence alone. This underscores the need for professionals to focus not only on demonstrating their skills but also on building rapport and showing empathy in their interactions.

Hence, building and nurturing professional relationships requires a combination of effective small talk, timely follow-up, consistent engagement, and authentic interactions. These strategies, supported by research, form the foundation for meaningful and lasting connections in the corporate world.

Leveraging Military and Law Enforcement Networks for Corporate Success

Leveraging existing networks from military and law enforcement backgrounds can be a powerful strategy for transitioning into and thriving within corporate roles. These networks, forged through shared experiences and a deep sense of camaraderie, often serve as invaluable resources during and after the transition to the civilian workforce. One of the most effective ways to leverage these networks is by reconnecting with former colleagues who have successfully transitioned into corporate roles and tapping into broader veteran networks designed to support this transition.

Reconnecting with former colleagues is a crucial step in leveraging military and law enforcement networks. These relationships are often built on trust, loyalty, and shared experiences, making them a natural starting point for building a professional network in the corporate world. To begin this process, it's essential to take stock of your current contacts and identify those who have already made the transition. Reaching out to these individuals can provide valuable insights into the challenges and opportunities of moving from a military or law enforcement background to a corporate environment. When reconnecting, it's important to approach these former colleagues with a clear intention. Start by expressing genuine interest in their career journey and any advice they might have. For instance, you might say, *"I've been exploring opportunities in the corporate sector and noticed that you've successfully transitioned from military service to [specific role]. I would love to hear about your experience and any tips you might have for someone starting down this path."* This approach not only opens the door for a meaningful conversation but also shows respect for their achievements and insights.

In many cases, former colleagues are more than willing to help, offering mentorship, making introductions, or providing referrals to job opportunities within their networks. These connections can be particularly valuable when navigating industries or roles that are less familiar. By staying in touch and offering your support in return, you can maintain and strengthen these relationships over time, turning them into long-term professional alliances.

In addition to individual connections, tapping into broader veteran networks can significantly enhance your ability to transition into and succeed in corporate roles. Many organizations and associations are specifically designed to support veterans as they move into civilian careers. These networks often provide resources such as job boards, mentorship programs, and networking events that connect veterans with employers who value their unique skills and experiences.

For example, the Veterans Employment Initiative (VEI), established by the White House and several key corporations, aims to help veterans find meaningful employment in the private sector. VEI and similar programs not only connect veterans with job opportunities but also provide training and resources to help them adapt to corporate environments. Engaging with such initiatives can provide both practical support and a sense of community during the transition process.

Another strategy for leveraging these networks is to participate in veteran-focused events and workshops. These gatherings offer opportunities to meet other veterans who have successfully transitioned into corporate roles and to learn from their experiences. Whether it's a job fair, a skills workshop, or a networking event, participating in these activities can broaden your network and expose you to new opportunities. Moreover, these events often feature representatives from companies actively seeking to hire veterans, giving you a chance to connect directly with potential employers. Fred Smith, the founder and CEO of FedEx, is a highly respected business leader whose military background played a pivotal role in shaping his career. After graduating from Yale University in 1966, where he famously wrote a paper outlining the idea of an overnight delivery service, Smith joined the U.S. Marine Corps.

During his time in the Marines, Smith served as a platoon leader and forward air controller in Vietnam. His experience in the military, particularly in logistics and coordination, gave him firsthand insights into the importance of reliable and efficient transportation systems—knowledge that would later become the foundation for FedEx.

In 1971, leveraging both his education and military experience, Smith founded Federal Express (later FedEx) with the revolutionary concept of overnight shipping. He envisioned a system where packages could be transported quickly and reliably across long distances, initially focusing on delivering urgent documents and items.

Under Smith's leadership, FedEx grew into a global logistics giant known for its innovation in the shipping and logistics industry. Smith's military training in leadership, decision-making under pressure, and logistics proved invaluable in turning his idea into one of the world's largest courier companies.

Today, FedEx is a multi-billion-dollar corporation, handling millions of shipments daily, and Smith's vision and leadership have been widely credited with revolutionizing the global shipping industry. Tapping into these networks also involves understanding and utilizing the common language and values shared among veterans. In many ways, the camaraderie and teamwork that define military service continue to resonate in the corporate world, particularly in industries that value leadership, discipline, and resilience. By emphasizing these shared values, veterans can more effectively connect with others who have made the transition and who understand the challenges and opportunities that come with it. It's also important to contribute to these networks actively. Whether by offering mentorship to other veterans who are earlier in their transition journey or by sharing your own experiences at events or online forums, giving back to the community can strengthen your network and enhance your professional reputation. Contributing to veteran networks not only helps others but also reinforces your connections and keeps you engaged with the broader veteran community.

Leveraging military and law enforcement networks in this way can significantly ease the transition into corporate roles, providing both emotional support and practical resources.

By reconnecting with former colleagues and engaging with veteran networks, you can access a wealth of knowledge and opportunities that might otherwise be difficult to find.

This approach not only helps in securing employment but also in building a long-term career in the corporate world. These networks serve as a bridge between the familiar structure of military service and the more fluid, often complex environment of the corporate sector, making them an invaluable resource for veterans looking to make their mark in a new arena.

Maintaining and Growing Professional Networks

Maintaining and growing professional networks over time requires consistent effort and strategic use of available tools and opportunities. As your career progresses, staying connected with your network and continuing to expand it can provide ongoing benefits, including new job opportunities, collaborations, and valuable industry insights. Here are some key strategies to help you maintain and grow your professional networks effectively:

Utilize social media Effectively:

➢ Regularly engage with your network on platforms like LinkedIn by liking, commenting on, and sharing posts that resonate with your professional interests. This keeps you visible to your connections and demonstrates your active involvement in the industry.

➢ Keep your profile updated with your latest accomplishments, skills, and career milestones. A well-maintained profile ensures that you present a professional image and that your contacts can easily see your current role and expertise.

➢ Periodically reach out to connections with personalized messages, whether to congratulate them on a new role or to share an article they might find interesting. This personal touch helps keep your relationships warm and demonstrates genuine interest in their professional journeys.

Join and Participate in Professional Associations:

➢ Becoming a member of industry-specific professional associations can provide access to a wealth of networking opportunities, including conferences, webinars, and discussion forums. These platforms allow you to connect with others in your field and stay informed about industry trends.

➢ Actively participate in association events, whether virtual or in-person. Engaging in these activities not only helps you meet new people but also positions you as an active and informed member of your professional community.

➢ Consider volunteering for leadership roles within these associations. Serving on committees or boards can significantly raise your profile within the industry and allow you to build deeper relationships with influential figures.

Attend Industry Events and Conferences:

➢ Make it a habit to attend key industry events, conferences, and seminars regularly. These gatherings are excellent opportunities to meet new contacts, learn about the latest developments in your field, and reconnect with existing network members.

➢ Before attending an event, set specific networking goals, such as meeting certain individuals or learning about a particular topic. Having a clear purpose will help you make the most of your time and ensure that you build meaningful connections.

➢ Follow up with new contacts after the event to solidify the relationship. A simple message referencing your conversation at the event can help establish a connection that could lead to future collaborations or opportunities.

Stay Connected Through Regular Communication:

➢ Schedule regular check-ins with key contacts in your network. Whether it's a quarterly coffee catch-up or a quick email to share an update, consistent communication helps keep the relationship alive and demonstrates your commitment to maintaining the connection.

➢ Share valuable information, such as industry reports, articles, or job leads, with your network. Providing value helps reinforce your relationships and positions you as a resourceful and knowledgeable professional.

➢ Be responsive to your network's needs. Whether someone reaches out for advice, a referral, or collaboration, being available and willing to help fosters goodwill and strengthens your professional ties.

Expand Your Network Intentionally:

➢ As you progress in your career, make it a point to expand your network by connecting with professionals in related industries or new areas of interest. This diversification can open up new opportunities and provide fresh perspectives.

➢ Approach new connections with a genuine interest in their work and experiences. Building relationships based on mutual respect and curiosity leads to more meaningful and lasting connections.

➢ Attend events outside of your immediate industry or comfort zone. Engaging with a broader range of professionals can introduce you to new ideas and potential career paths you might not have considered.

By employing these strategies, you can ensure that your professional network remains a valuable asset throughout your career. Maintaining and growing your network takes time and effort, but the benefits of staying connected and visible within your industry are well worth it.

Without question, mastering networking and relationship-building is crucial for thriving in the corporate world. By understanding and adapting to the more fluid nature of corporate relationships, leveraging existing networks, and consistently engaging with professional contacts, you can unlock numerous opportunities for career growth. Remember, the effort invested in building meaningful connections pays off through new opportunities, collaborations, and career advancements. Embrace the proactive approach to networking, and you'll find that these relationships become invaluable assets throughout your career.

Chapter 7: Education and Certifications

"Education is the most powerful weapon which you can use to change the world."

— Nelson Mandela

In today's dynamic and increasingly complex corporate environment, the significance of education and certifications in the field of corporate security cannot be overstated. As threats become more sophisticated and technology continues to advance, professionals in this sector must equip themselves with the knowledge and skills necessary to protect organizations from a wide range of risks. Higher education and relevant certifications are not just a means to gain technical expertise; they are essential for career advancement, strategic decision-making, and leadership in security management. This chapter explores the evolving educational requirements in corporate security, the importance of certifications, strategies for continuing education while working, and a guide to choosing the right educational path to align with individual career goals.

Exploring Educational Requirements in Corporate Security

In the field of corporate security, the educational requirements have evolved significantly over the years. While experience and a background in military or law enforcement were once considered sufficient, the growing complexity of threats and the increasing integration of technology in security operations have made higher education a critical component for success. Degrees in fields such as business administration, cybersecurity, and risk management are increasingly valued by employers and often serve as key differentiators in a competitive job market.

Business administration is one of the most sought-after degrees in corporate security. The reason for this lies in the multifaceted nature of corporate security roles, which often require a deep understanding of business operations, financial management, and strategic planning. A degree in business administration equips security professionals with the skills needed to align security strategies with broader business objectives, ensuring that security measures support the overall goals of the organization. According to a report by the U.S. Bureau of Labor Statistics, individuals with a business administration degree are more likely to advance into senior management roles within security departments, where they oversee budgets, manage teams, and contribute to high-level decision-making processes.

Moreover, a business administration degree provides a strong foundation in leadership and organizational behavior, which are essential skills in the corporate environment. Security professionals who understand the intricacies of corporate culture and can navigate complex organizational structures are better equipped to implement effective security policies and gain buy-in from other departments. This knowledge is particularly valuable in larger organizations, where security decisions often have far-reaching implications across multiple business units. Cybersecurity is another critical area where educational qualifications play a significant role. As corporate security increasingly involves protecting digital assets from cyber threats, a degree in cybersecurity has become almost indispensable for professionals in this field.

Cybersecurity degrees focus on the technical aspects of protecting information systems, including network security, encryption, and threat detection. The need for such expertise is underscored by the growing frequency and sophistication of cyberattacks. According to Cybersecurity Ventures, cybercrime is expected to cost the world $10.5 trillion annually by 2025, highlighting the urgent need for skilled cybersecurity professionals who can defend against these threats.

A cybersecurity degree not only provides the technical skills required to safeguard corporate networks but also emphasizes the importance of compliance with regulations such as the General Data Protection Regulation (GDPR) and the Health Insurance Portability and Accountability Act (HIPAA). Knowledge of these regulations is crucial for corporate security professionals, as non-compliance can result in hefty fines and damage to the organization's reputation. Furthermore, cybersecurity programs often include coursework on incident response and disaster recovery, preparing graduates to effectively manage and mitigate the impact of security breaches.

Risk management is another field of study that has gained prominence in the realm of corporate security. A degree in risk management focuses on identifying, assessing, and mitigating risks that could potentially harm an organization. This includes not only physical security threats but also financial, operational, and reputational risks. The interdisciplinary nature of risk management makes it particularly relevant to corporate security, as it requires a holistic understanding of the various factors that can affect an organization's security posture.

According to the Risk Management Society (RIMS), organizations with a formal risk management framework are better equipped to anticipate and respond to security incidents, reducing the potential impact on their operations. A degree in risk management provides professionals with the tools to develop and implement such frameworks, ensuring that security measures are proactive rather than reactive. Additionally, these programs often cover the principles of crisis management and business continuity, both of which are critical in maintaining organizational resilience in the face of security challenges. The value of formal education in corporate security is further supported by the increasing demand for certifications that require a foundational understanding of these fields. For example, the Certified Protection Professional (CPP) certification, offered by ASIS International, is widely recognized as a benchmark of excellence in corporate security.

Achieving this certification requires a combination of professional experience and knowledge in areas such as security principles, risk management, and business operations—all of which are covered in business administration, cybersecurity, and risk management degree programs. According to ASIS International, professionals with a CPP certification earn, on average, 20% more than their non-certified counterparts, highlighting the financial benefits of pursuing advanced education and certifications in the field.

In addition to these specific degrees, many corporate security professionals also pursue advanced degrees, such as a Master of Business Administration (MBA) with a focus on security management or an MBA in cybersecurity. These programs are designed to provide a deeper understanding of the strategic aspects of corporate security, preparing professionals for leadership roles within their organizations. An MBA with a focus on security management, for instance, combines traditional business courses with specialized security training, equipping graduates with the skills needed to manage complex security operations within a corporate framework. The versatility of an MBA also allows security professionals to transition into other areas of management, further broadening their career prospects.

The shift toward requiring higher education in corporate security reflects the changing nature of the field. As companies face more sophisticated threats and operate in increasingly complex environments, the need for security professionals who can think strategically and integrate security with business objectives has grown. Employers now look for candidates who not only have the practical experience but also the educational background to understand and navigate these challenges.

Furthermore, the emphasis on education in corporate security is not just about gaining technical skills or theoretical knowledge. It is also about developing critical thinking, problem-solving, and communication skills that are essential for success in the corporate world. These skills are often honed through rigorous academic programs that challenge students to analyze complex issues, develop innovative solutions, and effectively communicate their ideas to stakeholders at all levels of the organization.

Importance of Relevant Certifications in Corporate Security

My educational journey began with a degree in Justice Studies, focusing on Terrorism and Homeland Security. This provided a solid foundation for understanding the broader security landscape, but I quickly realized that succeeding in corporate security required more than traditional security training. I needed to expand my skill set to adapt to the unique challenges of corporate environments.

Instead of opting for widely recognized certifications like the CPP, I chose to pursue specialized certifications that were more relevant to the environments I was working in. A pivotal moment came during my tenure at Valero Energy. The threats we faced extended beyond physical security breaches. To enhance our response strategies and add value to the team, I decided to broaden my training. I became certified as an industrial firefighter and a hazmat technician. This decision stemmed from a need to understand the specific risks associated with industrial settings, such as chemical spills, fires, and other hazardous situations that traditional security training did not cover.

These certifications allowed me to approach security from a more comprehensive perspective. For instance, my knowledge of fire behavior and hazardous material response helped me grasp the interconnected nature of various emergency response protocols. This broader perspective was invaluable when working on security assessments or crisis management plans. It enabled me to identify vulnerabilities and recommend mitigation strategies that others might overlook.

A memorable instance that highlighted the value of this specialized training occurred when we were reviewing the emergency response plans for a major refinery. My background as a hazmat technician allowed me to question and refine our approach to chemical spill scenarios. I could communicate effectively with the fire and safety teams, bridging the gap between security and operational safety. This not only improved the overall robustness of our emergency plans but also enhanced my credibility across departments, demonstrating that I could contribute beyond the traditional scope of security.

To balance these pursuits with full-time work, I utilized company-supported training programs and sought certifications that offered flexible learning options. I made it a point to integrate new knowledge into my daily role, whether by revising emergency protocols or conducting cross-functional training sessions. This hands-on approach reinforced what I learned and showcased its value to my team and superiors.

By focusing on specialized, environment-specific certifications and training, I was able to carve out a niche that went beyond conventional security functions. This approach not only broadened my expertise but also highlighted the importance of continuously adapting and expanding one's skill set to address the evolving landscape of threats in any corporate environment.

Certifications have become increasingly vital in the field of corporate security, serving as key indicators of a professional's expertise, commitment, and credibility. These certifications not only validate the skills and knowledge required to excel in various aspects of security management but also enhance career prospects by distinguishing certified professionals from their peers. Among the most recognized and respected certifications in the industry are the Certified Protection Professional (CPP),

Certified Information Systems Security Professional (CISSP), and other specialized certifications tailored to corporate security needs.

The Certified Protection Professional (CPP) certification, offered by ASIS International, is one of the most esteemed credentials in the field of corporate security. The CPP certification is designed for experienced security professionals who demonstrate advanced competency in security management, including the implementation of security solutions, business continuity, and risk management strategies. Earning the CPP requires passing a comprehensive exam that covers seven domains: security principles and practices, business principles and practices, investigations, personnel security, physical security, information security, and crisis management.

The significance of the CPP certification lies in its holistic approach to security management, making it a valuable asset for professionals who aspire to leadership roles within their organizations. According to ASIS International, professionals with the CPP designation often see enhanced career opportunities and earning potential. The CPP is not just a testament to one's knowledge but also a demonstration of a commitment to ongoing professional development, as maintaining the certification requires continuous education in the field of security. Another critical certification in the corporate security landscape is the Certified Information Systems Security Professional (CISSP). Administered by the International Information System Security

Certification Consortium (ISC)², the CISSP certification is specifically designed for professionals who specialize in information security. As cyber threats have become a significant concern for businesses, the CISSP certification has gained prominence as a benchmark for cybersecurity expertise. The CISSP covers eight domains, including security and risk management, asset security, security engineering, communications and network security, identity and access management, security assessment and testing, security operations, and software development security.

The CISSP certification is often regarded as the "gold standard" for information security professionals and is highly sought after by employers across various industries. A study by (ISC)² found that professionals with a CISSP certification earn an average of 25% more than their non-certified counterparts, highlighting the financial benefits of obtaining this credential. The rigorous exam and experience requirements for the CISSP also ensure that certified professionals possess both the theoretical knowledge and practical experience needed to effectively manage and secure an organization's information systems.

In addition to the CPP and CISSP, several other certifications are particularly relevant to corporate security. The Physical Security Professional (PSP) certification, also offered by ASIS International, is designed for individuals who specialize in the physical aspects of security. This certification focuses on threat assessment, risk analysis, and the design and implementation of physical security measures. The PSP is ideal for professionals who are responsible for securing physical assets, such as buildings, infrastructure, and people. It provides a thorough understanding of how to evaluate security vulnerabilities and implement appropriate safeguards to protect against threats.

The Certified Information Security Manager (CISM) certification, offered by ISACA, is another valuable credential for corporate security professionals, particularly those involved in information security management. The CISM certification is geared toward individuals who design and manage an enterprise's information security program. It emphasizes the alignment of security strategies with broader business goals, making it particularly relevant for professionals who operate at the intersection of IT security and business management. CISM-certified professionals are equipped to manage and govern information security programs, conduct risk assessments, and develop incident response strategies.

For those focused on risk management within the corporate security domain, the Certified in Risk and Information Systems Control (CRISC) certification, also offered by ISACA, is an essential credential. CRISC is designed for professionals who identify and manage risks through the development and implementation of information systems controls. This certification covers four domains: IT risk identification, IT risk assessment, risk response and mitigation, and risk and control monitoring and reporting. CRISC-certified professionals are particularly valuable to organizations because they possess the skills to anticipate, evaluate, and respond to risks that could impact the organization's objectives. Another notable certification is the Certified Ethical Hacker (CEH), which is administered by the EC-Council. The CEH certification is designed for security professionals who specialize in ethical hacking, penetration testing, and vulnerability assessment. With the rise of cyber threats, organizations increasingly seek professionals who can think like hackers to identify and address security weaknesses before they can be exploited by malicious actors. The CEH certification equips professionals with the tools and techniques used by hackers, enabling them to strengthen an organization's defenses against cyberattacks.

For security professionals involved in corporate investigations, the Professional Certified Investigator (PCI) certification from ASIS International is highly relevant. The PCI certification is designed for individuals who conduct investigations involving fraud, misconduct, and other violations within an organization. It covers key areas such as case management, investigative techniques, and legal aspects of investigations. Professionals with PCI certification are well-equipped to handle complex investigations, ensuring that they are conducted thoroughly, ethically, and under legal standards.

In addition to these specific certifications, there are also industry-specific credentials that can be valuable for corporate security professionals working in particular sectors. For example, the Healthcare Security and Safety Certification (CHSS) is designed for security professionals in the healthcare industry, where protecting patient information and ensuring the safety of healthcare facilities are critical concerns. Similarly, the Certified Protection Officer (CPO) certification is geared toward security officers and supervisors who require a broad understanding of security principles and practices.

Certifications in corporate security not only validate an individual's expertise but also demonstrate a commitment to staying current with industry best practices and emerging threats. As the security landscape continues to evolve, professionals who invest in obtaining and maintaining relevant certifications are better positioned to meet the challenges of modern corporate security and advance their careers in this dynamic field. These certifications provide a structured path for continuous learning and professional growth, ensuring that certified individuals remain at the forefront of security management and are well-prepared to protect their organizations in an increasingly complex world.

Strategies for Continuing Education While Working

Continuing education is crucial for professionals in corporate security, especially in an ever-evolving field where staying updated with the latest trends, technologies, and best practices is essential. Balancing ongoing education with full-time work can be challenging, but several strategies can help professionals maintain their education without disrupting their careers. These strategies include leveraging online learning platforms, enrolling in part-time degree programs, and taking advantage of corporate training opportunities.

Utilize Online Learning Platforms

Online learning platforms such as Coursera, Udemy, and LinkedIn Learning offer a wide range of courses in areas relevant to corporate security, such as cybersecurity, risk management, and leadership. These platforms provide the flexibility to learn at your own pace, making it easier to balance education with work responsibilities.

Many online courses offer certifications upon completion, which can be added to your professional profile to demonstrate ongoing education and skill enhancement. This not only boosts your credentials but also shows your commitment to continuous learning.

Enroll in Part-Time Degree Programs

Part-time degree programs, such as those offered by many universities, allow professionals to pursue advanced education without having to leave their jobs. These programs are typically designed to accommodate working professionals, with classes held in the evenings, on weekends, or online.

By enrolling in a part-time degree program, you can gradually work toward an advanced degree, such as a Master's in Business Administration (MBA) with a focus on security management or a Master's in Cybersecurity. This enables you to enhance your qualifications and career prospects while continuing to earn a full-time income.

Take Advantage of Corporate Training Opportunities

Many companies offer in-house training programs or partnerships with educational institutions to provide employees with opportunities for professional development. These programs often focus on areas critical to the company's needs, such as leadership training, compliance, or advanced security techniques.

Participating in corporate training not only helps you develop new skills but also aligns your learning with the organization's strategic goals. This can make you a more valuable asset to your company and position you for potential promotions or new roles.

Leverage Tuition Reimbursement Programs

Some employers offer tuition reimbursement as part of their employee benefits package. This means the company will cover part or all of the cost of further education, provided it is relevant to your role or future career path. Taking advantage of this benefit can significantly reduce the financial burden of continuing education. Before enrolling in a program, ensure that it aligns with your employer's criteria for reimbursement, and communicate your educational goals with your manager to gain support for your professional development.

Create a Structured Study Schedule

Balancing work and education requires careful time management. Establishing a structured study schedule helps you allocate specific times during the week for coursework, studying, and assignments. This approach ensures that your education doesn't interfere with your work responsibilities or personal life.

Using tools like calendars, planners, or digital apps can help you keep track of deadlines and manage your time effectively. Sticking to a consistent study routine also reduces stress and improves your ability to retain new information.

Engage in Professional Networks and Study Groups

Joining professional networks or study groups related to your field of study can enhance your learning experience. These groups provide opportunities to discuss coursework, share resources, and gain different perspectives on complex topics. Networking with peers who are also pursuing continuing education can offer moral support and motivation, helping you stay committed to your educational goals while working full-time.

Focus on Microlearning

Microlearning involves short, focused bursts of learning, often in the form of brief videos, articles, or podcasts. This approach is particularly effective for busy professionals who might not have time for extended study sessions but still want to keep learning.

By integrating microlearning into your daily routine, such as during commutes or breaks, you can gradually build knowledge and skills without overwhelming your schedule. This method keeps you engaged in continuous learning without requiring significant time commitments.

These strategies collectively offer a practical and flexible approach to continuing education while working full-time. By incorporating these methods into your routine, you can stay current in your field, advance your career, and achieve your long-term professional goals without sacrificing your current job responsibilities.

Guide to Choosing the Right Educational Path

Choosing the right educational path is a critical decision for anyone looking to advance in the field of corporate security. Given the range of options available—from degrees and certifications to short-term courses and specialized training—selecting the best path requires careful consideration of your individual career goals, the time and resources you can commit, and the potential return on investment (ROI) for each option. Below is a guide to help you navigate this decision-making process.

Clarify Your Career Aspirations

The first step in choosing the right educational path is to clearly define your career goals. Ask yourself where you see your career in the next five to ten years. Are you aiming for a leadership position, such as Chief Security Officer (CSO) or Director of Corporate Security? Or are you more interested in becoming a specialist in a particular area, such as cybersecurity or risk management? Understanding your long-term objectives will help you identify the qualifications and skills necessary to reach them.

For example, if you aspire to a leadership role, pursuing an MBA with a focus on security management might be more beneficial than a technical certification. Conversely, if your goal is to become a cybersecurity expert, a specialized certification like the Certified Information Systems Security Professional (CISSP) would be more appropriate.

Assess Time Commitment and Flexibility

Once your career goals are clear, consider how much time you can realistically commit to furthering your education. Full-time degree programs can be intense and may require you to take time off work or significantly adjust your schedule. On the other hand, part-time programs or online courses offer more flexibility, allowing you to balance work and study.

If you have significant work responsibilities or personal commitments, a part-time degree program or an online learning platform might be the best choice.

These options provide the flexibility to learn at your own pace, often allowing you to complete coursework in the evenings or on weekends. Alternatively, if you're able to dedicate yourself full-time to your studies, a traditional on-campus program could offer a more immersive learning experience.

Consider the Return on Investment (ROI)

Evaluating the ROI of your educational choices is essential, particularly when considering the financial and time investments involved. ROI can be measured by how the education will impact your earning potential, career advancement opportunities, and job security. Researching industry trends and salary benchmarks for your desired role can help you determine whether the education will pay off in the long run.

For example, obtaining a CPP or CISSP certification might involve significant upfront costs, but these are highly respected credentials that can lead to higher salaries and better job prospects. Similarly, advanced degrees like an MBA can be expensive, but they often open doors to senior management positions with substantial financial rewards.

Explore Available Resources and Support

Before making a decision, explore the resources and support systems available to you. Many employers offer tuition reimbursement programs, scholarships, or professional development funds that can offset the cost of further education. Additionally, consider whether your chosen educational path offers career services, networking opportunities, or mentorship, as these can be invaluable in helping you achieve your career goals.

Align Education with Current and Future Industry Trends

Finally, ensure that your chosen educational path aligns with current and future trends in corporate security. The industry is rapidly evolving, particularly with advancements in technology and an increasing focus on cybersecurity. Opting for programs that incorporate emerging topics, such as artificial intelligence in security or the latest in risk management strategies, will keep you ahead of the curve and ensure that your skills remain relevant. By following this decision-making framework, you can choose an educational path that not only aligns with your career aspirations but also provides the flexibility, support, and ROI necessary to achieve long-term success in the field of corporate security.

In conclusion, in the ever-evolving landscape of corporate security, continuous learning and professional development are critical to staying ahead of emerging threats and advancing in your career. By carefully considering your career aspirations, time commitment, and return on investment, you can select an educational path that best aligns with your goals and keeps you competitive in the job market.

As Warren Buffett wisely stated, *"The best investment you can make is in yourself."* In the context of corporate security, this investment in education and certifications is not only about securing your future but also about ensuring the safety and resilience of the organizations you protect.

Chapter 8: Job Search Strategies

"Success is not final; failure is not fatal: It is the courage to continue that count."

— Winston Churchill

Navigating the job market can be daunting, especially for those transitioning from military or law enforcement careers into the corporate sector. The landscape of job security has shifted dramatically, influenced by technology, economic changes, and evolving work patterns.

Understanding these shifts and effectively tailoring your job search strategy is crucial for success. This chapter will explore contemporary trends in the corporate job market, provide practical advice on customizing resumes and cover letters, and offer strategies to tackle common challenges faced during job searches. Whether you're facing age discrimination, a lack of industry-specific experience, or gaps in employment, this guide aims to equip you with actionable tools for a successful transition.

Overview of the Corporate Security Job Market

The concept of job security in the corporate market has evolved considerably in recent years. It is significantly shaped by economic fluctuations, technological advancements, and shifting employment patterns.

Traditionally, job security meant long-term employment with a single company, often accompanied by benefits and a clear career progression. However, today, it presents a more complex and uncertain picture.

In the current corporate environment, job security is increasingly tied to an individual's ability to adapt and remain relevant in a rapidly changing job market. This is largely due to the accelerated pace of technological innovation, which has redefined the skills and competencies valued by employers.

For instance, automation and artificial intelligence have begun to replace routine tasks in industries ranging from manufacturing to finance. As a result, roles that once offered long-term stability are now vulnerable to obsolescence. Employees in such positions are finding that job security now depends on their willingness and ability to reskill and upskill to meet the demands of new, technology-driven roles.

Moreover, the rise of the gig economy and contract-based work has further complicated the notion of job security. Many companies in tech, media, and creative industries are relying more on freelance or contract workers rather than full-time employees. This shift allows organizations to remain agile and reduce overhead costs, but it also places the burden of job security on individuals. The gig economy poses challenges for workers, with income uncertainty and limited benefits making financial stability an ongoing battle.

While some workers appreciate gig work's flexibility and autonomy, others are concerned about the lack of long-term security and the absence of traditional employee benefits like health insurance and retirement plans.

Another significant factor influencing job security in the corporate market is the trend toward mergers and acquisitions (M&A). To remain competitive and expand their market share, many companies engage in M&A activities, which can lead to restructuring and downsizing. Employees often find themselves at risk of redundancy as overlapping functions are eliminated to streamline operations and reduce costs. Even in cases where layoffs are not immediate, the uncertainty accompanying such corporate changes can lead to decreased morale and a fear of job insecurity among employees.

Globalization also plays a critical role in shaping job security. When expanding internationally, companies often seek to optimize their operations by outsourcing or offshoring certain functions to regions with lower labor costs. Jobs in industries like manufacturing, customer service, and information technology are being moved to countries with cheaper workforces. Employees in developed markets face more job competition, needing new skills or lower wages to stay employed.

Economic downturns and market volatility further exacerbate job insecurity. Recessions and financial crises can lead to widespread layoffs, and hiring freezes as companies struggle to maintain profitability. During uncertain times, high-performing employees may be at risk of losing their jobs due to factors beyond their control. The COVID-19 pandemic, for example, resulted in significant job losses across various sectors, highlighting the vulnerability of even seemingly stable positions to unexpected economic shocks.

On the other hand, certain new trends offer some degree of hope for job security in the corporate market. The increasing emphasis on diversity, equity, and inclusion (DEI) within organizations is prompting companies to retain a more diverse workforce, recognizing that different perspectives drive innovation and better business outcomes.

Additionally, the growing importance of sustainability and corporate social responsibility (CSR) is creating new roles within organizations focused on environmental, social, and governance (ESG) initiatives. With companies striving to meet regulatory requirements and consumer expectations for ethical business practices, expert employees may find themselves in more secure positions, as these roles are becoming integral to corporate strategy. Furthermore, the demand for jobs in technology and healthcare continues to rise, driven by ongoing digital transformation and an aging population. Professionals in fields such as software development, cybersecurity, and healthcare services are likely to enjoy greater job security due to the essential nature of their work and the difficulty of automating these roles.

Tailoring Resumes and Cover Letters for Corporate Positions

When transitioning from military or law enforcement backgrounds, tailoring resumes and cover letters for corporate positions can enhance how your skills and experiences are perceived by civilian employers. The key is to translate military achievements and responsibilities into language that resonates with the corporate world, focusing on skills that are transferable and relevant to the job at hand.

For me, transitioning from military and law enforcement to corporate roles requires a thoughtful and strategic approach. Early on, I realized the importance of translating military achievements into language that resonates with corporate employers. Instead of focusing on rank and command roles, I emphasized the transferable skills—such as leadership, crisis management, and strategic planning—that are highly valued in the business world.

I recall a specific instance when I tailored my resume for a corporate security director position. I consciously replaced military jargon with terminology familiar to the corporate sector, opting for phrases like "led cross-functional teams" instead of "commanded troops." I focused on highlighting outcomes that would resonate with a corporate audience, including cost savings, efficiency improvements, and risk mitigation.

When preparing for interviews, I made it a point to research not just the company but also its culture, aiming to demonstrate how my experience in high-pressure environments could address corporate challenges. In one interview, I opened by recounting a critical crisis scenario I had managed in the military and then smoothly transitioned to how those exact skills applied to the corporate crisis management role I was seeking.

Example 1: Leadership Experience

Military: "Commanded a platoon of 30 soldiers, responsible for executing missions in high-pressure environments."

Corporate: "Led a team of 30 personnel, driving successful project execution in high-pressure environments. Demonstrated strong leadership and decision-making skills that ensured team cohesion and mission success under tight deadlines."

In the corporate version, the language shifts from military-specific terms like "platoon" and "missions" to more universally understood corporate language such as "team" and "project execution." This makes the experience more relatable to hiring managers in the business world.

Example 2: Crisis Management

Military: "Managed emergency response during a combat situation, ensuring the safety of all unit members while coordinating with external units."

Corporate: "Oversaw emergency response operations, coordinating with cross-functional teams to ensure the safety of all personnel and maintain operational continuity during crises."

This change highlights the transferable skills of crisis management and coordination, which are directly applicable to roles in corporate security, operations, and even project management.

Example 3: Strategic Planning

Military: "Developed and executed strategic operations plans, resulting in the successful completion of critical missions."

Corporate: "Developed and implemented strategic plans that led to the achievement of key objectives, enhancing operational efficiency and driving organizational success."

The second version uses language that emphasizes the outcomes and the impact of strategic planning, which is critical in the corporate context where results and ROI are key considerations.

Tailoring Resumes: Practical Tips

When tailoring a resume for a corporate position, it's important to focus on the following elements:

> **Language and Terminology:** Avoid military jargon that may be unfamiliar to corporate recruiters. Instead, use terms that are commonly understood in the business world. For example, replace "commander" with "team

leader" or "manager" and "missions" with "projects" or "initiatives."

➢ **Transferable Skills**: Highlight skills that are directly transferable to the corporate role you are applying for. These often include leadership, strategic planning, project management, crisis management, and risk assessment.

➢ **Quantifiable Achievements**: Where possible, include specific outcomes that demonstrate your effectiveness in previous roles. Corporate employers are often looking for measurable results, such as "improved operational efficiency by 20%" or "reduced costs by 15%."

➢ **Customization for Each Role**: Tailor your resume for each job application by emphasizing the experiences and skills most relevant to the specific role. This might mean reordering bullet points or adding specific examples that align with the job description.

Crafting Cover Letters: Bridging the Gap

Your cover letter is an opportunity to explain how your background aligns with the company's needs and to provide context for your transition from military or law enforcement to the corporate world.

➢ **Opening:** Start with a strong statement that captures the hiring manager's attention. For example, "With over 15 years of experience in high-stakes environments, I bring a unique blend of strategic leadership and crisis management expertise that is directly applicable to the challenges faced by [Company Name]."

> **Middle:** Use this section to highlight specific achievements from your military or law enforcement career, explaining how they are relevant to the corporate role. For instance, "In my previous role, I was responsible for leading cross-functional teams in the development and execution of complex strategic initiatives. This experience has equipped me with the skills necessary to drive project success and improve operational efficiency at [Company Name]."

> **Closing:** End with a strong closing statement that reiterates your enthusiasm for the role and your fit with the company's needs. "I am excited about the opportunity to bring my leadership skills and strategic planning experience to [Company Name], and I look forward to discussing how I can contribute to your team's success."

Interview Strategies: Translating Experience in Real-time

When it comes to interviews, preparation is key. Your goal is to demonstrate how your military or law enforcement experience has prepared you for the corporate world.

➢ **Research the Company and Role:** Understand the company's culture, values, and the specific challenges they face. This allows you to tailor your responses to demonstrate how your background is not just relevant but an asset.

➢ **Narrative Approach:** Use storytelling to make your experiences relatable. For example, instead of simply stating that you managed a crisis, describe a specific scenario: "During a critical operation, I led a team through a high-stakes situation where timing and coordination were crucial. This experience mirrors the kind of crisis management that [Company Name] might face in its operations."

➢ **Relate Military Experience to Corporate Challenges:** Draw direct parallels between your previous roles and the responsibilities of the corporate position. For example, "In the military, I was responsible for ensuring mission success under tight deadlines and resource constraints—skills that are directly transferable to managing corporate projects with strict budgets and timelines."

➢ **Practice Common Interview Questions:** Be ready to discuss how your skills translate into the corporate world, and prepare for behavioral questions that ask you to demonstrate how you've handled specific situations in the past.

By effectively tailoring your resume, crafting a compelling cover letter, and using strategic approaches in interviews, you can successfully translate your military or law enforcement experience into a narrative that resonates with civilian employers. This not only helps you stand out as a candidate but also demonstrates your value in a corporate setting.

Effective Interview Techniques for Transitioning Professionals

Effective interview techniques are crucial for professionals transitioning from military or law enforcement backgrounds into corporate roles. One of the key challenges these individuals face is addressing potential employer concerns about "militarized thinking" or a perceived lack of corporate experience. Employers may worry that candidates from a military background might struggle with the more flexible, collaborative environments typical of corporate settings or that they may lack the specific business acumen required for the role.

It's important for transitioning professionals to highlight how their military experiences have instilled valuable skills like adaptability, leadership, and strategic thinking—traits that are highly transferable to corporate environments.

Research supports the effectiveness of this approach. A study conducted by the Institute for Veterans and Military Families (IVMF) at Syracuse University found that 68% of employers reported that veterans often display higher levels of leadership and teamwork skills compared to their civilian peers. This aligns with the reality that military training emphasizes rapid decision-making, resilience under pressure, and a mission-focused mindset, all of which are assets in a corporate setting.

In interviews, it's beneficial to address potential concerns head-on. For example, candidates can acknowledge the difference in work environments while also emphasizing how their experience in high-stakes situations has prepared them to handle corporate challenges with calm and precision.

According to a report by the Society for Human Resource Management (SHRM), 77% of employers consider problem-solving skills crucial when evaluating candidates, and military professionals are often well-equipped in this area due to their extensive training in crisis management and strategic operations.

By preparing to discuss how their skills are applicable in a corporate context and backing these claims with evidence, transitioning professionals can effectively counter any concerns about their fit in the corporate world. This strategy not only reassures employers but also positions the candidate as someone who brings a unique and valuable perspective to the role.

Strategies for Overcoming Common Job Search Challenges

Job seeking can be a stressful and uncertain process. Whether you're a recent graduate, someone hoping to change careers, or even a seasoned professional hoping to change employers, job hunting can pose challenges throughout your career.

Overcoming Age Discrimination

➢ **Highlight Relevant Experience:** Emphasize how your extensive experience brings valuable insights that younger candidates may lack. Showcase your ability to mentor others and your deep understanding of industry dynamics, which can be a significant asset to any organization.

➢ **Stay Current with Technology:** Demonstrate your familiarity with current technologies and industry trends. Employers often associate age with a lack of tech-savvy, so showing your competence in relevant tools and platforms can dispel this myth.

➢ **Focus on Soft Skills:** Highlight soft skills like leadership, communication, and conflict resolution. These skills often improve with experience and are highly valued in corporate settings, making them key selling points for more seasoned professionals.

➢ **Be Flexible and Open to Learning:** Convey your willingness to adapt to new environments and learn continuously. Employers value candidates who are open to growth and change, regardless of age.

Addressing Lack of Industry-Specific Experience

➢ **Identify Transferable Skills:** Clearly articulate how your skills from previous roles apply to the industry you're targeting. For example, leadership, strategic planning, and crisis management are universally valuable across industries.

➢ **Pursue Additional Certifications:** Obtain certifications relevant to your target industry. This not only demonstrates your commitment to transitioning but also equips you with the specific knowledge needed for the new field.

➢ **Network within the Industry:** Build connections with professionals in your desired industry. Attend industry-specific events, join professional associations, and engage on LinkedIn to learn about the field and make valuable contacts.

➢ **Use Case Studies and Examples:** During interviews, use specific examples from your past roles to demonstrate how you've successfully adapted to new challenges. Employers will appreciate your ability to quickly learn and apply new knowledge.

Managing Gaps in Employment During Transition

➢ **Be Honest but Strategic:** Address employment gaps directly, but frame them in a positive light. Explain that the gap was a period for acquiring new skills, completing relevant training, or planning a thoughtful career transition.

➢ **Highlight Productive Use of Time:** Emphasize any activities you undertook during the employment gap, such as volunteering, consulting, or continuing education. This shows that you remained active and committed to personal and professional development.

➢ **Modify Your Resume:** Consider using a functional resume format that focuses on skills and accomplishments rather than a chronological work history. This can help minimize the visibility of employment gaps and draw attention to your strengths.

➢ **Prepare a Strong Explanation:** Be ready to discuss the employment gap confidently in interviews. Focus on how the time was spent improving yourself or preparing for the next stage of your career, and link this directly to the value you bring to the role.

Leveraging Mentorship and Support Networks

➢ **Seek Out a Mentor:** Find a mentor within the industry or field you're transitioning into. A mentor can provide guidance, share industry insights, and help you navigate challenges specific to your transition.

➤ **Join Professional Groups:** Participate in professional organizations related to your desired industry. These groups can offer networking opportunities, industry-specific knowledge, and potential job leads.

➤ **Engage with Alumni Networks:** Leverage alumni networks from any educational institutions you've attended. Alumni connections can be particularly helpful in providing job leads, advice, and support during your transition.

Building Confidence and Resilience

➤ **Practice Interviewing:** Regularly practice your interviewing skills, focusing on articulating your strengths and addressing potential concerns. Confidence in your ability to communicate your value can significantly improve your job search outcomes.

➤ **Set Realistic Goals:** Break down your job search into manageable goals, such as applying to a certain number of jobs each week or attending networking events. Achieving these smaller milestones can keep you motivated and reduce the stress of the overall process.

> ➤ **Stay Positive and Persistent:** Understand that transitioning to a new role or industry can take time. Stay positive, maintain a routine, and keep pushing forward, even when faced with setbacks. Persistence is key to overcoming job search challenges.

Utilizing Professional Resources

> ➤ **Consider Career Counseling:** Engage with career counseling services to help refine your job search strategy, improve your resume, and prepare for interviews. These services can offer personalized advice tailored to your unique situation.

> ➤ **Use Job Search Platforms Effectively:** Maximize the use of online job search platforms by setting up alerts for relevant roles, customizing your profile to highlight your transition goals, and actively networking within these platforms.

Implementing these strategies can help professionals transition effectively and navigate the challenges of entering the corporate world. Successfully navigating a job search in today's evolving corporate landscape requires adaptability and a strategic approach. By understanding current trends and effectively translating your unique experiences into corporate language, you can overcome barriers and showcase your value. Tailoring your resume, mastering interview techniques, and addressing potential challenges such as age discrimination or gaps in employment can significantly enhance your job search efforts. Leveraging mentorship and maintaining resilience will further support your journey.

Chapter 9: Understanding Corporate Hierarchy and Politics

Understanding corporate hierarchy and office politics is essential for professionals transitioning from military or law enforcement to the corporate world. Unlike the rigid structures and clear-cut command in the military, corporate environments often feature fluid hierarchies and complex power dynamics. Navigating these nuances requires more than just adapting to a new set of rules; it demands an understanding of informal influence, alliance-building, and perception management. This chapter explores these differences, offering strategies to effectively identify decision-makers, assert oneself appropriately, and manage conflicts while remaining true to one's principles.

Comparing Corporate Structures to Military and Law Enforcement Hierarchies

The structure, decision-making processes, and power dynamics in corporate environments can be vastly different from what one might be accustomed to in more regimented settings like the military. Navigating these differences effectively is key to success in a corporate career. In the corporate world, hierarchies are typically more fluid and less rigid than in the military or law enforcement. While both environments have clearly defined roles and chains of command, the way authority is exercised and decisions are made in corporate settings often involves more collaboration and consensus-building. In the military, decisions are usually made by high-ranking officers and are expected to be executed without question, reflecting a top-down approach that prioritizes discipline, efficiency, and order. In contrast, corporate decision-making often involves multiple stakeholders at various levels of the organization, including employees, managers, and executives, all of whom may have a say in the outcome.

This difference can sometimes lead to a slower, more deliberative process, but it also allows for a diversity of perspectives and can lead to more innovative solutions.

One key difference between corporate and military hierarchies is the level of formality and adherence to protocol.

In the military, ranks and titles carry significant weight, and there is a strong emphasis on respect for authority and the chain of command. Orders are given and followed without much room for debate, and there is a clear understanding that the hierarchy must be maintained to ensure the effectiveness of the unit. In corporate settings, the emphasis is often on collaboration and teamwork, with a greater degree of informality in interactions between different levels of the hierarchy. While respect for authority is still important, it is often balanced with a focus on building relationships and fostering open communication across the organization. This can be challenging for those used to the strict hierarchical structures of the military, where questioning or challenging authority is typically discouraged. Corporate structures can vary widely depending on the size and nature of the organization. They generally include several layers, from entry-level employees to middle management and up to senior executives and the board of directors.

These layers may be fewer in smaller companies, with individuals often wearing multiple hats and the lines of authority being more blurred. Larger corporations, on the other hand, may have more complex hierarchies with clearly delineated roles and responsibilities.

These structures are often designed to facilitate efficient decision-making and the management of resources across various departments, such as finance, marketing, operations, and human resources. Unlike the military, where the hierarchy is primarily functional, corporate hierarchies are often influenced by politics, with power dynamics playing a significant role in how decisions are made and who gets promoted.

Power dynamics in corporate environments are often more subtle and complex than in the military. While military rank is earned through a combination of time, performance, and leadership abilities, corporate power can be influenced by factors such as networking, political savvy, and the ability to build alliances. In corporate settings, power is not always tied directly to one's position in the hierarchy. Individuals who are effective at navigating office politics can often wield significant power, even if they do not hold a formal leadership title. Decision-making in corporate environments is also influenced by these power dynamics. In the military, decisions are typically made quickly and with a clear chain of responsibility. The focus is on achieving the mission with minimal delay, and the decision-making process is designed to support this goal.

Corporate decision-making can be slower and more complex, often involving input from multiple stakeholders and requiring a careful balancing of competing interests. For example, a decision to launch a new product might involve input from marketing, finance, operations, and legal teams, each of which has its priorities and concerns. Reaching a consensus that satisfies all parties can take time, and the process often involves negotiation, compromise, and sometimes even political maneuvering. Furthermore, corporate decision-making is often influenced by external factors such as market conditions, regulatory requirements, and shareholder expectations. In the military, decisions are typically driven by operational needs and strategic objectives, with less direct influence from external stakeholders.

In a corporate setting, however, leaders must consider how their decisions will impact the company's bottom line, its reputation, and its relationships with customers, investors, and regulators. This broader scope of consideration can make corporate decision-making more complex and nuanced than what one might experience in a military environment.

Another important aspect of corporate hierarchies is the role of middle management, which serves as a bridge between senior executives and front-line employees. Middle managers are responsible for implementing the strategies and directives set by the top leadership while also managing the day-to-day operations and addressing the concerns of their teams. This position requires a delicate balance of leadership, communication, and problem-solving skills, as middle managers must navigate the sometimes conflicting demands of upper management and their subordinates. In the military, the equivalent might be the role of a non-commissioned officer (NCO), who is tasked with ensuring that orders from higher-ups are carried out while maintaining the morale and effectiveness of the troops.

However, in the corporate world, the scope of middle management can be broader, and the ability to drive results through influence rather than direct command.

Unwritten Rules of Corporate Politics

Corporate politics is a complex and often subtle aspect of professional life that extends beyond the formal structures of hierarchy and decision-making. Understanding and navigating these unwritten rules can be crucial for career success, particularly for those transitioning from more regimented environments like the military or law enforcement. Unlike the clear-cut chain of command and straightforward decisions, corporate politics involves informal influence, alliance-building, and perception management. Adapting to corporate hierarchies and office politics proved to be one of the most challenging aspects of my transition from the military to the corporate world. In the military, decisions are straightforward, and leadership roles are clear-cut. Conversely, in the corporate environment, power dynamics are more nuanced, where influence often outweighs rank.

I remember early in my corporate career when I felt extremely frustrated with how slowly decisions were made. Accustomed to the military's decisive nature, I struggled with the layers of approval and the subtle, unspoken politics. A pivotal moment came during a project when I was overlooked for input on a critical security issue because I hadn't involved the right stakeholders from the start.

That experience taught me the value of building alliances. I began identifying key individuals—those who held influence, regardless of their position on the organizational chart. I made an effort to engage with them outside of formal meetings through coffee chats and informal conversations. This approach helped me build rapport and understand what motivated them, allowing me to align security initiatives with their goals.

When conflicts emerged, I drew on my crisis management training. Rather than confronting issues head-on, I focused on mediation and finding common ground, always framing discussions in terms of the broader objectives and shared goals.

For instance, when faced with a disagreement over budget allocations for security upgrades, instead of resisting, I collaborated with the finance team to demonstrate the long-term return on investment. This approach transformed a potential conflict into a collaborative success. These personal experiences and strategies have not only shaped my corporate journey but also offered valuable insights for others navigating similar transitions.

Informal influence in the corporate world refers to the ability to affect decisions and outcomes without relying on formal authority. While titles and positions matter, individuals who are adept at leveraging their relationships, knowledge, and communication skills can often wield significant power within an organization. This type of influence is usually built over time through trust, credibility, and the ability to consistently add value.

For example, a mid-level employee who consistently provides insightful solutions to complex problems might become a go-to person for advice, thereby gaining influence that extends beyond their official role. This informal power can be as critical—if not more so—than formal authority, particularly in organizations that value collaboration and consensus.

Alliance-building is another key component of corporate politics. In many ways, it's about creating a network of allies who support your goals and can help you navigate the organizational landscape. Alliances can be built across departments, with peers, and even with those at higher or lower levels in the hierarchy. The goal is to create a support system that can offer guidance, share information, and advocate on your behalf when needed. Building alliances requires emotional intelligence, the ability to understand others' motivations and the skill to align your interests with theirs.

Perception management is the third pillar of navigating corporate politics. How you are perceived by others—colleagues, superiors, and subordinates—can significantly impact your career. This involves not just managing your image but also being aware of how others' perceptions can shape your opportunities within the organization.

For example, being seen as a reliable problem-solver can lead to more challenging assignments, while being perceived as difficult to work with can limit your career growth, regardless of your actual performance. Perception management is about being mindful of how your actions, communication style and even your body language are interpreted by others. It also involves understanding the broader corporate culture and aligning your behavior with its values and expectations. In the corporate world, the importance of perception cannot be overstated. For instance, someone who is consistently visible in meetings, contributes thoughtfully and builds rapport with key stakeholders is likely to be perceived as a leader, even if they do not hold a formal leadership title. On the other hand, someone who does excellent work but does so quietly, without ensuring that their contributions are recognized, might be overlooked when opportunities for advancement arise. Managing perception is about striking a balance between self-promotion and genuine contribution, ensuring that your efforts are noticed and valued by those who matter.

Navigating the unwritten rules of corporate politics is an essential skill for career success. It requires a blend of strategic thinking, emotional intelligence, and a deep understanding of the organization's culture and dynamics. While these skills may seem daunting to those more familiar with formal structures and clear chains of command, they are crucial in a corporate environment where informal influence, alliances, and perception often dictate the real power dynamics. By mastering these aspects of corporate politics, professionals can better position themselves for success, ensuring that their contributions are recognized and their careers progress in line with their ambitions.

Strategies for Navigating Office Dynamics

Navigating office dynamics effectively is crucial for success in the corporate world. Understanding how to identify key decision-makers, knowing when to assert oneself, and learning how to diplomatically disagree with superiors are essential skills that can significantly impact your career. Here are some strategies to help you maneuver through the complexities of office politics and power structures.

Identifying Key Decision-Makers

In any organization, decision-making power doesn't always align with formal titles. Key decision-makers might not be the highest-ranking individuals but could still wield substantial influence.

Identifying these individuals requires keen observation and networking. Start by mapping out the organization's hierarchy and noting who is involved in various decision-making processes. Pay attention to who gets consulted, who has the ear of senior leaders, and who seems to influence project outcomes. Often, these are people who are well-connected across departments or those who have a reputation for expertise in their area. Networking is also crucial. Engage in conversations with colleagues at all levels to gather insights about who holds sway in different areas. Attend company events, participate in cross-departmental meetings, and seek out informal opportunities to build relationships.

Knowing When to Assert Yourself

Assertiveness is about standing up for yourself and expressing your ideas and needs clearly and respectfully. However, knowing when and how to assert yourself is key to maintaining a positive work environment and ensuring that your contributions are recognized. Assess the situation before speaking up. Consider the timing and the context. If you have a strong idea or solution, ensure that the discussion is open and that it's an appropriate time to present your thoughts. Avoid interrupting or dominating conversations, especially in meetings where others may have different perspectives. It's also essential to build credibility before asserting yourself. Establish a track record of reliability and competence so that when you do speak up, your input is taken seriously. According to research by the Harvard Business Review, credibility plays a significant role in how assertive communication is received. Building a reputation as a knowledgeable and reliable employee enhances the effectiveness of your assertiveness.

Diplomatically Disagreeing with Superiors

Disagreeing with superiors can be tricky but is sometimes necessary to ensure that the best decisions are made. The key is to approach disagreements with diplomacy and respect.

Start by framing your disagreement in a way that acknowledges the superior's perspective while presenting your views. Use phrases like, *"I understand your point of view, but have you considered…"* This approach demonstrates respect for their authority while introducing alternative ideas. Focus on the issue, not the person. Keep the discussion objective and based on facts rather than personal opinions. This helps prevent the conversation from becoming confrontational. For example, if you disagree with a decision about a project, present data or evidence supporting your position and explain how your suggestion could lead to better outcomes.

Techniques for Resolution and Strategies for Team Integration

Building alliances and managing conflicts effectively is key to thriving in the workplace while maintaining your principles. Here are some practical tips and techniques for achieving these goals:

Building Alliances

> **Understand Organizational Dynamics**: Take the time to observe and understand the power structures and informal networks within your organization. Identify key influencers and decision-makers, regardless of their formal titles. This awareness will help you navigate interactions more effectively.

> **Network Strategically**: Engage with colleagues from different departments and levels. Attend company events, participate in cross-functional meetings, and seek out informal gatherings. Building relationships outside of your immediate team broadens your support network and increases your influence.

> **Show Genuine Interest**: Build relationships by showing genuine interest in your colleagues' work and career goals. Engage in conversations about their projects, ask questions, and offer help where you can.

This demonstrates that you value their contributions and are willing to support them.

> **Provide Value**: Be proactive in offering assistance and sharing your expertise. By contributing to others' success, you create goodwill and establish yourself as a valuable resource. For instance, if you have specialized knowledge or skills, use them to help colleagues with their projects.

> **Communicate Effectively:** Practice open and transparent communication. Keep others informed about your work and progress, and be receptive to feedback. This fosters trust and ensures that your contributions are visible.

Managing Conflicts

> **Address Issues Early:** Don't let conflicts fester. Address issues as soon as they arise to prevent them from escalating. Approach conflicts with a solution-oriented mindset and aim to resolve them constructively.

> **Listen Actively:** When conflicts arise, listen actively to understand the other person's perspective. Avoid interrupting and focus on their concerns. This shows respect and helps in identifying common ground.

- ➤ **Stay Objective:** Keep discussions focused on the issue at hand rather than personal attributes. Avoid personal attacks and use facts and evidence to support your position. For example, if there's a disagreement over a project deadline, discuss the project requirements and timelines rather than question individual performance.

- ➤ **Seek Win-Win Solutions:** Aim for solutions that satisfy both parties' needs. Collaborate to find compromises that address the core concerns of everyone involved. For example, if there's a disagreement over resource allocation, work together to prioritize tasks and find a balanced solution.

- ➤ **Utilize Mediation:** If a conflict is particularly challenging, consider involving a neutral third party to mediate. A mediator can facilitate a constructive dialogue and help both parties reach an agreement.

- ➤ **Reflect on Your Principles:** When resolving conflicts, ensure that you remain true to your principles. Stand firm on values that are important to you, but approach disagreements with respect and flexibility. For instance, if you value transparency but face pressure to withhold information, find a way to balance openness with the need for confidentiality.

- ➤ **Follow-Up:** After resolving a conflict, follow up with the involved parties to ensure that the resolution is working and to address any lingering issues. This demonstrates a commitment to maintaining a positive working relationship.

Implementing these strategies can help build strong alliances and handle conflicts effectively without compromising your principles. Developing these skills enhances your professional relationships while positioning you as a valued team player committed to fostering a collaborative and respectful work environment.

Mastering the art of navigating corporate hierarchy and politics can transform career trajectories and enhance workplace effectiveness. By learning to identify key influencers, assert ideas tactfully, and manage conflicts constructively, professionals can excel in the corporate environment. Embracing these skills not only fosters career growth but also cultivates a collaborative and supportive work culture.

As John C. Maxwell aptly puts it, *"Leadership is not about being in charge. It is about taking care of those in your charge."* Applying this principle to corporate dynamics will lead to lasting success and professional fulfillment.

Chapter 10: From Command to Influence

Navigating the complexities of leadership requires more than just authority; it demands presence, credibility, and the ability to influence without direct power. This is especially true in corporate environments, where leaders must adapt to diverse teams, manage competing priorities, and communicate effectively across departments. Mastering executive presence and strategic communication enables leaders to inspire trust, build lasting relationships, and drive success.

Differences Between Military Command and Corporate Leadership

Military command and corporate leadership are two forms of authority that operate within fundamentally different frameworks while both focused on guiding and motivating people toward achieving specific objectives. The distinctions between these systems stem from the environments in which they function, the structures that support them, and how authority is earned and exercised.

Hierarchical Structure vs. Collaborative Framework

One of the most significant differences between military command and corporate leadership is the nature of their organizational structures. The military operates within a rigid, hierarchical framework where rank determines authority, and directives flow top-down.

In this environment, soldiers are trained to follow orders from superiors, often with little room for negotiation or discussion. This structure is essential in the military, where quick decisions, clarity, and unified action can mean the difference between success and failure and, sometimes, life and death. On the other hand, corporate organizations tend to follow a more collaborative framework. While companies still have hierarchies, the flow of communication and decision-making is generally more fluid. Authority in the corporate world is often shared or delegated across multiple levels of management, allowing for feedback, suggestions, and innovation from employees at various levels. Unlike the military, where orders must be followed without question, corporate leaders are expected to earn the trust and buy-in of their teams through persuasion, vision, and the demonstration of competence.

Authority and How It's Earned

In the military, authority is closely tied to rank, often earned through time served, training, and demonstrated competence. Promotions are based on a clearly defined set of criteria, and rank comes with a standardized set of responsibilities.

Once an officer achieves a certain rank, they are automatically granted authority over those with lower ranks, and this authority is non-negotiable. Soldiers are trained to follow orders from those of higher rank, irrespective of personal opinions or disagreements, because the chain of command is seen as critical to operational success. In contrast, authority in the corporate world is not always as clear-cut. While corporate leaders are often appointed based on qualifications and experience, their authority can be more fluid and subjective. Managers may have the formal authority to direct a team. Still, their effectiveness depends on their ability to influence and persuade employees, build relationships, and foster a sense of shared purpose. In many cases, corporate leaders must continually earn their authority by proving their competence, leading by example, and demonstrating integrity. An employee in a corporate setting may challenge a manager's decision or propose an alternative course of action, reflecting the less rigid nature of corporate authority.

Decision-Making: Command vs. Consensus

Another critical difference between military and corporate leadership lies in the decision-making process. In the military, higher-ranking officers often make decisions swiftly and rely on their experience and training to make the best possible choices under pressure. This centralized decision-making process is crucial in the military because it ensures a coordinated response to rapidly changing situations.

In many cases, there is no time for consultation or debate, and soldiers are expected to implicitly trust the judgment of their commanding officers. In the corporate world, decision-making is often more decentralized and collaborative. Leaders are encouraged to consult with their teams, gather input from different departments, and seek external advice before making important decisions. This approach allows for more diverse perspectives and helps organizations remain agile in a constantly evolving business environment.

However, this collaborative process can also slow decision-making, especially in larger organizations where multiple stakeholders must be consulted.

Motivation and Discipline

Military command relies heavily on discipline as a form of motivation. Soldiers are trained from the beginning of their careers to adhere to a strict code of conduct and to obey orders without hesitation. The consequences of disobedience or failure to meet expectations can be severe, ranging from formal reprimands to more serious legal consequences under military law. This strict discipline ensures that all military members are aligned with the organization's goals and that they can perform under extreme pressure.

In contrast, corporate leadership emphasizes intrinsic motivation and personal development more. While discipline is still important in corporate settings, it is often enforced through policies, performance reviews, and incentives rather than strict codes of conduct. Corporate leaders are expected to inspire and motivate their teams by fostering a positive work environment, offering opportunities for career growth, and recognizing individual contributions. Employees are motivated not just by the desire to avoid punishment but by the prospect of personal and professional advancement, recognition, and a sense of belonging to a larger mission.

Flexibility vs. Standardization

Flexibility is another key difference between military and corporate leadership. The military relies on standardized procedures and protocols to ensure that operations are carried out consistently and efficiently, regardless of the specific individuals involved. This standardization allows military units to function seamlessly, even when personnel are reassigned or replaced. Regardless of their position, every soldier is trained uniformly, ensuring little room for deviation from established procedures.

Corporate organizations, on the other hand, tend to value flexibility and adaptability. While there are certainly standardized processes in place, particularly in areas such as compliance and operations, corporate leaders are often encouraged to think creatively and make decisions that are tailored to the unique circumstances of their teams or markets. This flexibility allows companies to innovate, respond to changes in the business environment, and differentiate themselves from competitors.

Mastering Influence Techniques for Leading Without Direct Authority

Influencing without direct authority is critical in today's interconnected and increasingly collaborative work environments. Unlike traditional hierarchical systems, where authority is clearly defined and enforced, modern organizations often rely on cross-functional teams, where individuals must work together without a clear power structure. Leaders must rely on persuasion, negotiation, and consensus-building in these situations to move initiatives forward. Mastering these techniques allows professionals to navigate complex organizational landscapes and drive results without formal authority.

The Importance of Influencing Without Authority

Early in my corporate career, I learned a valuable lesson about the power of listening as a tool for influence. During a major security upgrade project, I found myself in a position where I didn't have direct authority over the IT department. Yet, their cooperation was crucial to the project's success.

Rather than pushing my agenda or forcing a solution, I took the time to listen to their concerns and understand their challenges. By framing the security upgrades as solutions to some of their existing pain points, I was able to build rapport and gain their support without needing any formal directive. This experience taught me that influence often begins with empathy and understanding the perspective of others. Influencing without direct authority is essential for several reasons.

First, many organizations today adopt flatter, more decentralized structures where decision-making is distributed across teams. In such environments, it's rare for one person to have all the power needed to implement changes unilaterally. Instead, success depends on collaborating effectively and gaining support from diverse stakeholders. Second, as teams become more cross-functional, working across departments is common. Marketing teams need input from product development, sales teams require collaboration with customer service, and finance needs to engage with operations. In these scenarios, no one department can dictate terms to the others. This makes it vital for professionals to influence their peers, aligning different goals and perspectives to achieve a common objective.

Lastly, influencing without authority builds trust and fosters collaboration, two key elements of successful organizations. Leaders who rely solely on their positional power often fail to cultivate lasting relationships, while those who can influence through respect, credibility, and understanding gain lasting allies. This not only leads to more successful outcomes but also helps create a more positive, productive workplace culture.

Techniques for Persuasion, Negotiation, and Building Consensus

Influencing without direct authority requires a different skill set than simply giving orders. To be successful, leaders must excel in three key areas: persuasion, negotiation, and consensus-building.

Persuasion

When it comes to persuasion, I've always believed in aligning my objectives with the goals of those I'm trying to influence. It's not just about what I want to achieve but about how my proposal can help others succeed.

By being transparent about my intentions and demonstrating how a particular action benefits me and the broader team or organization, I've found that people are much more receptive to my ideas. This approach fosters trust and encourages collaboration, showing that I'm considering the bigger picture, not just my individual needs.

Several techniques can help make your arguments more persuasive:

> **Understand Your Audience:** Persuasion begins with knowing what motivates the people you're trying to influence. Take the time to understand their concerns, priorities, and goals. This allows you to frame your proposal to align with their interests, increasing the likelihood they will support your initiative.

> **Build Credibility:** People are likelier to listen to and follow someone they trust. Building credibility involves consistently delivering results, being transparent, and demonstrating expertise in your area. Over time, this establishes you as a reliable and knowledgeable figure that others will respect and follow, even without formal authority.

> **Use Data and Evidence:** Facts and figures can be incredibly persuasive, especially when dealing with analytical or data-driven individuals. Presenting clear,

well-researched evidence to support your ideas can help sway even the most skeptical colleagues.

> **Tell a Story**: While data is important, don't underestimate the power of storytelling. People naturally draw to narratives that illustrate a compelling vision or provide emotional resonance. Sharing success stories, anecdotes, or hypothetical scenarios can help make your proposal more relatable and engaging.

Negotiation

Negotiation is fundamental when working across departments or teams where priorities may differ. When you don't have formal authority, you need to find mutually beneficial solutions that allow both sides to feel like they've gained something. Effective negotiation involves:

> **Active Listening:** Before negotiating, it's crucial to understand the needs and concerns of the other party. Active listening involves fully focusing on what they say, asking clarifying questions, and acknowledging their perspective. This shows respect and creates an atmosphere of collaboration.

> **Identify Common Ground:** Once you understand each other's positions, focus on identifying areas of overlap. Highlighting shared objectives can help shift the

conversation from competing interests to how both sides can work together to achieve common goals.

> **Offer Solutions, Not Demands:** When negotiating, it's essential to offer solutions considering the other party's needs. Rather than making demands, frame your suggestions as ways to help both sides. This increases the likelihood of reaching a compromise that everyone can agree on.

> **Be Willing to Compromise:** Influencing without authority requires flexibility. You may not get everything you want in a negotiation, but be prepared to give and take. Offering concessions on less important points can help you secure agreement on critical issues.

In my experience in negotiation, I often rely on the "Yes, and..." technique to build on the ideas of others rather than dismissing them. This approach keeps the conversation constructive and collaborative, making it easier to find common ground.

For example, if a colleague proposes a cost-saving measure that might compromise security, instead of rejecting the idea outright, I would say, "Yes, I see how that could save costs, and I think we can also enhance security by..." This method ensures that the other person feels heard and valued while allowing me to introduce my perspective in a way that feels like a natural extension of their idea. It's a simple but effective way to keep negotiations positive and solution-focused.

Building Consensus

Consensus-building is a more collaborative approach to decision-making that focuses on aligning the interests of different stakeholders. When building consensus, the goal is to ensure that everyone involved feels heard, understood, and aligned with the final decision.

- ➢ **Engage Early and Often:** Building consensus starts by involving stakeholders early in the process. The sooner you bring others into the conversation, the more invested they will feel in the outcome. Regular communication also helps prevent misunderstandings and resistance later.

- ➢ **Foster Open Dialogue:** Creating an environment where people feel comfortable sharing their opinions is key to building consensus. Encourage open discussion, solicit input from all relevant parties, and ensure that different viewpoints are considered. This creates a sense of ownership and commitment to the final decision.

- ➢ **Find the Win-Win:** True consensus is achieved when everyone feels they've gained something. Look for opportunities to create win-win scenarios where each stakeholder's priorities are addressed somehow. Even if not every desire can be fully met, acknowledging and integrating different perspectives can lead to a solution that satisfies the majority.

In a world where formal authority is often dispersed, the ability to influence without direct power is essential. By mastering the techniques of persuasion, negotiation, and consensus-building, professionals can drive results and achieve their goals across departments and teams. These skills help individuals lead more effectively and foster a culture of collaboration, trust, and shared success.

Developing Executive Presence and Credibility in Corporate Settings

Executive presence and credibility are essential for corporate success, and these qualities are rooted in how effectively you can lead, communicate, and inspire trust. They aren't simply about holding a leadership title but about projecting confidence, carrying yourself in important moments, and building trust over time through consistent, reliable actions.

In the corporate world, executive presence often depends on how well you handle high-pressure situations. It's not about being the loudest person in the room but about being the person others turn to when clarity and steady leadership are needed.

When faced with difficult decisions, the ability to stay calm, offer thoughtful solutions and demonstrate confidence goes a long way in establishing that presence. At the same time, credibility is built through the consistency of your behavior by proving that you can deliver results and that your actions align with the values you promote.

One of the best examples of someone who has mastered executive presence and credibility is Indra Nooyi, the former CEO of PepsiCo. Nooyi is widely known for her calm but commanding presence, particularly during corporate transformation and challenges. When she first became CEO in 2006, PepsiCo was a highly profitable company, but Nooyi saw that the future of the business required a significant shift. She recognized the growing demand for healthier products. She led the company toward that vision, boldly investing in more nutritious food and beverages while maintaining PepsiCo's traditional snack business. Nooyi didn't just dictate these changes from the top. She engaged with employees, board members, and external stakeholders, carefully explaining her vision and its necessity for the company's long-term success. One of her most famous initiatives was "Performance with Purpose," which focused on sustainability and healthier product offerings. This was not immediately popular with some stakeholders who feared it could negatively impact profits. Still, Nooyi's ability to communicate the bigger picture and align her goals with broader corporate and societal trends earned her respect and credibility. She consistently demonstrated executive presence through her strategic communication—by explaining the rationale behind her decisions clearly, persuasively, and with a calm assurance that made others confident in her leadership. She wasn't afraid to face resistance or tough questions, always prepared with data and a clear vision of how PepsiCo's transformation would benefit the company in the long run.

Another key factor in Nooyi's success was her authenticity. Even as one of the most powerful women in business, she maintained a reputation for being approachable and transparent, often sharing personal insights about her journey and struggles. This openness built trust within her organization, external partners, and the public. Nooyi's example shows that executive presence is not about being authoritative but about being genuine and consistent, ultimately building more profound credibility over time.

"Leadership is hard to define, and good leadership even harder. But if you can get people to follow you to the ends of the earth, you are a great leader."
Indra Nooyi

Her leadership at PepsiCo demonstrated that executive presence is more than just commanding attention—it's about earning it by being prepared, thoughtful, and clear in your communication and following through on your vision with tangible results. She made tough decisions that transformed the company, and by aligning her vision with the broader goals of the organization and its stakeholders, she was able to build trust and influence without ever needing to resort to a top-down leadership style.

Nooyi's career is a testament to how mastering executive presence and credibility can elevate a leader's impact in a corporate setting, especially when leading transformative change. Her legacy at PepsiCo shows how these traits, combined with strategic communication and authenticity, can guide a company through challenging transitions and leave a lasting mark.

My Personal Narrative

When I first transitioned into corporate settings, I was used to the direct, no-nonsense communication style from my previous experiences, much like those from military environments where communication is clear, concise, and action-oriented.

However, I quickly realized that in the corporate world, how you present yourself can be just as important as what you present. It became clear that building influence required more than just being efficient and straightforward; it demanded a certain level of finesse in communication and presence.

I began to observe the executives I admired, paying close attention to how they spoke and carried themselves in meetings, particularly how they handled difficult questions or challenging moments. One executive I respected always took a brief pause before answering any question, which struck me as a way to collect his thoughts and project a sense of calm and control. I adopted that same technique, realizing that pausing before responding gave me time to craft a thoughtful, deliberate answer rather than reacting impulsively.

To build my executive presence, I focused on three key areas: clarity, confidence, and consistency. Clarity in communication became essential, which meant learning to remove any unnecessary jargon or complexity and speak in straightforward terms that resonated with my audience. Focusing on the audience's specific concerns and using language they understood made my ideas more impactful.

I learned that confidence isn't just about being assertive or speaking loudly. True confidence comes from knowing your subject matter deeply and backing up your statements with relevant data, experiences, or examples. When I said this, I made sure I had facts to support my positions and presented them in a way that demonstrated my knowledge and conviction.

Consistency was another key element that I worked on. Over time, I realized that people trust you when you are reliable—when you consistently deliver on your promises and maintain a professional demeanor.

This wasn't just about being reliable in completing tasks but also about how I presented myself in every interaction, big or small. By maintaining a consistent tone and approach, I built credibility and trust within my teams and with senior leadership.

When it came to presentations, I learned to modify my approach based on who I spoke to. Rather than using a one-size-fits-all method, I would always start by framing the discussion around what my audience cared most about. If I were presenting to the finance team, I would focus on ROI, cost-benefit analysis, or financial metrics that mattered to them. On the other hand, if my audience were the HR team, I would shift the focus to how the initiative would impact employee morale, safety, or engagement. Tailoring the message to each specific audience made my presentations more relevant and demonstrated that I understood their priorities, making my arguments more persuasive. Through these experiences, I better understood how to navigate corporate dynamics and how executive presence is truly built over time. It's not just about what you say but how you say it and how well you align your message with the needs and concerns of those around you.

Strategies for Leading Cross-Functional Teams

One of the biggest challenges I faced was during a company-wide security overhaul, where I led a cross-functional team of IT specialists, H.R. managers, and external contractors.

Each group had different priorities—I.T. focused on data security, HR on employee privacy, and contractors on meeting deadlines. It sometimes felt like herding cats, but I quickly learned to respect and leverage their diverse expertise. I created a shared vision of success that aligned with everyone's goals and clarified that every voice mattered. To manage the differences, I adopted a collaborative approach, encouraging input from all parties and setting clear, common goals that outlined how each team's contributions were essential. Regular check-ins helped keep everyone aligned, and celebrating small wins along the way maintained morale. Communication became a challenge in virtual settings, so I over-communicated key updates and used collaborative tools like shared dashboards for transparency. I scheduled informal virtual coffee breaks to build rapport, which helped foster personal connections and trust within the team.

Here are a few strategies for leading cross-functional teams, addressing challenges like diverse expertise levels, competing priorities, and virtual team management.

> ➤ **Emphasize clear communication:** Establishing open and transparent communication channels is crucial when leading cross-functional teams. Regular updates, clearly defined goals, and a shared understanding of roles help to prevent misunderstandings and keep everyone aligned.

> ➤ **Align team goals with organizational objectives:** Ensure all team members understand how their tasks contribute to the broader organizational goals. This alignment helps keep competing priorities in check and encourages collaboration toward a common purpose.

➤ **Leverage diverse expertise:** Recognize and appreciate the team's different expertise levels. Encourage members to share their knowledge and skills, fostering an environment of mutual learning and respect that enhances the team's overall performance.

➤ **Address competing priorities through prioritization frameworks:** Use structured frameworks like RACI (Responsible, Accountable, Consulted, Informed) or MoSCoW (Must Have, Should Have, Could Have, Won't Have) to address and balance competing priorities effectively. These methods help clarify roles and determine what needs immediate attention.

➤ **Foster collaboration and trust across virtual teams:** Managing virtual teams presents unique challenges, such as ensuring collaboration and trust across distances. Utilize digital tools to maintain engagement, foster regular communication, and create opportunities for virtual team-building activities to strengthen connections.

➤ **Provide flexibility and accountability:** Recognize the need for flexibility, particularly in virtual settings. Allow team members autonomy in completing tasks but ensure accountability by setting clear deadlines and expectations.

➤ **Resolve conflicts quickly and fairly:** Conflicts may arise in cross-functional teams due to different perspectives or priorities. Address these issues early by mediating discussions, finding common ground, and ensuring that all voices are heard and respected.

Celebrate team successes and individual contributions: Acknowledge collective and individual achievements to maintain morale and motivate the team. Recognizing successes keeps the team engaged and committed to the shared goals. In conclusion, in today's fast-paced corporate landscape, leading cross-functional teams effectively is crucial for any successful leader. Balancing diverse expertise, competing priorities, and the challenges of virtual teams requires strong communication, flexibility, and a collaborative approach.

By fostering trust, leveraging each team member's strengths, and maintaining clear goals, leaders can overcome these challenges and achieve long-term success. As the saying goes, "Leadership is not about being in charge. It's about taking care of those in your charge." With the right strategies, leaders can truly make an impact.

Chapter 11: Risk Management in the Corporate World

"I have learned that nothing is certain except for the need to have strong risk management, a lot of cash, the willingness to invest even when the future is unclear, and great people."

- Jeffrey R. Immelt

In the corporate world, effective risk management is critical to ensuring long-term success and sustainability. Organizations today face many risks, from financial and reputational threats to cybersecurity and operational disruptions. By implementing comprehensive risk management frameworks, such as ISO 31000 and COSO ERM, companies can proactively assess, mitigate, and respond to potential risks before they escalate.

This chapter explores how businesses across various industries have successfully navigated risks by adopting structured, forward-thinking strategies, highlighting the importance of adaptability and resilience in a dynamic market.

Comparing Risk Assessment in Military and Corporate Environments

When transitioning from military or law enforcement environments to the corporate world, one of the most striking differences is how risk is assessed and managed. In military settings, risk assessment is often a matter of life or death, with a clear focus on immediate physical threats and operational readiness. Decisions must be made quickly and precisely, often following a top-down approach. On the other hand, corporate environments deal with a much broader spectrum of risks, including financial, reputational, and compliance threats, alongside physical risks. This difference in scope and how risks are handled can be quite an adjustment for someone transitioning between these two worlds.

In the military, the primary goal of risk assessment is to eliminate or neutralize imminent threats to personnel and mission objectives. The decision-making process is typically swift and hierarchical. Commanders at higher levels assess the situation and provide clear directives, followed immediately by those on the ground. The risks are tangible, and the consequences of inaction or wrong decisions are often severe.

Soldiers and law enforcement officers are trained to respond to immediate dangers like enemy attacks, natural disasters, or other crises that directly impact lives and mission success. The focus is overwhelmingly on mitigating physical threats and ensuring operational continuity in the field.

A 2020 study titled *"Flexibility and Resilience in Corporate Decision Making: A New Sustainability-Based Risk Management System in Uncertain Times"* from the *Global Journal of Flexible Systems Management* highlights how corporate risk management has evolved to focus on resilience, flexibility, and long-term sustainability in decision-making[1]. Unlike the reactive, threat-focused approach in military risk assessments, corporate environments emphasize proactive strategies that account for financial, reputational, and operational risks. This study demonstrates the importance of assessing and mitigating risks that may not have immediate physical consequences but could lead to significant long-term impacts, such as a company's financial stability or public reputation.

I distinctly remember how this approach shaped my thinking during my military service. Risk assessments revolved around real-time decisions—whether to move forward with an operation, whether a route was safe, or how to react to unforeseen dangers like enemy fire or hostile terrain. Everything was geared toward quick, decisive action to protect lives and complete the mission. There was a defined chain of command, and once a decision was made at the top, it was implemented without question. The urgency was palpable because the risks were immediate, visible, and potentially fatal.

However, when I transitioned to the corporate world, I found that risk assessment operates under a very different set of principles. Corporate risk is broader, encompassing physical dangers and financial, reputational, and legal threats. While physical safety is always a priority, the focus is more on

---

[1] Settembre-Blundo, D., González-Sánchez, R., Medina-Salgado, S., & García-Muiña, F. E. (2021). Flexibility and resilience in corporate decision making: a new sustainability-based risk management system in uncertain times. Global Journal of Flexible Systems Management, 22(Suppl 2), 107-132.

prevention and long-term planning. It's about foreseeing potential issues before crises and mitigating risks to protect the company's assets and reputation over time.

I vividly recall a situation early in my corporate career when a data breach was discovered. Coming from a military background, I initially saw the incident as minor since there was no immediate operational impact. However, I quickly learned that the potential reputational damage was immense.

The breach could erode customer trust and damage the company's standing in the marketplace, even though no sensitive data had been compromised. This was a turning point for me, as it highlighted the stark differences between military and corporate approaches to risk. In the corporate world, the lack of immediate physical danger doesn't diminish the severity of the threat. The impact of financial losses, customer dissatisfaction, or legal repercussions can be just as damaging to an organization's long-term survival as physical threats are in a military setting.

One of the critical differences in risk management between the military and corporate sectors is how proactive the corporate world is in assessing risk. Military operations tend to be reactive because threats are identified, neutralized, or eliminated. It's a constant cycle of identifying and removing danger to ensure safety and mission success. In corporate environments, however, the emphasis is often on prevention. Companies invest significant time and resources in identifying potential risks before they materialize—whether through market analysis, customer feedback, financial forecasting, or regulatory compliance checks. The goal is to prevent the risk from ever becoming a reality.

Corporate risk management also tends to involve more collaboration across departments. Financial risk, for instance, may include input from finance, legal, and compliance teams, all working together to create a holistic view of the potential threats to the organization.

This approach contrasts with the more centralized decision-making process in the military, where risk is assessed, and decisions are made within the chain of command. The process is often slower in the corporate world, with more room for discussion, debate, and negotiation. While this can sometimes feel inefficient, it reflects the complexity of managing risks.

Another key difference is the role that reputation plays in corporate risk management. In the military, the primary focus is on protecting lives and completing the mission. In contrast, companies are deeply concerned with how risks affect their brand and customer relationships.

The potential for reputational damage can drive significant decisions, as companies know that public trust can be fragile. A single misstep—whether a product recall, a data breach, or a scandal—can have long-lasting consequences for a business, even if it doesn't immediately impact operations. This difference in priorities was another adjustment for me. While I was used to assessing threats regarding physical danger and immediate action, I had to learn to think about the long-term implications of a decision on the company's reputation, stock price, and customer loyalty.

Risk assessments now involve looking at everything from social media backlash to regulatory fines. It became clear that corporate risk management required quick thinking in a crisis and a deep understanding of how various types of risks interact and affect the broader business landscape.

Expanding Key Risk Management Frameworks in Business

Risk management is essential to corporate strategy, helping organizations anticipate, mitigate, and respond to potential threats. Two widely recognized frameworks that guide businesses in managing risks effectively are ISO 31000 and COSO ERM (Enterprise Risk Management).

These frameworks provide structured approaches to identifying, assessing, and addressing risks, ensuring that companies can make informed decisions and maintain operational stability. This chapter delves into both frameworks, explaining how they work and how they can be applied in practical business scenarios.

ISO 31000: A Global Standard for Risk Management

ISO 31000, developed by the International Organization for Standardization (ISO), is a comprehensive risk management framework designed to provide a uniform approach to risk management applicable to organizations of all sizes and industries. The framework offers a set of guidelines, principles, and processes that help businesses manage risks systematically and effectively.

One of the core principles of ISO 31000 is that risk management should create and protect value for the organization. This means that risk management efforts should not only protect the organization from threats but also contribute to the achievement of objectives. For example, in a manufacturing company, adopting ISO 31000 might focus on improving production processes to reduce the risk of defects, enhancing product quality and customer satisfaction. Another important aspect of ISO 31000 is its emphasis on integrating risk management into the organization's governance and decision-making processes. Rather than treating risk management separately, ISO 31000 encourages companies to embed risk awareness across all departments and functions. This holistic approach ensures that risks are considered in strategic planning, operational activities, and performance evaluations.

This might mean that a company's IT department considers potential cybersecurity risks when planning new technology initiatives. In contrast, the finance department assesses financial risks when planning investments or mergers. Applying ISO 31000 in Practical Situations: ISO 31000 provides a flexible structure that can be adapted to various industries. For example, in the construction industry, companies might use ISO 31000 to assess safety risks on job sites, develop mitigation strategies such as enhanced worker training or improved equipment, and monitor outcomes to ensure continuous improvement. In the banking industry, the framework can help institutions evaluate market risks, such as interest rate fluctuations, and establish protocols to protect their financial stability.

By encouraging a proactive and continuous approach to risk management, ISO 31000 allows companies to protect themselves from immediate threats and build resilience for the future. Companies implementing ISO 31000 are better equipped to anticipate emerging risks and adapt to a rapidly changing business environment, whether related to regulatory changes, new technologies, or evolving customer demands.

COSO ERM: A Structured Approach to Enterprise Risk Management

The COSO ERM framework, developed by the Committee of Sponsoring Organizations of the Treadway Commission, offers a more detailed and structured approach to enterprise-wide risk management.

COSO ERM focuses on integrating risk management with corporate governance, ensuring that all risks are managed in alignment with an organization's strategic objectives. Unlike ISO 31000, which provides broad principles, COSO ERM offers specific guidelines on how organizations should identify, assess, and respond to risks.

One of the key elements of COSO ERM is its focus on the risk management process as a continuous, iterative process rather than a one-time assessment. The framework outlines steps organizations should follow to manage risks effectively. These steps include:

> **Risk identification:** Companies must first identify potential risks impacting their operations or objectives.

> **Risk assessment:** After identifying risks, organizations evaluate each risk's likelihood and potential impact.

> **Risk response:** Based on the assessment, companies develop strategies to avoid, mitigate, transfer, or accept the risks.

> **Monitoring and reporting:** Continuous monitoring ensures that risk management strategies remain effective and responsive to changing conditions.

Applying COSO ERM in Practical Situations: In practical applications, COSO ERM is often used by businesses operating in heavily regulated industries, such as finance, healthcare, and energy. For example, a financial services company might use

COSO ERM to manage credit risk by identifying potential risks to its loan portfolio, assessing the likelihood of borrowers' default, and establishing mitigation strategies such as diversifying the portfolio or tightening credit approval criteria.

Another practical application of COSO ERM is in managing reputational risk. For instance, a company facing a potential public relations crisis might use the framework to identify the root causes of the issue, assess the potential damage to the company's brand, and develop a response plan, such as issuing public statements, engaging with customers, and addressing the underlying issues that led to the crisis. COSO ERM is also highly valuable in managing compliance risks, significant in industries subject to strict regulatory oversight. A pharmaceutical company, for instance, could use COSO ERM to ensure compliance with FDA regulations by regularly assessing risks related to product safety, conducting audits, and developing strategies to address any compliance gaps.

Comparing ISO 31000 and COSO ERM

While both ISO 31000 and COSO ERM provide robust frameworks for risk management, they differ in several ways. ISO 31000 is more flexible and offers general guidelines that can be tailored to a wide range of industries and organizational sizes. It is less prescriptive, allowing businesses to adapt the framework to their needs.

On the other hand, COSO ERM is more structured and detailed, making it particularly useful for larger organizations with complex risk profiles or those operating in regulated industries. In terms of application, ISO 31000 is ideal for organizations looking for a broad risk management framework that can be easily integrated into their operations. Its flexibility makes it suitable for small businesses or industries where risk is less regulated. With its more detailed approach, COSO ERM is often favored by larger companies or those in sectors like finance, where risk management must align with stringent regulatory requirements. Effective risk management ensures companies can navigate uncertainties, protect their assets, and maintain their reputation in an increasingly complex business environment. As both frameworks emphasize, risk management is not just about avoiding threats—it's about enabling the organization to achieve its objectives with greater confidence and resilience.

Communicating Risk to Non-Security Stakeholders

"Risk comes from not knowing what you're doing."
— **Warren Buffett.**

Effectively communicating risk to non-security stakeholders is essential for professionals managing security in corporate environments. Many stakeholders, such as executives or board members, may not have a technical background, making it challenging to understand the importance and implications of cybersecurity initiatives. To bridge this gap, it's crucial to translate technical security concepts into business language that resonates with their priorities, such as financial impact, legal risks, and return on investment (ROI). A notoriously famous real-life example of communicating risk effectively to non-security stakeholders comes from Target Corporation. In 2013, Target experienced a massive data breach that exposed the personal information of 40 million credit card holders and 70 million customer records[2]. The breach caused significant reputational and financial damage, with costs estimated in the hundreds of millions of dollars.

Before the breach, there were warnings from their security system about vulnerabilities, but the risk wasn't communicated effectively to the leadership in business terms[3]. The technical teams struggled to translate these concerns into a language that the board and executives, focused on sales and business growth, could prioritize.

Had the security risks been framed in terms of potential financial losses, reputational harm, and legal consequences, it is possible the breach could have been prevented or mitigated more effectively. This event highlights the importance of making non-technical stakeholders understand security risks in business

---

[2] https://www.forbes.com/sites/maggiemcgrath/2014/01/10/target-data-breach-spilled-info-on-as-many-as-70-million-customers/
[3] https://www.sipa.columbia.edu/sites/default/files/2022-11/Target%20Final.pdf

language to ensure proactive decision-making. This breach ultimately led to a significant shift in how corporations handle cybersecurity communication, making it a well-known example of risk management.

The Importance of Translation

In many corporate settings, discussions around security tend to focus on technical jargon—talk of firewalls, encryption, and vulnerabilities, for example, may not resonate with non-technical stakeholders. These concepts, while critical, don't provide the business context that executives need to make informed decisions. To secure buy-in for security investments, professionals must shift the conversation from technical explanations to tangible business outcomes.

In my experience, one of the most significant challenges was explaining to the board the need for a major security investment. I initially focused on potential threats and vulnerabilities, detailing technical aspects like system weaknesses and potential cyberattacks.

However, it quickly became apparent that this wasn't enough. The board needed to understand the business implications of these risks. I pivoted to using a scenario-based approach, outlining what a data breach could mean regarding lost revenue, legal costs, and damage to customer trust. I secured their support by translating the risks into financial terms and illustrating how the investment would protect against these consequences. This experience underscored the importance of framing technical discussions in business terms.

Techniques for Translating Technical Concepts into Business Language

To communicate risk effectively, several techniques can help translate complex security concepts into language that non-technical stakeholders can understand and relate to:

➢ **Use Business-Oriented Scenarios:** One effective approach is to frame cybersecurity risks through real-world scenarios that stakeholders can relate to. For example, instead of discussing abstract threats like "malware," explain how a cyberattack could lead to operational disruptions, revenue loss, or reputational damage. Drawing parallels to high-profile incidents involving competitors or other companies within the same industry can also help make the risks more relatable and urgent.

➢ **Emphasize Financial Impact and ROI:** Business leaders are naturally concerned with the bottom line, so translating security risks into potential financial outcomes can effectively communicate the importance of cybersecurity initiatives. This involves discussing how a lack of investment in security could lead to costly breaches, regulatory fines, and lost business. Additionally, emphasizing the ROI of security investments— how a security measure can prevent much larger losses in the future—helps frame the discussion regarding risk mitigation and financial prudence.

> **Use Analogies and Comparisons:** Analogies are an excellent way to explain technical concepts to non-experts. One analogy I've found particularly useful is comparing cybersecurity to a home security system. Just as no one questions why you lock your doors or install a security system to protect your home, cybersecurity measures protect the organization's digital assets. This comparison helps stakeholders understand that just as physical security is a necessity, digital security is equally critical in today's business environment.

> **Visual Tools Like Risk Heat Maps:** Visual aids can simplify complex information and make grasping risks easier. Risk heat maps are a powerful tool for illustrating the likelihood and impact of different risks, categorizing them in a way that is easy for stakeholders to understand. A heat map allows business leaders to see at a glance which risks are high-priority and require immediate attention. This visual representation of risks helps make abstract concepts more concrete and provides a clear, actionable view of the organization's risk landscape.

> **Provide Concrete Examples and Case Studies:** Another effective technique is referencing real-world examples of companies that suffered major losses due to security breaches. For instance, pointing to high-profile data breaches resulting in multimillion-dollar fines or losing customer trust can make the

discussion more tangible. When stakeholders see how similar companies were affected by neglecting security, they are more likely to understand the importance of preventive measures.

> **Tailor the Message to the Audience's Concerns:** Different stakeholders have different priorities, so it's essential to tailor the message to address their specific concerns. For example, when presenting to a finance team, focus on the cost implications of security risks and the financial benefits of preventive measures. When speaking to the legal team, emphasize compliance risks and potential liabilities. By aligning the message with the stakeholder's priorities, you increase the likelihood of gaining their support for security initiatives.

Demonstrating ROI for Security Initiatives

Demonstrating the ROI is one of the most critical elements of securing buy-in for security initiatives. Business leaders often require a clear justification for any significant investment, and cybersecurity is no exception. Showing how security measures can reduce risk exposure and prevent costly incidents is key to making a compelling business case.

For example, when investing in a new cybersecurity solution, you might present data showing that the cost of a breach, including lost business, legal fees, and reputational damage, far outweighs the cost of the proposed investment. By breaking down the numbers and presenting a clear picture of how the security initiative will save the company money in the long run, you can help stakeholders see the value of the investment.

Case Studies in Successful Risk Mitigation

One of my most memorable successes at a previous company was implementing a comprehensive active shooter response plan. We partnered with local law enforcement and conducted multiple drills to ensure every employee knew their role in an emergency. Initially, there was significant resistance due to concerns about disrupting business operations. However, by framing the initiative as an essential investment in employee safety, we eventually gained support across the organization. The importance of the plan became clear when we faced a real threat. The coordinated response developed during those drills was credited with preventing what could have been a tragic outcome.

One of the most valuable lessons learned was the importance of involving all stakeholders from the very beginning. When people feel they have a role and a voice in the process, they are more likely to support the initiative and take ownership.

Another key lesson was the need for continuous improvement. After the incident, we conducted after-action reviews to assess what went well and what needed refinement. This demonstrated that risk management isn't a one-time event but an ongoing process of evaluation and adjustment to ensure the best possible outcome in the future. Now, we will discuss real-world examples of companies that have effectively navigated and mitigated various risks. These case studies, from industries as diverse as retail, energy, and technology, demonstrate the power of proactive risk management strategies in safeguarding businesses against financial, reputational, and operational threats.

Each example highlights the importance of foresight, flexibility, and a comprehensive approach to handling risks, providing valuable lessons for organizations looking to strengthen their risk management practices.

Walmart's Supply Chain Resilience

Walmart is a prime example of a company that implements robust risk mitigation strategies, particularly in its supply chain management. The retailer faced significant disruptions during natural disasters, such as Hurricane Katrina. In response, Walmart developed a comprehensive risk management strategy that included building redundancies into its supply chain, adopting advanced data analytics to forecast potential disruptions, and establishing contingency plans for various scenarios.

By leveraging technology and improving communication, Walmart has maintained continuity during crises, ensuring its products are delivered to consumers even in adverse conditions. This proactive approach to risk management has made Walmart's supply chain one of the most resilient in the retail industry.

BP's Response to the Deepwater Horizon Spill

The Deepwater Horizon oil spill in 2010 was one of the most catastrophic environmental disasters in history. However, the aftermath also demonstrates effective risk mitigation strategies. While BP initially struggled with its response, it eventually implemented extensive safety and risk management measures to prevent future occurrences.

BP revamped its safety protocols, increased investments in technological innovations to monitor drilling operations, and enhanced its crisis management plans. Although the spill was a lesson in the consequences of ineffective risk management, BP's reforms afterward exemplified how companies can respond to massive risks and implement lasting changes to mitigate future risks.

Coca-Cola's Water Stewardship Program

In its operating regions, Coca-Cola faced significant reputational and operational risks related to water scarcity. Recognizing that water is a vital resource for production, Coca-Cola launched an ambitious risk mitigation strategy focusing on water stewardship.

The company committed to returning the equivalent amount of water it uses in its beverages to communities and nature. Coca-Cola achieved its goal through partnerships with local governments and NGOs, implementing water-saving technologies, and improving water-use efficiency across all operations. This strategy mitigated operational risks and helped secure the company's reputation as a responsible corporate citizen.

Target's Post-Breach Cybersecurity Overhaul

After its infamous 2013 data breach, Target significantly overhauled its cybersecurity strategies. The company implemented new technologies and security protocols, such as enhanced encryption, tokenization of customer data, and increased monitoring for suspicious activities.

Target also hired a Chief Information Security Officer (CISO) and began educating employees and stakeholders about cybersecurity risks. These efforts helped Target recover from the breach and significantly reduced the likelihood of future cyber threats. This case study illustrates the importance of learning from failures and adapting risk management strategies to address evolving threats.

Toyota's Risk Management During the 2011 Earthquake

Toyota's supply chain was severely disrupted during Japan's 2011 earthquake and tsunami. However, Toyota had already implemented a robust risk management strategy that helped it mitigate some of the disaster's impact.

The company had built close relationships with its suppliers, ensuring open lines of communication and the ability to respond quickly to crises. Toyota also diversified its supplier base and maintained multiple manufacturing locations globally, which helped spread the risk. These strategies enabled Toyota to recover more quickly than many competitors, demonstrating the importance of resilience and diversification in risk mitigation.

These case studies emphasize the effectiveness of forward-thinking risk management strategies in mitigating potential threats and responding to crises.

From supply chain resilience and environmental stewardship to cybersecurity and disaster recovery, companies that adopt comprehensive risk management frameworks are better equipped to handle unforeseen challenges and maintain operational continuity. By studying these examples, organizations can learn to implement proactive risk management practices that protect their assets, reputation, and long-term viability.

As corporate environments evolve, managing risks effectively is essential for maintaining operational stability and protecting a company's reputation. Whether mitigating supply chain disruptions, responding to cybersecurity threats, or managing compliance risks, the most successful companies view risk management as an ongoing, dynamic process. Learning from these examples, businesses can cultivate resilience and ensure their long-term success.

Peter Drucker famously said, *"The greatest danger in times of turbulence is not the turbulence itself, but to act with yesterday's logic."*

Embracing proactive risk management enables companies to navigate uncertainties with confidence.

Chapter 12: Crisis Management and Business Continuity

"It takes 20 years to build a reputation and five minutes to ruin it. If you think about that, you'll do things differently."
- Warren Buffett

Crises are inevitable for any organization, whether due to external events like natural disasters or internal challenges such as operational failures or cyberattacks. While a crisis can severely disrupt business operations, having a well-structured crisis management plan can significantly mitigate its impact. Effective crisis management isn't just about solving problems as they arise; it requires a proactive approach that includes preparation, communication, and quick, decisive action.

Leaders who excel in crises focus on safeguarding the organization's reputation, maintaining stakeholder confidence, and ensuring business continuity while keeping their teams resilient and motivated.

Principles of Crisis Management

Crisis management involves identifying, assessing, and resolving any event or situation that threatens an organization's functioning or reputation. The primary goals are to minimize damage, ensure swift recovery, and maintain or restore stakeholder confidence. Key principles include:

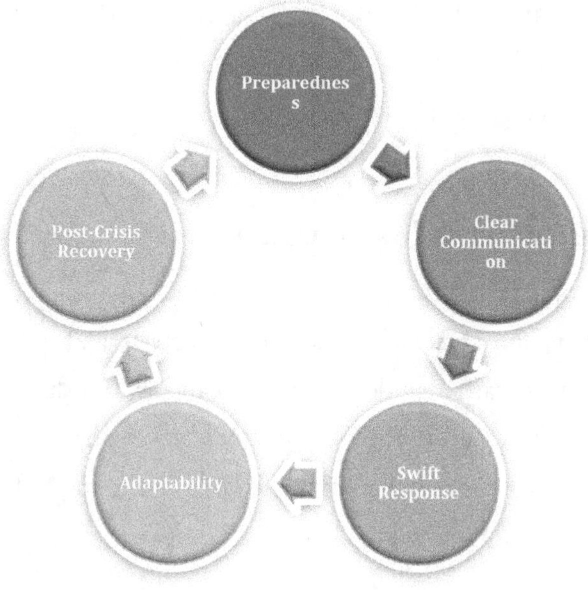

➢ **Preparedness:** Organizations need proactive crisis planning, including risk assessments and scenario planning, to anticipate potential crises.

➢ **Clear Communication:** A vital component of timely, transparent, and consistent messaging to internal and external stakeholders.

➢ **Swift Response:** Fast, effective action is critical to controlling the situation before it escalates.

➢ **Adaptability:** Flexibility to adjust the response as new information emerges.

> **Post-Crisis Recovery:** Evaluation of the response, identification of lessons learned, and rebuilding stakeholder trust.

Corporate Crisis Management

In corporate settings, crisis management typically involves safeguarding the company's reputation, profitability, and stakeholder trust. Crises can include financial scandals, product recalls, cyber-attacks, or PR disasters. The focus is on managing external perceptions and internal communications and ensuring business continuity with minimal impact on operations.

Johnson & Johnson's Tylenol Crisis (1982)

In one of the most studied cases of corporate crisis management, Johnson & Johnson faced a major crisis when seven people in Chicago died after taking Tylenol capsules laced with cyanide[4]. The company's swift and transparent response became an example of effective crisis management. Key actions included:

---

[4]https://www.ou.edu/deptcomm/dodjcc/groups/02C2/Johnson%20&%20Johnso
n.htm

➢ **Immediate product recall:** Johnson & Johnson pulled 31 million bottles of Tylenol off shelves[5], even though the contamination was limited to one area.

➢ **Public safety first:** The company focused on customer safety over short-term profit, winning public trust.

➢ **Open communication:** They maintained constant, honest communication with the public and media, including press conferences and full cooperation with law enforcement.

➢ **Post-crisis innovation:** They introduced tamper-proof packaging after the crisis, setting a new industry standard for product safety.

Military and Law Enforcement Crisis Management

Military and law enforcement crisis management approaches differ significantly from corporate settings. They focus more on operational control, situational containment, and public safety rather than reputation. The goal is to neutralize threats swiftly and efficiently, often involving coordinated teams and tactical operations.

---

[5] https://www.nytimes.com/2002/03/23/your-money/IHT-tylenol-made-a-hero-of-johnson-johnson-the-recall-that-started.html

Differences from Corporate Settings

> **Command Structure:** Military and law enforcement rely on hierarchical command structures where decision-making is centralized and immediate actions are taken without external stakeholder considerations.

> **Public Safety Focus:** Unlike corporations, where reputation is paramount, the focus is on minimizing physical harm and ensuring security during crises like terrorist attacks, hostage situations, or large-scale civil disturbances.

> **Reputation as a Secondary Concern:** While the corporate world prioritizes brand image, law enforcement is more concerned with executing legal authority and public order, often only considering reputational damage in the aftermath.

While corporate and military/law enforcement approaches share the core principles of preparedness, communication, and adaptability, they diverge significantly in focus and application.

Corporate crisis management is shaped by stakeholder communication and brand protection, while military and law enforcement strategies emphasize immediate control and public safety. The contrast between Johnson & Johnson's Tylenol response and tactical law enforcement interventions underscores the differences between reputation management and operational command in crises.

The Value of Military and Law Enforcement Experience in Crisis Management

Military and law enforcement personnel are often thrust into environments where failure can have catastrophic consequences. These experiences develop key crisis management skills such as rapid decision-making, calm under pressure, and adaptive leadership—all of which are crucial in corporate settings during times of crisis. The transition from the battlefield or the streets into the boardroom may seem like a leap, but the skills learned in military and law enforcement roles can enhance how corporations respond to crises, helping them navigate complex challenges with agility and precision.

Rapid Decision-Making Under Pressure

"A good plan, violently executed now, is better than a perfect plan executed next week."
- General George S. Patton

Decisions must often be made in the heat of the moment in military and law enforcement operations. Whether a commanding officer decides how to respond to an ambush or a police officer determines the safest way to handle a volatile suspect, the ability to act quickly and decisively is essential. Importantly, these decisions are often made with incomplete information, a ticking clock, and high stakes—sometimes life or death. This skill directly translates to corporate crisis management, where indecision can exacerbate problems. For instance, during a product recall or a cybersecurity breach, a corporation may not have all the details about what has gone wrong, but waiting too long to act can lead to irreparable damage to the brand, financial losses, or loss of customer trust.

An individual with a military background is trained to assess a situation swiftly, prioritize the available options, and move forward with the best possible solution. They understand the importance of quickly taking control of a situation and know how to lead their teams through uncertain circumstances. This skill is critical in corporate environments, where delays can worsen a crisis.

The Deepwater Horizon Crisis

The Deepwater Horizon oil spill in 2010 provides an example of how decision-making under pressure could have potentially mitigated the crisis. When the drilling rig exploded, spilling millions of barrels of oil into the Gulf of Mexico, it became one of the worst environmental disasters in U.S. history. The explosion took the lives of 11 workers stationed on the rig and unleashed roughly 3.19 million barrels (134 million gallons) of oil into the Gulf, which flowed for 87 days[6]. BP, the company responsible for the rig, was criticized for its delayed response and lack of decisive action. While the technical challenges of stopping the spill were immense, the public's perception of the company's slow reaction time led to a significant loss of trust and financial damage.

A leader with military or law enforcement experience may have approached the situation differently. These individuals are conditioned to act in the face of uncertainty, knowing that even an imperfect action is often better than no action. In the military, hesitation can cost lives, and this mindset of "do something now, adjust later" is invaluable when dealing with corporate crises where hesitation can cost a company its reputation.

Maintaining Composure and Cool-Headed Leadership

Military and law enforcement personnel are trained to stay calm in chaos. Whether it's a police officer managing a crowd in the wake of a violent protest or a soldier leading their team under fire, maintaining composure is critical. This calm demeanor is just as important in a corporate crisis. Employees, customers, and shareholders often look to leadership for reassurance during a crisis. If a company's leaders panic, it sends ripples of fear and

---

[6] https://www.nrdc.org/bio/zanagee-artis/fourteen-years-after-deepwater-horizon-drilling-still-threat#:~:text=On%20April%2020%2C%202010%2C%20barrels,which%20flowed%20for%2087%20days.

uncertainty throughout the organization and can amplify the problem. However, a leader with military or law enforcement training knows how to control their emotions, maintain a calm exterior, and project confidence even when the situation is dire.

This cool-headed leadership can help steady a company during times of crisis. When a CEO or senior management team remains calm and communicates a clear plan of action, it helps to calm employees and stakeholders, reducing panic and restoring a sense of order.

Adaptive Leadership in Dynamic Environments

Another key lesson learned in military and law enforcement settings is the ability to adapt to rapidly changing circumstances. Plans rarely survive their first encounter with reality, and soldiers and law enforcement officers know they must be ready to adjust their strategies on the fly.

This adaptability is often honed through intensive training and real-world experience, where unpredictable events unfold, requiring immediate adjustments. In corporate crises, this ability to be flexible and adjust course quickly can mean the difference between success and failure. For instance, a company might enter a crisis with a set plan, but new information can change the situation's dynamics. A data breach may reveal that more sensitive data has been compromised than initially thought, or a product defect may escalate into a widespread public relations issue. Leaders with military and law enforcement experience understand that the original plan may need to be abandoned or modified as new information comes to light.

The Importance of Communication

Communication is paramount in both military and corporate crisis management. Military leaders are trained to keep their teams informed, providing clear instructions even when under stress. In law enforcement, communication is equally critical—officers must relay information to dispatchers, fellow officers, and sometimes the public while managing an unfolding situation.

This same communication principle applies in corporate crises, where stakeholders need clear and consistent information to understand the nature of the crisis and how it is being handled. Without timely updates, rumors and misinformation can spread, further damaging a company's reputation. A leader with military experience understands the importance of providing clear, concise updates, both internally and externally. They know how to manage the flow of information, ensuring that employees, customers, and the public are kept informed while preventing panic. This experience can be invaluable in managing the narrative of a corporate crisis, where effective communication can help contain the situation and reassure stakeholders that the company is in control.

Rudy Giuliani's Leadership Post-9/11

One of the most famous examples of crisis communication is Mayor Rudy Giuliani's leadership following the 9/11 terrorist attacks. As Mayor of New York City, Giuliani demonstrated remarkable calm and effective communication in the immediate aftermath of the attacks. His military-style approach to providing clear, authoritative updates helped calm a city in chaos[7]. Giuliani's ability to maintain composure, offer reassurances, and outline clear steps for recovery earned him widespread praise and helped restore confidence in the city's recovery efforts.

In corporate crises, effectively communicating with stakeholders—whether through press conferences, internal communications, or social media—can help control the narrative and prevent the crisis from spiraling out of control. Military and law enforcement personnel develop skills in high-pressure environments—rapid decision-making, calm leadership, adaptability, and clear communication—directly transferable to corporate crisis management. In both settings, the stakes are high, and the need for swift, decisive action is paramount. The ability to stay calm under pressure, adapt to changing circumstances, and communicate clearly can help corporations survive crises and emerge stronger on the other side. Hiring leaders with military or law enforcement experience can be a game-changer for companies looking to improve their crisis management strategies. These individuals bring with them a wealth of

---

[7] https://www.jba.af.mil/News/Commentaries/Display/Article/338041/

knowledge about managing complex, high-stakes situations, and their unique experiences can help guide companies through their toughest challenges, ensuring a swift and effective response when disaster strikes.

The Importance of Business Continuity Planning

Business continuity planning (BCP) is critical for organizations aiming to ensure operational resilience during crises. A well-prepared BCP provides a roadmap for businesses to maintain essential functions, minimize disruption, and recover quickly, no matter the type of crisis. While many companies focus on natural disasters and infrastructure failures, the rise of cyberattacks has made data security and continuity planning vital components of any corporate strategy.

One notable example of effective business continuity planning in a cyber crisis is Marriott International's response to the 2018 data breach. Marriott, one of the largest hotel chains in the world, faced a massive cyberattack that exposed the personal data of approximately 500 million customers[8]. Despite the severity of the breach, Marriott's business continuity planning allowed the company to manage the crisis effectively, minimizing operational disruptions and working toward a swift recovery. This case demonstrates how business continuity planning, particularly in the context of data security, can save a company

---

[8] https://www.csoonline.com/article/567795/marriott-data-breach-faq-how-did-it-happen-and-what-was-the-impact.html

from long-term damage and ensure smooth operational recovery.

Background: The 2018 Data Breach

In November 2018, Marriott International disclosed that it had suffered one of the largest data breaches in history. Hackers had infiltrated the systems of Starwood Hotels, a subsidiary of Marriott. They gained unauthorized access to sensitive information, including names, addresses, phone numbers, passport numbers, and credit card details. Shockingly, the breach had been ongoing since 2014, long before Marriott acquired Starwood in 2016. The breach impacted the personal data of up to 500 million guests worldwide, triggering immediate concern from customers, regulators, and the media. Faced with this massive crisis, Marriott's leadership was tasked with both managing the immediate fallout of the breach and ensuring the company's ability to continue its operations. This is where Marriott's business continuity planning came into play.

Step-by-Step Business Continuity Response by Marriott

Risk Assessment and Identification

A risk assessment is the first step in any robust business continuity plan. For Marriott, the breach revealed vulnerabilities in their data security systems that had been overlooked for years.

This risk assessment was not just a post-crisis activity; Marriott's internal audits and evaluations before the breach had identified cybersecurity as a critical risk, given the size of their customer base and the vast amounts of sensitive data they handled.

This proactive identification of data security as a key risk had already led Marriott to establish continuity strategies for dealing with data breaches, even before the 2018 incident occurred. Although the breach had a catastrophic impact, the company had been prepared with protocols to mitigate the fallout, including systems for rapidly informing affected customers and preventing further data loss.

Immediate Response and Containment

Once the breach was discovered, Marriott's continuity plan was activated. A critical aspect of any BCP is the immediate response and containment of the crisis. Marriott's response focused on three key areas: stopping the breach, assessing the damage, and protecting customer data from further exposure.

Marriott's cybersecurity teams quickly mobilized to isolate the affected systems and stop the unauthorized access. In coordination with external experts, they investigated the scope of the breach and determined the attackers' methods. The company also worked closely with regulatory bodies and law enforcement to ensure that all legal requirements were met and the breach was properly reported to authorities. Containment in this phase was crucial for preventing the crisis from escalating. Marriott's BCP ensured that protocols were in place to handle large-scale data breaches, allowing the company to react quickly and decisively rather than being paralyzed by the situation.

Communication Strategy

One of the most important aspects of business continuity planning is having a clear and effective communication strategy. During a crisis, timely and accurate communication can be the difference between maintaining public trust and creating long-lasting damage to a company's reputation.

Marriott's BCP included a communication plan designed for situations like this, ensuring that stakeholders—customers, employees, and investors—were informed promptly. The company publicly announced the breach in November 2018, giving details about the extent of the data compromised and offering guidance to customers on steps to protect themselves.

They set up a dedicated website and call center to handle customer inquiries, giving affected individuals access to information about what had occurred and how they could check whether their data had been compromised.

Marriott also offered free identity theft monitoring for those whose information was most at risk. By taking these steps, Marriott aimed to minimize panic and maintain transparency throughout recovery. Internally, Marriott communicated regularly with employees, especially those working in IT and customer service, ensuring they were well-equipped to answer customer concerns and manage the breach's day-to-day impact on business operations.

Business Operations and Continuity

Despite the magnitude of the breach, Marriott's business continuity planning allowed the company to keep its global operations running smoothly. One of the primary goals of a BCP is to ensure that essential business functions continue, even when a crisis threatens to disrupt normal operations.

Marriott's hotels remained open, and guests could still make reservations, check in, and access services without interruptions. The company's ability to continue operating was due in part to the segregation of systems within it—core customer-facing operations were not directly affected by the breach, which was largely confined to the Starwood reservation system.

In addition, Marriott's continuity planning ensured that alternative measures were in place to manage potential disruptions. This included data recovery systems, redundant backups, and failover protocols that allowed the company to protect key operations from being compromised by the breach. These systems were essential in maintaining operational integrity and providing uninterrupted customer service worldwide.

Recovery and Lessons Learned

After the initial crisis response, the next critical phase of Marriott's business continuity plan was the recovery and evaluation process. This phase involved assessing the breach's impact, strengthening security measures, and rebuilding trust with customers and stakeholders.

Marriott invested heavily in cybersecurity following the breach, implementing more stringent controls, upgrading data encryption systems, and enhancing its security monitoring capabilities to prevent future incidents. The company also reviewed its acquisition practices, ensuring that due diligence on cybersecurity was a central part of evaluating future mergers or acquisitions.

Post-crisis recovery also included settling regulatory penalties and customer lawsuits. Marriott cooperated with various regulatory agencies worldwide, addressing the concerns of privacy advocates and law enforcement authorities. In 2019, Marriott faced a £99 million fine from the UK Information Commissioner's Office for violating GDPR requirements. While financially damaging, these actions were part of the company's full transparency and recovery process.

Perhaps most importantly, Marriott worked to rebuild customer trust. Through enhanced data security and a commitment to improved privacy standards, Marriott sought to reassure its guests that their information would be safe moving forward. By incorporating these lessons into its long-term strategy, Marriott strengthened its resilience and prepared itself for future challenges. Marriott International's response to the 2018 data breach is a powerful example of the importance of business continuity planning.

While the breach was a significant crisis, Marriott's ability to contain the situation, communicate effectively, and continue business operations demonstrated the value of a robust BCP. The company's post-crisis recovery also highlighted the importance of learning from the experience to strengthen security and rebuild customer trust.

This case study illustrates that no company is immune to crises, but those with well-thought-out continuity plans are better equipped to weather the storm, limit damage, and recover quickly. In today's world, where cyberattacks and data breaches are increasingly common, having a comprehensive business continuity plan is more important than ever for organizations looking to safeguard their operations and reputation.

Strategies for Leading Organizations Through Crises

Successfully guiding an organization through a crisis requires more than addressing immediate challenges. It involves managing communication, maintaining relationships with key stakeholders, and ensuring the internal team remains resilient and motivated. A leader must focus on short-term damage control and long-term recovery, balancing the immediate need for action with the ongoing task of safeguarding the organization's future. Below are strategies for leading organizations effectively through crises, focusing on managing media relations, coordinating with legal teams, and maintaining employee morale.

Managing Media Relations

In any crisis, the media is critical in shaping public perception of an organization. Handling media relations effectively can make the difference between controlling the narrative and allowing it to spiral out of control.

> **Be transparent and proactive:** One of the most important strategies for managing media relations during a crisis is transparency. Avoid withholding information, as this can lead to speculation and damage the organization's reputation. Instead, release factual updates regularly and address issues head-on. When the organization is seen as forthright, it helps build trust with the media and the public.

> **Designate a spokesperson**: Appoint a single, well-prepared spokesperson to handle all media interactions. This ensures consistent messaging and prevents mixed signals from being sent to the public. The spokesperson should be someone who can remain calm under pressure,

communicate clearly, and reflect the organization's values.

➤ **Prepare key messages:** Before public communication, develop a clear set of key messages that align with the organization's crisis management goals. These messages should emphasize accountability, empathy, and steps the organization takes to resolve the situation. Having these messages prepared in advance ensures that the organization remains on message even in the face of difficult questions from the media.

➤ **Respond quickly:** In the age of social media and 24-hour news cycles, speed is essential. Delayed responses can lead to rumors and misinformation taking root. Even if not all the facts are available, it is important to acknowledge the situation, provide available information, and commit to giving updates as the situation evolves.

➤ **Monitor media coverage:** Monitor the media's coverage of the crisis closely. This will help the organization identify any misinformation or negative trends that need to be corrected. It also allows the leadership team to adjust its messaging as necessary to address concerns raised by the public or media outlets.

Coordinating with Legal Teams

Crises often have legal implications, whether they involve compliance issues, potential lawsuits, or regulatory violations. Coordinating effectively with legal teams is essential to protect the organization and ensure the response adheres to legal requirements.

> **Involve legal early:** As soon as a crisis unfolds, the legal team should be looped in. This allows them to assess the situation from a legal perspective and advise on actions to minimize legal risks. Waiting too long to involve legal counsel can result in missteps that complicate the situation later.

> **Balance transparency with legal concerns:** While transparency is critical, there are often legal considerations that need to be considered when deciding what information to share publicly. The legal team should work closely with communication teams to ensure that statements are honest but do not inadvertently increase the organization's liability.

> **Prepare for potential lawsuits:** In many crises, especially those involving data breaches, product recalls, or safety incidents, lawsuits are a distinct possibility. The legal team should begin preparing for potential legal actions early on, ensuring that records are kept, key

actions are documented, and the organization is prepared to defend itself if needed.

> **Adhere to regulatory requirements:** Many industries are heavily regulated, and failure to comply with reporting requirements can worsen a crisis. For instance, a data breach may require notification to affected individuals or regulatory bodies within a certain timeframe. Legal teams should ensure that all necessary regulatory steps are being followed.

> **Guide public statements:** The legal team should review all public statements to ensure they do not inadvertently admit liability or create further legal complications. While the organization needs to communicate openly, it must do so without exposing itself to unnecessary legal risks.

Maintaining Employee Morale

During a crisis, employees are often the first to feel the effects, both in terms of workload and emotional stress. Leaders must prioritize maintaining morale to keep the organization running smoothly and prevent long-term impacts on employee engagement and retention.

> **Communicate regularly with employees:** Employees should never be left in the dark during a crisis. Regular updates from leadership are crucial to keep everyone

informed about the situation, the steps being taken to address it, and how it may impact them personally. Clear and honest communication fosters a sense of trust and stability within the workforce.

➤ **Show empathy and support:** Crises can create a stressful work environment. Leaders should acknowledge a crisis's emotional toll on employees and offer support where possible. This might include providing additional resources, such as access to counseling services, or simply making it clear that leadership understands the challenges employees are facing.

➤ **Involve employees in the recovery process:** Employees often feel more empowered and less anxious when they are part of the solution. Leaders should involve key employees in the recovery planning process, encouraging them to contribute ideas and play active roles in helping the organization move forward. This also reinforces a sense of purpose and teamwork.

➤ **Recognize and reward efforts:** Crises often require employees to go above and beyond their normal duties. Recognizing these efforts—whether through public acknowledgment, bonuses, or other incentives—can go a long way in maintaining morale and showing employees that their hard work is appreciated.

> ➢ **Ensure workload balance:** While crises often lead to increased workloads, leaders should monitor this carefully to prevent burnout. If necessary, bring in additional support or adjust priorities to ensure employees are not overwhelmed. Burned-out employees can quickly become disengaged, leading to long-term productivity and morale issues.

Leading an organization through a crisis is a complex challenge that requires quick decision-making, clear communication, and compassionate leadership. Effectively managing media relations helps shape public perception and prevent misinformation, while close coordination with legal teams ensures that the organization's actions are legally sound.

Finally, maintaining employee morale is critical to keeping the organization functioning and ensuring that the workforce remains engaged and motivated, even under pressure.

By focusing on these key strategies—transparent media relations, coordinated legal efforts, and a strong emphasis on employee well-being—leaders can guide their organizations through even the most challenging crises and emerge stronger on the other side.

In conclusion, successfully navigating a crisis requires more than just addressing immediate concerns—it's about creating a path to recovery while maintaining trust and stability.

Leaders who are transparent with the media, coordinate effectively with legal teams, and prioritize employee well-being can guide their organizations through the most challenging situations. Strong communication, swift decision-making, and adaptability are critical elements in surviving a crisis and emerging stronger from it. By mastering these strategies, organizations can not only minimize damage but also enhance their long-term resilience and credibility in the eyes of both internal and external stakeholders.

Chapter 13: Technology and Cybersecurity

"Security is a process, not a product."

- Bruce Schneier

In today's interconnected world, the integration of technology in both physical and digital security is more important than ever. Cyberattacks, data breaches, and physical intrusions are no longer isolated threats—they are intertwined, creating a complex risk landscape that requires security professionals to be agile and informed. As security technology evolves, so too must the strategies that protect organizations from these blended threats.

Leveraging artificial intelligence, machine learning, and big data, security professionals can now take a more proactive approach, identifying and mitigating risks. This chapter explores the latest advancements in security technology and essential principles that every security professional must know.

Evolving Role of Technology in Modern Corporate Security

The role of technology in corporate security has evolved dramatically in recent years, leading to a convergence of physical and digital security systems. This shift has fostered the development of a more integrated and holistic security approach, where advanced cybersecurity frameworks now supplement traditional physical measures like CCTV systems and access control. In my experience, this convergence is not just a theoretical ideal but a practical necessity in today's security landscape. In previous roles, I have worked extensively with AI-driven video analytics integrated into physical security systems.

For instance, integrating advanced AI algorithms with CCTV systems significantly enhanced our ability to proactively identify potential threats. Instead of relying solely on human operators to monitor surveillance footage, AI analyzed real-time video feeds, identifying unusual behaviors, such as loitering in restricted areas or unauthorized access attempts. These analytics were configured to trigger alerts automatically, allowing security teams to respond quickly.

The integration of these AI systems with cybersecurity protocols was a game-changer. Unusual physical behaviors often correlate with digital security risks, so we developed a system where physical security breaches trigger alerts in our cybersecurity framework. For example, if a surveillance system detected suspicious behavior in a restricted area, it would automatically trigger cybersecurity teams to monitor digital access points or network activity. This holistic approach allowed us to address potential threats before they escalated into full-scale incidents.

The Convergence of Physical and Digital Security

As businesses adopt cutting-edge technology in their daily operations, the line between physical and digital security becomes increasingly blurred. Traditionally, physical security involves locks, cameras, and guards, while digital security protects networks and data from hackers and cyber threats. However, the growing sophistication of cyberattacks and physical threats has necessitated a more unified approach.

Modern corporate security now requires the integration of both physical and digital security systems to address the growing number of blended threats. For instance, a cybercriminal may hack into a company's network and disable security cameras or access control systems, compromising digital and physical assets. Conversely, an intruder gaining unauthorized physical access to a facility could steal sensitive data stored on servers, which would typically fall under the purview of cybersecurity teams.

Companies are now integrating digital surveillance systems with cybersecurity frameworks to mitigate these risks. For example, many businesses are adopting IP-based security cameras and Internet of Things (IoT) devices, which can transmit data across networks, making them potential targets for cyberattacks. This increases the need for securing physical devices like one would secure digital assets by implementing firewalls, encryption, and intrusion detection systems.

AI and Machine Learning in Corporate Security

The application of AI and machine learning has transformed the corporate security landscape. AI-driven video analytics have revolutionized physical security by enabling more precise threat detection. These systems can recognize unusual patterns or behaviors, such as unauthorized access, crowd gathering, or even subtle signs of stress in individuals, which could indicate a potential security threat.

Machine learning algorithms learn from the data they process, improving their accuracy. In a corporate setting, this can mean that security systems constantly learn and refine their ability to detect threats. For instance, a video surveillance system can learn what constitutes "normal" behavior within a specific environment and flag deviations from this baseline as potential security risks.

In cybersecurity, AI is also employed to enhance threat detection and response. AI-powered systems can sift through massive amounts of data, identifying abnormal traffic patterns, phishing attempts, or malware more quickly and accurately than human analysts. In some cases, AI systems can even initiate responses to these threats autonomously, such as quarantining infected systems or blocking suspicious network activity before damage occurs.

The Rise of Cyber-Physical Systems and IoT

The rise of cyber-physical systems (CPS) and Internet of Things (IoT) devices has introduced both opportunities and challenges in corporate security. These systems, which involve integrating physical processes with digital networks, offer increased efficiency and automation in building security, manufacturing, and logistics. However, they also create additional points of vulnerability. IoT devices, for example, have enabled it to remotely monitor and control physical systems like HVAC units, access control systems, and surveillance cameras. While these devices offer significant convenience, cybercriminals often target them due to weak security protocols. Many IoT devices lack robust encryption or password protection, making them an entry point for hackers looking to compromise physical and digital systems.

To address these vulnerabilities, companies must adopt a holistic approach to security that includes securing not only their networks and data but also their physical infrastructure. This means implementing stringent security measures at every level of the organization, from access control systems and surveillance cameras to digital networks and cloud storage. Encryption, multi-factor authentication, and regular security audits are essential tools for protecting these interconnected systems.

Cloud-Based Security Solutions

With the growing adoption of cloud-based services, more businesses are moving their security operations to the cloud. Cloud-based security solutions offer several advantages, including scalability, flexibility, and cost-efficiency. Cloud platforms enable organizations to store and analyze large amounts of data from physical security systems like video surveillance, access control, and alarm systems.

Additionally, cloud-based systems provide real-time access to security data from any location, allowing security teams to monitor operations remotely. This particularly benefits organizations with multiple sites or facilities, as it enables centralized monitoring and control of all security operations.

Furthermore, the cloud offers enhanced data redundancy and disaster recovery capabilities, ensuring that critical security data is not lost during a physical or digital attack.

However, migrating security operations to the cloud also introduces new risks. Cloud environments can be vulnerable to cyberattacks, and organizations need to implement comprehensive cloud security protocols. This includes encryption of sensitive data, strong access controls, and ongoing monitoring for potential threats.

The Role of Big Data in Security

Big data analytics has become a powerful tool in corporate security, enabling organizations to process and analyze vast amounts of data from physical and digital systems.

Organizations can gain a more comprehensive view of their security posture by integrating data from video surveillance, access control, and cybersecurity systems.

Big data allows security teams to identify patterns and trends that may indicate a potential threat. For example, data analytics can reveal patterns of behavior that precede a security breach, such as repeated access attempts at odd hours or unusual network activity. This proactive approach allows security teams to address potential threats before they escalate into major incidents. Furthermore, big data analytics can enhance post-incident investigations by providing detailed insights into the timeline and sequence of events leading up to a breach. This helps organizations identify vulnerabilities and take corrective actions to prevent future incidents.

A Holistic Security Approach

The evolving nature of corporate security requires a holistic approach that integrates physical and digital security measures. Rather than treating these as separate entities, organizations must recognize the interdependencies between physical and cyber threats. A comprehensive security strategy involves collaboration between physical security teams, cybersecurity experts, and IT departments. This ensures that all security aspects are covered, from securing access points to monitoring network traffic.

Cross-functional communication and regular security audits are essential for identifying potential vulnerabilities and ensuring that security protocols are up-to-date.

The role of technology in modern corporate security continues to grow, and the convergence of physical and digital security is becoming the norm. By leveraging advanced technologies like AI, machine learning, IoT, and big data, companies can develop a more proactive and integrated approach to security. The result is a more resilient organization that can anticipate and respond to threats, ensuring business continuity and protecting valuable assets.

Basic Cybersecurity Principles Every Security Professional Should Know

In today's increasingly interconnected world, cybersecurity has become a core concern for businesses across industries. With the growing prevalence of cyberattacks, from data breaches to ransomware, security professionals must be well-versed in the fundamental principles of cybersecurity to protect their organizations. Understanding key concepts such as threat intelligence, incident response, and data protection regulations is essential for developing a comprehensive cybersecurity strategy that addresses both present and emerging threats. This chapter will explore these basic principles and outline the foundational knowledge every security professional should possess.

Threat Intelligence

Threat intelligence refers to gathering, analyzing, and interpreting information about current and potential cyber threats. By understanding the tactics, techniques, and procedures (TTPs) that cybercriminals use, organizations can better defend against attacks. Threat intelligence encompasses external data (such as information from cybersecurity firms and global threat databases) and internal data (such as network traffic logs and incident reports).

Threat intelligence is typically divided into three main categories:

> **Strategic intelligence** provides a high-level overview of the threat landscape, often focusing on trends that may affect the organization over time. This type of intelligence helps executives and decision-makers understand the risks they face.

> **Tactical intelligence** focuses on specific threats, such as the techniques cyber criminals are using or vulnerabilities they are targeting. This information is

critical for frontline security teams to develop appropriate defenses.

➤ **Operational intelligence** involves real-time data on ongoing or imminent threats. For example, if a company receives information about a specific attack targeting its industry, it can immediately adjust its security measures to counter the threat.

Properly implemented, threat intelligence helps security professionals anticipate potential attacks and take preventative measures. It also informs the development of robust security protocols and aids incident response by providing context on attackers' behaviors. By incorporating threat intelligence into daily operations, organizations can significantly reduce their risk of cyberattacks.

Incident Response

An effective incident response plan is essential for minimizing the damage caused by a cyberattack. Incident response refers to the structured approach to handling a cybersecurity breach, including detection, containment, eradication, recovery, and post-incident review. Organizations that fail to prepare for a cyber incident adequately often scramble to mitigate damage after an attack.

Key Stages of Incident Response:

Preparation: The preparation phase involves creating an incident response plan, forming an incident response team, and training staff to recognize potential cyber threats. A strong preparation phase also includes setting up detection systems and establishing communication protocols during an incident.

> **Detection and Analysis:** In this phase, organizations detect the occurrence of a security event. Detection tools include intrusion detection systems (IDS), security information and event management (SIEM) systems, and log analysis. Once a potential incident is identified, a thorough analysis is conducted to determine the severity of the threat and whether it constitutes a genuine security breach.

> **Containment:** After detecting an incident, the primary goal is to contain the threat to prevent it from spreading. Immediate actions might include isolating infected systems, shutting down affected network segments, or blocking malicious IP addresses. Short-term containment may involve stopping the active threat, while long-term containment involves strengthening security measures to prevent recurrence.

> **Eradication:** Once the incident is contained, the root cause of the attack must be eradicated. This involves

removing malware, deleting malicious accounts, and patching vulnerabilities exploited during the attack.

> **Recovery:** After eradicating the threat, the affected systems can be restored to normal operation. This process includes ensuring that systems are fully functional, implementing additional security measures to prevent future attacks, and monitoring systems for signs of lingering threats.

> **Post-Incident Review:** The final step is to review the incident to determine what went wrong, what was done correctly, and how future incidents can be better managed. A detailed report of the incident, including lessons learned, helps the organization improve its overall cybersecurity posture.

A well-defined incident response process is crucial for mitigating the financial and reputational damage caused by cyberattacks. The faster an organization can detect, contain, and recover from an incident, the less impact it will have on business operations. Incident response also plays a vital role in regulatory compliance, as many data protection regulations require organizations to report breaches promptly.

Data Protection Regulations

In recent years, governments worldwide have introduced strict data protection regulations to safeguard individuals' privacy and ensure that organizations handle data responsibly. Security professionals must understand these regulations to ensure their organization remains compliant, avoiding fines and penalties while protecting sensitive data.

➤ **General Data Protection Regulation (GDPR):** Perhaps the most well-known data protection law, GDPR governs how organizations collect, store, and use personal data of individuals within the European Union (EU). Under GDPR, organizations must obtain explicit consent to collect personal data, notify authorities within 72 hours of discovering a data breach, and provide individuals with the right to access, correct, or delete their data. Non-compliance with GDPR can result in hefty fines of up to €20 million or 4% of global annual revenue, whichever is higher[9].

➤ **California Consumer Privacy Act (CCPA):** Similar to GDPR, the CCPA grants California residents greater control over their personal information. It requires businesses to disclose what personal data they collect, allows consumers to request deletion of their data, and gives them the right to opt out of the sale of their personal information. The CCPA also

---

[9] https://sprinto.com/blog/gdpr-fines/#:~:text=The%20fine%20for%20severe%20GDPR,principles%2C%20including%20conditions%20for%20consent

imposes fines for non-compliance, which can be as high as $7,500 per violation10.

➤ **Other Regulations:** Depending on the region and industry, organizations may also need to comply with other data protection regulations, such as the Health Insurance Portability and Accountability Act (HIPAA) in the United States, which governs the security of medical information or the Payment Card Industry Data Security Standard (PCI DSS), which sets requirements for handling payment card data.

Compliance and Best Practices

To ensure compliance with data protection regulations, organizations should adopt several best practices, including:

➤ **Data minimization:** Collect only the data necessary for business purposes and ensure that it is deleted once it is no longer required.

➤ **Encryption:** Encrypt sensitive data to protect it in case of a breach.

➤ **Access controls:** Limit access to sensitive data to only those who need it for their work and implement multi-factor authentication for added security.

---

[10] https://www.cookiehub.com/blog/what-are-the-penalties-for-violating-ccpa#:~:text=CCPA%20Fines,fine%20is%20%247%2C500%20per%20breach.

> ➤ **Regular audits:** Conduct regular audits of data handling practices to identify and fix potential compliance gaps.

Understanding and applying basic cybersecurity principles is essential for any security professional tasked with protecting their organization from the ever-evolving threat landscape.

Threat intelligence allows for proactive defense strategies, while incident response ensures that organizations are prepared to manage and recover from attacks. Additionally, data protection regulations are critical for compliance and safeguarding sensitive information. By mastering these core principles, security professionals can build a strong cybersecurity framework that minimizes risk and protects organizational assets and customer trust.

Bridging the Gap Between Physical and Digital Security

In my experience, effectively bridging the gap between physical and digital security requires more than just implementing advanced technology; it demands a holistic approach emphasizing cross-functional collaboration.

One strategy I have found particularly useful is fostering regular communication and collaboration between IT teams and physical security personnel. In one specific case, I was involved in upgrading an access control system where we integrated biometric verification with cybersecurity authentication processes. The goal was to ensure that access to sensitive areas within a facility was not just about physical presence but also tied to digital verification, thus securing both physical and digital assets simultaneously. This integration began with regular joint meetings between the IT department and physical security teams to assess potential vulnerabilities and opportunities for better synergy. By aligning our objectives, we could design a system that combined physical access controls, such as keycards or biometrics, with cybersecurity protocols, ensuring that even after physical entry, users still had to pass digital verification checks to access sensitive systems or data. For example, gaining entry to a restricted data center requires biometric authentication. Still, users also had to go through a multi-factor authentication process to access digital networks inside that facility.

The collaboration resulted in a more cohesive security posture, with both teams playing an integral role in detecting and addressing potential threats. This integrated approach helped us enhance security and streamline operations by reducing the complexity and fragmentation that often occur when physical and digital security measures are treated as separate entities. It became clear that to address modern security challenges, the lines between physical and digital security must blur, and seamless integration is key to mitigating risks from both areas.

The Convergence of Physical and Digital Security

Integrating physical and digital security is increasingly becoming necessary as organizations deal with an expanding array of threats. Traditionally, physical security focuses on safeguarding people, buildings, and assets through measures like locks, surveillance cameras, and security personnel, while digital security concentrates on protecting networks, data, and IT infrastructure from cyber threats. However, the need for a unified security strategy has grown as physical assets become digitized and cyber threats become more sophisticated.

One of the driving factors behind this convergence is the proliferation of IoT devices and interconnected systems. Physical security systems, such as access control, CCTV, and alarm systems, are now frequently connected to corporate networks. This integration makes these systems more vulnerable to cyberattacks, as hackers can exploit weaknesses in physical systems to gain access to digital networks. Conversely, cybercriminals can use compromised digital assets to disable physical security measures, exposing organizations to digital and physical threats.

Cross-Functional Collaboration

Bridging the gap between physical and digital security requires breaking down the traditional silos that exist between IT departments and physical security teams. Cross-functional collaboration between these two groups is essential to creating a cohesive and comprehensive security strategy. Often, these teams work in isolation, each focusing on their respective areas of expertise. However, potential vulnerabilities can go unnoticed without collaboration, and important security measures may be overlooked. Regular joint meetings between IT and physical security teams effectively align cybersecurity protocols with physical security measures. These meetings allow for sharing information, such as potential threats, new vulnerabilities, and security incidents, enabling both teams to respond more effectively to evolving risks.

For example, if IT discovers a network vulnerability that could impact physical security systems, such as surveillance cameras or access control devices, they can work with the physical security team to mitigate the risk before cybercriminals exploit it.

Moreover, cross-functional collaboration fosters a deeper understanding of each team's roles and responsibilities, helping to ensure that security measures are integrated rather than fragmented. IT teams can offer insights into securing physical systems from cyberattacks, while physical security teams can provide valuable input on protecting physical assets with digital components. This collaborative approach ensures that both teams are working toward the same goal: protecting the organization from all types of threats, whether physical, digital, or a combination of both.

Integrating Physical and Digital Security Technologies

Integrating technologies that address both types of threats is critical to bridging the gap between physical and digital security. Access control, surveillance, and alarm systems should be integrated with cybersecurity protocols to create a seamless security network.

For example, modern access control systems can incorporate biometric verification, such as fingerprint or facial recognition, and traditional methods, like keycards or passwords.

These systems can then be linked to the organization's cybersecurity infrastructure, requiring individuals to verify their identity physically and pass digital authentication checks before accessing sensitive areas or data. This integration ensures that unauthorized personnel cannot gain access to either physical or digital assets, even if they manage to breach one layer of security.

Surveillance systems can also benefit from this integrated approach. CCTV cameras connected to the corporate network should be secured against cyberattacks through encryption, network segmentation, and regular security updates.

Additionally, advanced video analytics can detect suspicious behavior and trigger alerts that notify physical security teams and IT departments of potential security breaches. These systems can be designed to flag physical threats and correlate them with digital activities, such as an employee attempting unauthorized access to a server room while their account is trying to log into a restricted network remotely.

Training and Awareness

Another key component in bridging the gap between physical and digital security is ensuring that staff across the organization know both types of threats and understand how they intersect. Security awareness training should cover common cyber risks like phishing, malware, and ransomware and highlight how physical security measures, such as securing access badges or safeguarding sensitive areas, play a critical role in overall security.

Employees should be aware that their actions can have digital and physical consequences. For example, leaving a computer unlocked in a secure area can lead to unauthorized individuals gaining access to the corporate network, just as failing to lock a door can result in someone physically entering a restricted space. By fostering a culture of security awareness, organizations can help reduce vulnerabilities caused by human error and ensure that employees are vigilant about both physical and digital risks. With these strategies, businesses can effectively bridge the gap between physical and digital security, safeguarding their assets and data from an increasingly complex threat landscape.

Staying Updated on Technological Advancements

In the rapidly evolving field of security technology, staying updated on the latest advancements is crucial for both personal development and organizational security. With new threats emerging constantly and innovations in both physical and cybersecurity becoming more sophisticated, professionals must remain proactive in learning and adapting. To do so, leveraging various resources that provide insights, education, and networking opportunities is important.

In my career, I've found that keeping up with the latest developments requires reading industry publications, attending key conferences, and taking advantage of online learning platforms. These resources offer theoretical knowledge and practical insights that can be applied in real-world security scenarios. Furthermore, by encouraging my teams to engage with these resources, I've been able to foster a culture of continuous improvement and innovation.

Recommended Publications

One of the most accessible ways to stay informed about advancements in security technology is through industry publications. These publications provide up-to-date news, in-depth analysis, and case studies from experts in the field.

> **Security Management Magazine:** Published by ASIS International, this magazine is a leading resource for

security professionals. It covers a wide range of topics, including physical security, cybersecurity, risk management, and loss prevention. I frequently rely on Security Management for its comprehensive articles on the latest industry trends and innovations.

➢ **Cybersecurity Insiders:** As the name suggests, Cybersecurity Insiders focuses on cybersecurity. It offers news, research reports, and insights from leading cybersecurity experts. With increasing physical and digital security convergence, staying informed about cybersecurity developments is essential for all security professionals.

Both publications provide valuable insights into emerging technologies and best practices, helping security professionals anticipate potential threats and opportunities.

Key Conferences

Attending industry conferences is another vital way to stay updated on technological advancements. Conferences bring together security professionals, technology providers, and thought leaders to discuss the latest innovations, share experiences, and explore future trends.

➢ **NRF Protect:** This is one of the premier events for security professionals, particularly retail ones. It focuses on asset protection and loss prevention but also covers broader security topics. The conference offers hands-on demonstrations of the latest security technologies, making it a valuable resource for professionals looking to stay informed.

- ➢ **ASIS Global Security Exchange (GSX):** Hosted by ASIS International, GSX is one of the largest global security conferences. It covers many topics, from physical security innovations to cybersecurity and risk management. Attending GSX has allowed me to network with industry leaders and learn about cutting-edge solutions from vendors and practitioners alike.

- ➢ **ISC West:** This conference is another important event in the security industry, particularly for physical security professionals. It showcases the latest security technology, from surveillance systems to access control, and offers educational sessions led by industry experts.

These conferences are invaluable for networking, learning from peers, and seeing firsthand how the latest technologies can be applied to enhance security measures.

Online Learning Platforms

In addition to publications and conferences, I've found that online learning platforms offer a convenient way to stay updated on emerging technologies and expand knowledge in specific areas. These platforms provide access to courses industry professionals teach, often allowing flexible learning schedules.

➢ **Coursera:** This platform offers specialized courses on emerging technologies, including AI in security and cybersecurity frameworks. Many courses are developed in partnership with top universities and organizations, providing high academic rigor while remaining accessible to working professionals.

➢ **LinkedIn Learning:** LinkedIn Learning provides many courses across many subjects, including security technology, incident response, and threat intelligence. It's particularly useful for learning practical skills that can be immediately applied in the workplace. I encourage my teams to use LinkedIn Learning for continuous professional development, as the courses are often short and focused on specific topics relevant to modern security challenges.

By engaging with these resources, security professionals can continuously enhance their knowledge, keeping pace with the fast-moving world of technology. Furthermore, these platforms make it easy to stay informed about foundational security principles and cutting-edge innovations.

In conclusion, the convergence of physical and digital security is no longer an option but is necessary to protect modern organizations from multifaceted threats. Businesses can build a more resilient security framework by embracing emerging technologies, such as AI, IoT, and cloud-based solutions. Staying updated through trusted resources like industry publications, conferences, and online platforms empowers security professionals to stay ahead of evolving risks. A commitment to continuous learning and cross-functional collaboration will ensure that organizations are prepared to navigate the challenges of the digital age, safeguarding both physical assets and critical data effectively.

Chapter 14: Legal and Ethical Considerations

Legal and ethical considerations are at the heart of corporate security management, shaping how companies protect their assets, data, and personnel while respecting the rights and privacy of employees and stakeholders. The growing complexity of regulatory environments and technological advances have introduced new challenges for security professionals. They must navigate a landscape where legal obligations, ethical principles, and security needs often intersect and sometimes conflict. Understanding these dynamics is crucial for creating robust policies that comply with the law and foster trust, transparency, and ethical integrity within the organization.

Balancing Employee Privacy with Security Measures

Balancing employee privacy with security measures is one of the most sensitive aspects of corporate security. The challenge lies in ensuring safety while not overstepping boundaries that may feel invasive to employees.

Recent studies and legal cases provide a comprehensive view of this evolving landscape, highlighting the complexities of integrating effective monitoring systems without compromising employee trust and morale. In my corporate job, one effective strategy I've implemented is transparency—openly communicating with employees about security measures and their reasons. For instance, we anticipated potential concerns when we introduced a new access control system using biometric data. To address these, we organized town hall meetings to explain how the system functioned, the rationale for its implementation, and the safeguards we had established to protect personal data. This proactive approach to communication alleviated fears and fostered a sense of trust among the staff.

Similarly, employees initially expressed apprehension about constant monitoring when we decided to enhance surveillance measures at one of our facilities. Understanding their concerns, we chose to involve them in the decision-making process.

We clearly articulated the specific risks we were aiming to mitigate and provided transparency regarding the storage and usage of the footage. By prioritizing honesty and clarity, we gained their support and cooperation. This experience underscored the importance of open dialogue and trust when implementing security measures that may impact personal privacy.

Legal Landscape and Compliance Challenges

The increasing reliance on remote work, accelerated by the COVID-19 pandemic, has fundamentally altered the dynamics of workplace monitoring. According to a recent analysis, employers are now more inclined to implement extensive monitoring systems on remote devices, driven by the need to manage workflows and protect sensitive data effectively. However, this has raised significant legal and ethical concerns regarding the extent of surveillance permissible under current privacy laws. In the United States, the Electronic Communications Privacy Act (ECPA) provides a framework for monitoring electronic communications, but it allows for exceptions if there is a legitimate business purpose or if the employee has given consent. The U.S. Supreme Court's ruling in *City of Ontario v. Quon* established that employees have a reduced expectation of privacy when using employer-provided devices. Despite these provisions, the lack of uniform federal regulation has led to a patchwork of state laws, complicating compliance efforts for businesses operating across multiple jurisdictions.

For instance, the Personal Information Protection and Electronic Documents Act (PIPEDA) Canada governs how private sector organizations collect, use, and disclose personal information in the course of commercial activities, including information about employees. Companies must obtain consent to collect personal data and be transparent about how this data will be used and stored. Employees have the right to access their data and request corrections. This law applies to federally regulated businesses and sets a high data protection and transparency standard.

Employee Perceptions and the Impact on Morale

Research indicates that pervasive surveillance can harm employee morale and trust. A study conducted by VMware found that approximately 70% of global business decision-makers have implemented or are planning to implement monitoring systems for remote workers[11]. While this is intended to enhance productivity and security, the intrusive nature of such monitoring can lead to a sense of distrust among employees, potentially decreasing their accountability and adherence to company policies.

Additionally, employees often perceive constant monitoring as an invasion of their privacy, especially when it extends beyond working hours. This can create a hostile work environment, increase turnover rates, and diminish job satisfaction. Ethical considerations are paramount here; while employers have a legitimate interest in safeguarding corporate assets and data, they must also respect the personal boundaries of their workforce.

Finding the Right Balance

To mitigate the negative consequences of surveillance, companies must adopt a balanced approach that prioritizes transparency, consent, and proportionality. Effective monitoring policies should be communicated to employees, emphasizing the scope, purpose, and limitations of the data being collected. For

---

[11] https://news.vmware.com/releases/virtual-floorplan

example, visible signage about surveillance and detailed explanations of monitoring practices can help alleviate concerns and promote a culture of transparency.

Moreover, monitoring should be limited to work-related activities during business hours, and any data collected should be relevant to business objectives. This approach complies with legal standards and respects employees' privacy, fostering a more positive work environment.

Future Considerations

As remote work continues to evolve, so will the legal and ethical challenges associated with employee monitoring. Businesses must stay abreast of changes in privacy laws and be proactive in reviewing and updating their monitoring policies. The path forward requires a nuanced understanding of business needs and employee rights, ensuring that security measures do not infringe upon individual privacy.

By maintaining this balance, companies can build a secure yet respectful workplace where employees feel valued and protected. This will enhance productivity and contribute to a stronger, more trusting organizational culture.

Ethical Challenges Unique to Corporate Security Roles

Corporate security professionals face a complex landscape where they must balance competing interests, including protecting company assets, ensuring public safety, and respecting employee privacy.

This often places them in ethically challenging situations where their actions and decisions can have profound implications. Below, we explore some unique ethical challenges they encounter, focusing on scenarios like balancing employee privacy with security needs and managing conflicts between corporate interests and public safety. Corporate security and public safety generally go hand in hand, but there are instances when conflicts emerge, necessitating a nuanced approach. Maintaining ethical integrity while adhering to both corporate policies and local regulations is crucial in these situations. For example, during a security upgrade project, our team faced a dilemma: we wanted to implement advanced monitoring systems, but local regulations prohibited certain surveillance technologies. To address this, we collaborated closely with our legal and compliance teams, adapting the system design to comply with local laws while achieving our security objectives.

One case occurred during a large-scale event we hosted. Concerns arose about overcrowding and its potential impact on public safety. Initially, our internal security team planned to manage the situation independently.

However, we soon realized that involving local law enforcement would enhance public safety and provide access to valuable external resources. This proactive collaboration prevented a potential crisis and fostered a positive relationship with the community and local authorities. By aligning our internal plans with external support, we successfully navigated the situation's complexities while upholding corporate and public safety standards.

Balancing Employee Privacy with Security Needs

One of the most significant ethical dilemmas in corporate security is balancing maintaining security and respecting employee privacy. Companies need to protect their assets, intellectual property, and sensitive data, which often necessitates monitoring employee activities. However, excessive surveillance can lead to an erosion of trust and a perception of a hostile work environment.

A survey from Gartner Insights showed that employee acceptance of monitoring surges to 70% when companies explain the scope and purpose of monitoring[12]. This monitoring can include tracking keystrokes, analyzing screen activity, and logging employee interactions on platforms like Microsoft Teams or Zoom. These systems aim to identify potential security risks and optimize workflow efficiency but also raise significant

---

[12] https://hbr.org/2024/02/surveilling-employees-erodes-trust-and-puts-managers-in-a-bind

concerns about employee privacy and trust within the organization. While intended to protect corporate interests, such measures can make employees feel that their privacy is being invaded, leading to lower morale and increased turnover. A key ethical question arises: to what extent should a company monitor its employees? Legally, companies are permitted to monitor work-related activities, especially on company-owned devices and networks. However, they must also navigate a patchwork of privacy laws, such as Brazil's Lei Geral de Proteção de Dados (LGPD), which grants employees rights over their data, including the right to access, rectify, and request the deletion of their data. Similarly, South Korea's Personal Information Protection Act (PIPA) imposes strict requirements on collecting, using, and storing personal data, giving employees the right to be informed about what data is being collected and how it is used. These regulations require companies to adopt transparent data practices and ensure compliance across different jurisdictions to protect employee privacy effectively.

To address these challenges, companies should adopt transparent policies that clearly outline the scope and purpose of monitoring activities. Employees should be informed about what is being monitored, how the information will be used, and what safeguards are in place to protect their privacy. Additionally, consent should be obtained wherever possible, and monitoring should be limited to work-related activities during business hours to avoid unnecessary intrusion into employees' personal lives.

Managing Conflicts Between Corporate Interests and Public Safety

Another complex ethical challenge arises when corporate security professionals must navigate conflicts between corporate interests and public safety. For example, in the aftermath of a data breach, a company might be tempted to minimize the incident to protect its reputation and avoid financial losses. However, this can have severe consequences for customers, employees, and the broader community, who may be exposed to risks such as identity theft or fraud.

The case of Equifax's 2017 data breach is a prime example. The company delayed disclosing the breach, which exposed the personal information of over 148 million people, including names, social security numbers, and credit card details[13]. The delayed response and subsequent breach handling were widely criticized, raising questions about the company's commitment to transparency and public safety over its financial interests.

Corporate security professionals must advocate for ethical decision-making, emphasizing the importance of timely and transparent communication during such incidents. This involves balancing the company's right to protect its reputation with its responsibility to safeguard the public. In practice, this means being honest about the scope of the breach, cooperating with authorities, and taking proactive steps to mitigate the impact on affected individuals. Moreover, corporate security roles often

---

[13] https://archive.epic.org/privacy/data-breach/equifax/

require coordination with law enforcement in cases involving potential threats to public safety. This can lead to conflicts of interest when the company's need to protect proprietary information clashes with the public's right to know. For instance, if a company becomes aware of a cyber threat targeting critical infrastructure, it has an ethical duty to report this to the authorities, even if doing so might expose its vulnerabilities.

Navigating Legal and Ethical Gray Areas

Corporate security professionals also encounter numerous legal and ethical gray areas. For instance, advanced surveillance technologies like facial recognition or AI-driven behavior analytics can help identify potential security threats. However, these technologies raise significant privacy concerns and potential biases.

Facial recognition, for example, has been criticized for its potential to misidentify individuals, particularly among minority groups. This can lead to discriminatory practices, whether intentional or not and poses a serious ethical dilemma for security professionals. Should a company implement a technology that could enhance security but may also infringe on individual rights and perpetuate biases?

To navigate these gray areas, corporate security teams should conduct thorough ethical reviews before implementing such technologies. This includes evaluating the potential risks and benefits, consulting with diverse stakeholders, and ensuring compliance with existing legal frameworks. Companies should also consider alternative, less intrusive methods of achieving their security objectives where appropriate.

The Role of Corporate Culture and Ethical Leadership

An organization's corporate culture and ethical leadership are crucial in shaping how security challenges are approached. Security professionals often operate within a framework defined by the company's values and the ethical tone set by senior management. A culture that prioritizes ethical behavior and transparency can empower security teams to make decisions that balance security needs with ethical considerations.

For instance, a company that values transparency and trust is more likely to adopt privacy-conscious monitoring policies and proactively communicate with employees about security measures. On the other hand, a company that prioritizes profit over ethical considerations may pressure its security teams to take actions that compromise employee privacy or public safety.

Corporate security professionals must advocate for a strong ethical framework within their organizations, promoting practices that align with both legal requirements and ethical principles.

This involves continuous education and training, fostering open dialogue about ethical dilemmas, and building a culture of accountability.

Strategies for Ensuring Compliance While Maintaining Effectiveness

Navigating the intricate landscape of corporate security and regulatory compliance requires a careful balance between adhering to legal requirements and achieving security objectives. A robust framework for ethical decision-making can guide organizations through complex situations, ensuring that they meet regulatory standards without compromising operational effectiveness. Below are some strategies that can help organizations strike this balance.

➤ Develop a Comprehensive Compliance Program: A well-structured compliance program is the foundation for aligning corporate security with legal requirements. It should include detailed policies and procedures covering all security aspects, from data protection to physical security measures. Regular audits and risk assessments should be conducted to identify potential vulnerabilities and ensure that all practices comply with applicable laws and regulations.

➤ Engage with Legal and Compliance Teams Early: It is crucial to involve legal and compliance experts from the outset of any security project. These teams can provide valuable insights into local, national, and international regulations that may impact the implementation of security measures. Early collaboration helps design systems and protocols that are both effective and compliant, minimizing the risk of legal repercussions down the line.

➤ Incorporate Ethical Decision-Making Frameworks: Ethical decision-making frameworks, such as utilitarianism or deontological ethics, can be integrated into corporate decision-making to ensure that actions align with legal and moral standards. For example, a utilitarian approach would consider the broader impact of a decision on all stakeholders, while a deontological perspective would emphasize adherence to ethical principles, regardless of the outcomes. Applying these frameworks can help security professionals navigate ethical dilemmas, such as balancing employee privacy with surveillance needs.

➤ Implement Transparent Communication Policies: Transparency is a key component of compliance and ethical integrity. Organizations should maintain clear and open communication with all stakeholders, including employees, customers, and regulatory bodies. This includes being transparent about the purpose and scope of surveillance measures, the collected data types, and how that data will be used. Transparent communication fosters trust and can preempt potential conflicts with stakeholders.

➤ Adopt a Risk-Based Approach to Compliance: A risk-based approach focuses on identifying and prioritizing the most significant compliance risks. Organizations can allocate resources more effectively and implement targeted controls by understanding the potential impact and likelihood of various compliance breaches. This approach **en**sures that high-risk areas receive the most attention while lower-risk areas are managed proportionately, optimizing security and compliance efforts.

➤ Leverage Technology for Automated Compliance: Modern technologies, such as AI and machine learning, can be used to automate many compliance processes. For example, AI can be used to monitor employee activities for compliance breaches, flagging suspicious behavior without the need for invasive surveillance. Similarly, machine learning algorithms can help analyze large volumes of data to detect patterns that might indicate non-compliance, allowing for proactive risk management.

➤ Regular Training and Awareness Programs: Continuous education is essential for maintaining a culture of compliance and ethical behavior. Regular training sessions should be conducted to ensure that all employees understand the importance of compliance and know the specific policies and procedures that apply to their roles. Training should also cover ethical decision-making, helping employees recognize and navigate ethical dilemmas they may encounter.

➤ Create a Culture of Accountability and Integrity: Building a corporate culture that values accountability and integrity is crucial for ensuring long-term compliance and ethical behavior. This involves setting the right tone at the top, where leaders model ethical behavior and prioritize compliance in their decision-making. Employees should feel empowered to report unethical behavior or potential compliance breaches without fear of retaliation. Establishing clear channels for whistleblowing and protecting those who raise concerns are vital components of such a culture.

➤ Foster Collaboration with External Stakeholders: In some cases, ensuring compliance while maintaining effectiveness requires collaboration with external stakeholders, such as industry regulators, law enforcement, and community organizations. For instance, collaborating with local law enforcement during large-scale events can enhance public safety and ensure that security measures comply with local regulations. This collaboration can also provide access to additional resources and expertise, helping to address complex security challenges more effectively.

➤ Conduct Post-Implementation Reviews: After implementing any security measure, it's important to conduct a post-implementation review to assess its effectiveness and compliance. This involves evaluating whether the measure achieved its intended security objectives and identifying any compliance issues that may have arisen. Feedback from this review should be used to refine the compliance program and inform future decision-making, ensuring continuous improvement.

By integrating these strategies, organizations can confidently navigate the complex landscape of corporate security and regulatory compliance. This approach helps meet legal obligations and promotes ethical behavior, fostering trust and credibility among stakeholders. A robust compliance framework and a commitment to ethical decision-making are essential for achieving security and compliance objectives in today's increasingly regulated environment.

Case Study: Navigating Complex Legal and Ethical Situations - The Apple vs. FBI Encryption Debate

One of the most well-known and complex cases in recent years that highlights the challenge of balancing legal, ethical, and security considerations is the 2016 conflict between Apple Inc. and the Federal Bureau of Investigation (FBI) over unlocking an iPhone belonging to one of the perpetrators of the San Bernardino terrorist attack.

Background

In December 2015, a terrorist attack in San Bernardino, California, resulted in 14 deaths and numerous injuries. The FBI recovered an iPhone 5C used by one of the attackers and sought access to the device to investigate potential links to other individuals and to prevent future attacks. However, the phone was locked with a passcode, and the data was encrypted, making it inaccessible without the password.

The Legal Dilemma

To access the data, the FBI requested Apple create a special version of its operating system to disable security features, such as the auto-erase function, after multiple failed password attempts. The FBI invoked the All-Writs Act of 1789, a federal statute that grants courts the authority to issue orders necessary to aid their jurisdiction, as the legal basis for compelling Apple to comply. Apple refused, arguing that creating such a tool would set a dangerous precedent, potentially allowing any government to demand similar access to all devices, thereby compromising the security and privacy of millions of users worldwide. The case quickly escalated into a highly publicized legal battle, with Apple filing a motion to vacate the court order.

Ethical Considerations

The ethical implications of this case were profound and multifaceted:

> **Privacy vs. Security**: At the heart of the debate was the balance between individual privacy and national security. Apple maintained that building a backdoor would not

only affect the particular device in question but could also be used to unlock any iPhone, potentially exposing sensitive personal information of millions of users to misuse and abuse.

➤ **Precedent for Future Cases**: Apple feared that complying with the order would set a legal precedent, opening the door for similar requests in the future, not just from the U.S. government but from any government. This could lead to a slippery slope where the privacy and security of all users would be jeopardized.

➤ **Trust and Integrity**: Apple's stance was also about maintaining the trust of its customers. The company has long positioned itself as a protector of user privacy, and complying with the FBI's request would have betrayed this commitment. This could have led to a loss of consumer trust and damaged Apple's brand integrity.

Resolution and Impact

In the end, the case did not reach a judicial conclusion. The FBI announced that it had unlocked the phone using a third-party tool, reportedly developed by a private company. This rendered the court order moot, and the case was dismissed. The fallout from the case, however, had a lasting impact:

➤ **Legal Precedents and Legislation**: The case sparked a national and international debate on encryption, privacy, and government access to digital data. It highlighted the need for clear legal frameworks and led to calls for legislation that would establish the limits of government access to encrypted devices.

➢ **Corporate Responsibility and Consumer Rights**: The case also underscored the role of technology companies in protecting consumer rights and their ethical responsibility in resisting authorities' overreach. It set a benchmark for how companies might handle similar requests in the future, reinforcing the notion that corporate responsibility includes defending user privacy.

➢ **Technological Developments**: Technology companies have continued to enhance encryption technologies in response to the case and similar pressures. Apple, for instance, has introduced even more robust security measures, making it technically impossible for the company to access encrypted data on its devices, even if ordered.

The Apple vs. FBI case remains a seminal example of the complex interplay between legal obligations, ethical considerations, and security needs.

It demonstrates the importance of establishing clear boundaries and frameworks for navigating such conflicts. For corporate security professionals, this case serves as a reminder of the need to carefully consider the broader implications of their actions, balancing compliance with ethical integrity and the long-term trust of their stakeholders. In conclusion, navigating the intricate balance between legal requirements and ethical responsibilities in corporate security is more essential than ever.

Companies must go beyond mere compliance and foster a culture of ethical decision-making that respects individual privacy and public safety.

This involves continuous monitoring of legal developments, engaging in proactive dialogue with stakeholders, and implementing security measures that are transparent and justifiable. By aligning legal obligations with ethical values, organizations can build resilient security frameworks that safeguard their assets and their stakeholders' trust, ultimately contributing to a more secure and ethically sound business environment.

Chapter 15: Global Security Considerations

Global security considerations have become increasingly complex as businesses expand across international borders. The interconnected nature of modern enterprises means that security professionals must be adept at navigating many factors, including diverse legal frameworks, cultural nuances, and varying threat landscapes. Ensuring the safety of assets, personnel, and data requires compliance with local regulations and an understanding of global trends in security risks, such as cyber threats and geopolitical instability. Effective global security management demands a strategic approach that integrates these diverse elements, aligning them with the organization's overarching security objectives.

Challenges of Security in a Globalized Business Environment

In today's interconnected world, businesses operate across diverse geographical locations, each with unique legal, cultural, and security challenges. In my previous role, we faced the challenge of installing surveillance systems in countries with stringent data privacy regulations. To navigate this, we collaborated extensively with legal experts familiar with each jurisdiction. Their guidance was invaluable in adjusting our processes to ensure data collection and storage complied with local laws. This often meant tailoring our technology deployments; in some cases, we had to install localized data servers or restrict certain features that were not permissible in specific countries. Additionally, I advocated for regular audits of our security systems to verify compliance, ensuring that our security measures remained practical and legally sound.

Likewise, when managing security operations across diverse geographical locations, I focus on creating a global security framework with core principles that can be adapted to local contexts. Consistency is crucial, but I recognize that each location has its unique risks and challenges. For instance, I managed security for sites in two vastly different regions—one in a politically unstable area and another in a highly regulated, peaceful country.

While the core strategies, such as perimeter protection and access control, were consistent, the unstable region required additional measures like enhanced security personnel and frequent risk assessments. I developed site-specific security plans, allowing us to maintain the same standard of protection despite the differing local conditions. Managing security in this globalized context is a complex task that requires a nuanced understanding of varying legal jurisdictions, cultural differences in risk perception, and the logistical challenges of protecting assets, personnel, and data across borders. Companies must develop adaptive strategies that account for these complexities while maintaining consistent security standards.

Varying Legal Jurisdictions

One of the most significant challenges for global businesses is complying with various legal requirements across different jurisdictions. Each country has laws governing data protection, surveillance, labor rights, and corporate responsibility. This legal fragmentation creates a complex regulatory environment that can be difficult to navigate, especially for companies that operate in multiple regions with conflicting laws.

For example, Japan's Act on the Protection of Personal Information (APPI) requires companies to obtain explicit consent from individuals before collecting sensitive personal data. It mandates strict controls over the transfer of personal information to third parties, especially when data is shared internationally. In contrast, India's Information Technology (Reasonable Security Practices and Procedures and Sensitive Personal Data or Information) Rules, 2011, impose specific obligations on companies collecting and processing sensitive personal data, such as financial and health information. Therefore, Companies operating in Japan and India must adapt their data management practices to comply with the specific requirements of each law, which can be both complex and resource-intensive, given the differences in consent and data transfer regulations.

Furthermore, countries like China have cybersecurity laws, which include strict data localization requirements, meaning that companies must store certain types of data within China's borders. These conflicting legal requirements can make it difficult for businesses to develop a coherent global data security strategy, forcing them to maintain separate data infrastructures and compliance programs for each jurisdiction.

Cultural Differences in Risk Perception

Cultural differences significantly influence how risks are perceived and managed in various regions, complicating the implementation of a unified security strategy. What one culture views as a minor security concern may be a significant issue in another. These differences can affect everything from how employees respond to security policies to how customers perceive a company's security measures.

For instance, in some Asian cultures, there is a high tolerance for surveillance as a trade-off for safety and security, making it easier for companies to implement comprehensive monitoring systems in workplaces. In contrast, European cultures, particularly in countries like Germany, place a high value on privacy and individual rights, leading to resistance against extensive surveillance measures. A global company trying to implement a standardized security protocol may face pushback in some regions while gaining acceptance in others, complicating the rollout of global security initiatives.

Moreover, the perception of cyber threats can vary significantly across cultures. In the United States, there is generally a high level of awareness and concern about cybersecurity, driven by frequent high-profile data breaches and regulatory pressures.

In contrast, in regions where cybercrime is less visible or publicized, companies may struggle to convince local management and employees of the need for stringent cybersecurity measures. These differences necessitate a localized approach to security education and awareness programs tailored to the specific cultural context of each region.

Managing Security Across Diverse Geographical Locations

The logistical challenge of managing security across multiple geographical locations cannot be overstated. Companies must ensure that physical security measures, such as access controls and surveillance systems, are effective in each location while also coordinating responses to security incidents. This can be particularly difficult when operating in regions with varying levels of infrastructure and security threats.

For example, a company with offices in North America and sub-Saharan Africa must contend with vastly different security environments. In North America, sophisticated electronic access control systems and high-definition surveillance cameras may be the norm, supported by reliable infrastructure and rapid response capabilities. In contrast, a lack of infrastructure, political instability, and higher crime rates in sub-Saharan Africa may necessitate a more robust physical security presence, including security personnel and emergency response plans. Moreover, geopolitical risks, such as terrorism, political unrest, and regional conflicts, can directly impact the security of employees and assets.

Multinational companies operating in politically unstable regions must develop comprehensive security plans that include evacuation procedures, crisis communication strategies, and close coordination with local authorities. This adds another layer of complexity to managing global security, requiring constant monitoring of geopolitical developments and the ability to rapidly adapt security measures as the situation evolves.

Strategies for Navigating the Global Security Landscape

To effectively manage these challenges, companies must adopt a flexible and adaptive approach to security that can be customized to meet the needs of each location while maintaining overall coherence. Here are a few strategies that companies can employ:

> **Localized Compliance Programs:** Develop compliance programs that are tailored to the specific legal requirements of each jurisdiction while ensuring alignment with the company's global policies. This may involve setting up separate data storage solutions,

modifying employee monitoring practices, or adjusting reporting structures to meet local regulations.

> **Culturally Sensitive Security Training**: Design security awareness and training programs considering cultural attitudes toward privacy and security. Tailor communication strategies to address local concerns and ensure employees understand the rationale behind security measures.

> **Integrated Security Management Systems**: Implement integrated security management systems that allow for centralized monitoring and coordination of security across all locations. These systems should be capable of adapting to local conditions, providing the flexibility to implement additional controls or modify procedures as needed.

> **Proactive Risk Assessment**: Conduct regular risk assessments that take into account local security threats, legal changes, and cultural factors. Use these assessments to continuously refine security policies and procedures, ensuring they remain effective and compliant.

Managing security in a globalized business environment is a multifaceted challenge that requires a deep understanding of varying legal jurisdictions, cultural nuances, and the logistical complexities of operating across diverse geographical locations. By developing adaptive strategies that account for these differences, companies can effectively safeguard their assets, data, and personnel while maintaining compliance with local regulations and fostering a culture of security and trust across all regions. This holistic approach is essential for navigating the complexities of today's global business landscape and ensuring the long-term security and success of the organization.

Cultural Considerations in International Security Operations

Managing security operations in a globalized business environment requires more than technical expertise and legal standards adherence. Cultural sensitivity plays a crucial role in effectively implementing security protocols and building productive relationships with local stakeholders. Misunderstanding or ignoring cultural nuances can hinder security operations and damage the trust and cooperation necessary for maintaining a secure environment. This chapter explores the importance of cultural considerations in international security operations, offering guidance on adapting security protocols to different cultural contexts and strategies for building rapport with local stakeholders.

The Importance of Cultural Sensitivity

Cultural sensitivity in security operations is vital because cultural norms and values deeply influence how security measures are perceived and accepted. What might be considered an acceptable security practice in one country could be seen as invasive or disrespectful in another. For instance, facial recognition technology might be readily accepted in some countries as a measure of enhanced security, while in others, it could be viewed as a severe breach of personal privacy and a potential tool for government overreach. Such differences necessitate a tailored approach to security operations that considers local attitudes and legal constraints.

Furthermore, security personnel need to be aware of local customs and etiquette to avoid unintentional offenses. For example, in some cultures, making direct eye contact can be seen as confrontational; in others, it is a sign of confidence and honesty. Similarly, the way security staff communicate, the language they use, and their body language can all impact how local employees and stakeholders perceive them.

Adapting Security Protocols to Local Contexts

Adapting security protocols to different cultural contexts requires a flexible framework that allows local customization while maintaining global security standards. This involves several key steps:

- ➢ **Conducting Cultural Risk Assessments:** Before implementing any security measures, it is essential to conduct a cultural risk assessment. This process involves understanding the local social and cultural environment, including prevalent attitudes toward authority, privacy, and security. For instance, visible security measures like extensive CCTV coverage might be met with resistance in countries with high levels of distrust in government or law enforcement. In contrast, such measures may be welcomed in countries where security threats are more prevalent.

➢ **Customizing Communication Strategies**: How security measures are communicated can significantly affect their acceptance. In some cultures, direct and explicit communication may be appreciated; in others, a more nuanced and indirect approach may be required. It is crucial to frame security protocols in a way that aligns with local values and concerns. For example, emphasizing community safety and the protection of personal data might resonate better in cultures that prioritize collective well-being over individual autonomy.

➢ **Adapting Operational Protocols**: While the core principles of security, such as access control, surveillance, and emergency response, remain consistent, the operational details should be adapted to local contexts. For instance, in regions where bribery and corruption are common, additional measures such as rotation of security personnel and strict financial oversight may be necessary to prevent internal security breaches. In countries with stringent privacy laws, data collection and storage protocols must be carefully designed to comply with local regulations.

➢ **Training and Awareness Programs**: Training programs should be customized to include cultural sensitivity training for security personnel. This helps them understand local customs, behaviors, and the cultural implications of their actions. For example, in some cultures, female security personnel might be preferred for screening female employees or visitors due to cultural norms regarding gender interactions.

Building Rapport with Local Stakeholders

When fostering strong partnerships with local teams and external stakeholders, I prioritize building trust and involving local teams in decision-making processes. This empowers them to adapt global security strategies to their specific needs and challenges. Additionally, maintaining strong relationships with external stakeholders, such as law enforcement and security vendors, is crucial for ensuring quick and effective responses during crises.

For instance, at a facility in a remote international location, I worked closely with local law enforcement, offering our site as a venue for their training exercises. This collaboration not only built goodwill but also established mutual understanding and trust. When we later faced a security threat, the pre-existing relationship allowed for smooth coordination and a swift response. This experience reinforced for me the critical role those local partnerships play in a successful global security strategy.

Building trust and rapport with local stakeholders is essential for effectively implementing security measures. This involves engaging with stakeholders, including local employees, community leaders, law enforcement agencies, and government officials. Here are some strategies for building productive relationships:

➢ **Engage Early and Often:** Establishing a relationship with local stakeholders is crucial before implementing any security measures. This involves regular meetings, open dialogues, and consultations to understand their concerns and expectations. For example, if a company plans to enhance security at a facility, engaging with local community leaders can help mitigate fears and misconceptions about the increased presence of security personnel.

➢ **Demonstrate Respect for Local Practices**: Respecting local customs and practices helps build goodwill. For instance, if a security protocol involves certain procedures that might conflict with religious practices (such as screenings during prayer times), it is important to find a compromise that respects these practices without compromising security.

➢ **Collaborate with Local Authorities**: Working in partnership with local law enforcement and security agencies can enhance the effectiveness of security measures. Local authorities often better understand the regional threat landscape and can provide valuable support during security incidents. However, it is important to be mindful of local political dynamics and avoid being seen as too closely aligned with controversial entities.

➢ **Implement Community-Based Security Programs:** In some regions, involving the local community in security initiatives can be highly effective. This could include community watch programs, security awareness workshops, or collaboration on local safety campaigns. Such initiatives enhance security and foster a sense of shared responsibility and trust between the company and the community.

To address these concerns, the company engaged with local stakeholders, including government officials and community leaders, to explain the purpose and scope of the surveillance system. They also worked with local legal experts to ensure full compliance with regional data privacy laws. The company modified its original plan by reducing the number of cameras in less critical areas and enhancing data encryption measures to protect privacy. This adaptive approach ensured compliance and built trust with the local community, demonstrating the company's respect for local norms and regulations.

Strategies for Managing Diverse Teams and Partnerships

Managing global teams and partnerships is a complex endeavor that requires a nuanced understanding of cultural dynamics, effective communication strategies, and the ability to align diverse operational practices under a cohesive framework. This task is even more challenging for security professionals, as they must ensure that security protocols are consistently implemented across various geographical locations while adapting to local contexts. This involves addressing challenges like remote team management, language barriers, and aligning security practices across different country operations.

Remote Team Management

Remote team management is one of the fundamental challenges in managing global security operations. Security teams are often dispersed across different time zones and locations, making it difficult to maintain constant communication and coordination. Effective remote management requires clear communication channels, well-defined roles and responsibilities, and technology to bridge the distance. To manage remote teams effectively, it's crucial to establish regular communication routines, such as weekly video calls or daily check-ins. These meetings help maintain a sense of connection and ensure all team members are aligned with current objectives and challenges. Additionally, leveraging collaboration tools like Microsoft Teams, Slack, or other secure communication platforms allows for real-time updates and information sharing, which is essential for timely decision-making and coordination.

Moreover, fostering a sense of inclusivity and shared purpose within the team is important. Remote teams can sometimes feel isolated, leading to disengagement. To counter this, managers should actively involve all team members in decision-making processes and recognize their contributions, regardless of their location. Creating opportunities for virtual team-building activities and celebrating achievements collectively can also help strengthen team cohesion and morale.

Overcoming Language Barriers

Language barriers present a significant hurdle in managing global teams and partnerships. Miscommunications due to language differences can lead to misunderstandings, reduced efficiency, and even security breaches. It's essential to establish a common language for communication, typically English, in multinational settings while also being mindful of the language capabilities of all team members.

Managing global security teams remotely presents unique challenges, such as navigating language barriers and adapting to varying local protocols. To effectively address these issues, I prioritize regular communication, setting clear expectations, and investing in team development.

It's essential to leverage local expertise while maintaining a strong leadership presence. I achieve this by conducting weekly calls and making regular in-person visits whenever feasible to ensure everyone stays aligned with our objectives. For instance, I once managed a team in a region where English wasn't the primary language. I introduced language training for the team to bridge the communication gaps and brought on local liaisons who could interpret and help convey our security protocols. This approach allowed us to uphold global standards while being sensitive to local nuances, ultimately improving team cohesion and operational efficiency.

One strategy to overcome language barriers is to provide language training for team members who need it. Offering English as a Second Language (ESL) courses or other language programs can help improve proficiency and reduce misunderstandings.

Additionally, translating key documents, such as security protocols and policies, into local languages ensures that all team members fully understand the guidelines and procedures they are expected to follow. Using clear and simple communication language can also help bridge the language gap. Avoiding jargon, idioms, or culturally specific references makes the information more accessible to non-native speakers. Encouraging team members to ask for clarification if they do not understand something and promoting a culture where it is acceptable to seek help with language issues can also reduce the risk of miscommunication.

Aligning Security Practices Across Different Country Operations

Aligning security practices across different countries is a delicate balancing act. While a global security framework provides consistency and coherence, it must be flexible enough to adapt to local laws, cultural norms, and operational realities. Each country may have unique security threats, regulatory requirements, and resource availability, all of which must be considered when implementing security measures.

The first step in aligning security practices is to establish a global security policy that outlines the core principles and objectives of the organization. This policy should serve as a foundation for building local security practices. It is important to communicate this policy clearly to all team members and stakeholders, emphasizing the need for local adaptation while maintaining the integrity of the overall security strategy.

Next, conducting a thorough risk assessment for each location is essential. This involves identifying specific threats and vulnerabilities that may differ from one region to another. For example, a site in a politically unstable region may require enhanced physical security measures. At the same time, a location in a highly regulated country may need to focus more on compliance with data protection laws. Tailoring security protocols to address these unique risks ensures that the global strategy remains relevant and effective.

Local laws and regulations are another critical consideration. Compliance with legal requirements is non-negotiable, but it can vary significantly from one country to another. For instance, data privacy laws in the European Union under the General Data Protection Regulation (GDPR) are far more stringent than in many other parts of the world. Security teams must work closely with legal and compliance departments to ensure that security practices in each location meet local regulatory standards without compromising the organization's overall security posture.

Collaboration with local stakeholders, including law enforcement, regulatory bodies, and security vendors, is crucial for aligning security practices. Local partners can provide valuable insights into regional security challenges and help implement culturally and operationally appropriate measures. Building strong relationships with these stakeholders facilitates smoother coordination and more effective security management.

Building a Cohesive Security Culture

A unified security culture is essential for ensuring security practices are consistently applied across all locations. This culture should be based on shared values such as integrity, vigilance, and responsibility. Promoting this culture requires continuous training and education tailored to each location's specific needs and contexts. Training programs should go beyond technical skills, including cultural sensitivity training, awareness of local security threats, and understanding local laws and regulations. Regular training sessions, workshops, and e-learning modules can help reinforce the security culture and keep team members informed about the latest developments and best practices.

Leadership plays a key role in building and maintaining this security culture. Security leaders must lead by example, demonstrating a commitment to security and ethical behavior in all their actions. They should also be accessible and approachable, encouraging team members to voice concerns and provide feedback on security practices. This open communication fosters a sense of ownership and accountability among all team members.

Resources for Developing Global Security Expertise

As global security operations become more complex, it is essential for professionals to continuously develop their skills and knowledge to navigate the evolving landscape effectively.

This chapter concludes with valuable resources for enhancing global security expertise, including international security associations, cross-cultural training programs, and global risk assessment tools. These resources provide a foundation for a robust understanding of global security challenges and best practices.

International Security Associations

➤ **ASIS International:** ASIS is one of the leading global organizations for security professionals, offering a wealth of resources, certifications, and networking opportunities. Their certifications, such as the Certified Protection Professional (CPP) and Physical Security Professional (PSP), are recognized worldwide. They help security professionals demonstrate their expertise in managing complex security operations across different regions.

➤ **International Security Management Association (ISMA):** ISMA is an exclusive network of senior security executives from major international companies. It provides members with a platform to share best practices, participate in executive education programs, and access research on global security trends. Membership is by invitation only, making it an elite resource for high-level security professionals.

➤ **Overseas Security Advisory Council (OSAC):** Established by the U.S. Department of State, OSAC promotes security cooperation between the U.S. government and American private-sector organizations operating abroad. It provides timely information on security threats and best practices through reports, briefings, and networking events.

> **International Association of Professional Security Consultants (IAPSC):** IAPSC is a global network of independent security consultants. It offers resources and training to help consultants stay current with industry standards and global security trends. The organization also provides a directory of consultants with specific regional and subject matter expertise.

Cross-Cultural Training Programs

> **Cultural Intelligence Center:** The Cultural Intelligence (CQ) Center offers training and assessment tools designed to help professionals develop cultural intelligence. These programs are essential for security teams operating in diverse environments, providing insights into understanding and managing cross-cultural interactions effectively.

> **Global Leadership Training by Berlitz:** Berlitz offers training programs focusing on developing global leadership skills, including managing cross-cultural teams, effective communication in multicultural settings, and adapting business strategies to different cultural

contexts. This training is valuable for security professionals who need to lead teams in various geographical regions.

➢ **Intercultural Communication Institute (ICI):** ICI provides training and resources to improve cross-cultural communication skills. Their programs are designed for professionals working in international settings and cover topics such as cultural adaptation, conflict resolution, and effective communication strategies across cultures.

Global Risk Assessment Tools

➢ **World-Check Risk Intelligence:** Offered by Refinitiv, World-Check provides comprehensive global risk intelligence, including information on individuals, organizations, and jurisdictions that pose potential risks. This tool helps security professionals conduct due diligence and assess threats in various regions, supporting informed decision-making.

➢ **Control Risks Global RiskMap:** Control Risks offers an annual RiskMap that provides a comprehensive overview of political and security risks worldwide. The interactive map includes assessments of countries and regions, helping security professionals understand the potential threats and vulnerabilities in specific areas.

> **International SOS and Control Risks Travel Risk Map:** This tool provides an overview of medical and security risks for travelers worldwide. It offers detailed information on potential threats and health risks in different countries, which is crucial for security teams managing travel and expatriate security.

> **Everbridge Critical Event Management:** Everbridge provides tools for managing critical events and assessing risks globally. Their platform offers real-time threat monitoring, communication, and response capabilities, enabling security teams to respond to incidents and mitigate risks quickly.

> **Global Incident Map:** This tool provides real-time information on various types of incidents, including terrorism, crime, and natural disasters, worldwide. Security professionals can use this resource to monitor global events and assess their potential impact on operations.

These resources provide valuable knowledge and skills and foster a network of professionals who can share insights and best practices. As the global security landscape continues to evolve, staying informed and connected through these resources is essential for maintaining effective security operations worldwide.

In conclusion, to navigate the complexities of global security, organizations must cultivate a deep understanding of the diverse factors that influence security operations across different regions. This includes staying informed about evolving legal requirements, fostering cultural sensitivity, and leveraging global partnerships. By utilizing resources such as international security associations, cross-cultural training programs, and advanced risk assessment tools, security professionals can develop the expertise needed to manage risks effectively in a globalized environment. Maintaining a proactive and adaptable approach will be key to safeguarding organizations and building resilient global operations as the security landscape continues to evolve.

Chapter 16: Executive Protection in the Corporate World

Executive protection in the corporate world goes beyond traditional security measures, encompassing a comprehensive approach that includes risk assessment, secure travel, and maintaining a professional yet discreet presence. As high-profile executives often symbolize their companies, their safety and public image are paramount. Adequate executive protection requires blending security seamlessly into the executive's professional life without disrupting their business activities or compromising their public persona. This nuanced balance distinguishes corporate executive protection from its military or law enforcement counterparts.

As Benjamin Franklin said, *"Reputation is everything. If it takes a thousand good deeds to build a good reputation, it takes only one bad one to lose it."*

Unique Aspects of Executive Protection in Business Settings

Executive protection (EP) in corporate environments differs significantly from VIP protection in military or law enforcement contexts. While the latter often emphasizes high visibility and tactical readiness, executive protection in business requires a delicate balance between ensuring security and maintaining the executive's ability to conduct business seamlessly. Here, we will explore the unique challenges and strategies of EP in corporate settings, drawing distinctions from its more rigid military counterpart and highlighting the necessity of integrating security measures with business facilitation.

Distinctions Between Corporate and Military Executive Protection

In military and law enforcement, the primary objective is tactical defense, often with a highly visible and assertive security presence. These operations are usually conducted in high-risk environments with immediate and tangible threats. However, corporate executive protection prioritizes discretion and flexibility. The goal is to ensure that the executive can maintain productivity and a professional image without the overt presence of a security detail.

In business contexts, security personnel must often blend into the background. Executives need to attend meetings, engage with stakeholders, and travel with minimal disruption. This requires the protection team to anticipate potential risks and plan accordingly, ensuring a safe environment without hindering the executive's freedom of movement or ability to interact freely.

As an executive protection professional, I had to ensure the safety of a senior executive attending multiple business meetings across different cities. The challenge was to provide comprehensive security without disrupting the executive's schedule or drawing attention. This required intensive advance work, including vetting locations, securing travel routes, and coordinating with local security teams while remaining as unobtrusive as possible. The executive needed to move freely and interact with stakeholders without feeling restricted by the security presence. This experience taught me the importance of blending into the background while maintaining a strong security posture.

Key Components of Effective Executive Protection in Business Settings

➤ **Advance Planning and Risk Assessment:** Successful executive protection begins with thorough planning. This involves conducting detailed risk assessments for every location the executive will visit, identifying potential threats, and establishing contingency plans. The planning phase is crucial for minimizing risks and ensuring a safe yet non-intrusive security presence.

➤ **Discretion and Professionalism**: In corporate settings, security must be effective and discreet. The security team's behavior, attire, and interactions should align with the professional environment, maintaining the executive's public image while providing robust protection. This often means choosing low-profile vehicles, wearing business attire, and avoiding visible security measures unless necessary.

➤ **Coordination with Local Resources**: Local law enforcement and private security services can be invaluable allies. Building strong relationships with these entities allows better coordination during events, travel, and response to emerging threats. This partnership is essential for navigating local legal environments and enhancing security.

Balancing Security with Business Facilitation

One of the primary challenges in corporate executive protection is balancing the need for security with the executive's business requirements. Unlike military environments, where security concerns often take precedence, the executive's ability to conduct business efficiently and without disruption is paramount in the corporate world.

➤ **Minimizing Disruptions:** Security measures should be designed to minimize disruptions. For example, using secure, fast-track routes through airports, arranging private meeting rooms with controlled access, and scheduling security briefings at convenient times all help reduce interference with the executive's schedule.

➤ **Enhancing Executive Productivity:** Security personnel should be seen as facilitators of the executive's work, not hindrances. This means understanding the executive's priorities and working to ensure that security measures align with their business needs. A proactive security team that anticipates and resolves issues before they impact the executive is invaluable.

➤ **Maintaining Public Image:** The executive's public image can be crucial to their business effectiveness. A heavy or obtrusive security presence can send the wrong message to clients and partners. The security team must be aware of this and strive to be as inconspicuous as possible, ensuring their presence is felt rather than seen.

Adapting Military Skills to Corporate Executive Protection

Many former military and law enforcement professionals transition into corporate executive protection. While their risk assessment, tactical response, and crisis management skills are invaluable, they must also adapt to the nuances of the corporate environment.

1. **Understanding Corporate Culture:** Corporate settings often require a more nuanced approach to communication and interaction. Former military personnel must adapt to less hierarchical structures and develop softer interpersonal skills. Understanding the corporate culture and the executive's personal preferences is essential for effective protection.

2. **Flexibility and Adaptability:** Corporate environments can be less predictable than military settings, with last-minute changes to travel plans, meetings, and events. The protection team must be flexible and capable of adapting to these changes while maintaining security protocols.

3. **Emphasizing Non-Physical Security Measures:** Besides physical protection, corporate EP often involves safeguarding sensitive information, ensuring secure communications, and protecting the executive's digital footprint. This requires integrating cybersecurity measures into the overall protection strategy, a skill set that may be new to those from a purely physical security background.

Executive protection in business settings requires a distinct skill set that blends traditional security measures with an understanding of corporate dynamics. Drawing on the strengths of military and law enforcement training, successful corporate EP professionals must adapt their approach to prioritize discretion, business facilitation, and a deep understanding of the executive's needs. By striking this balance, they can provide robust protection that allows the executive to operate freely and effectively without compromising their safety or productivity.

Balancing Security with Business Facilitation

In executive protection, the primary challenge is maintaining a high level of security without impeding the executive's ability to conduct business. This delicate balance requires comprehensive advance work, strategic planning for secure travel, and discreet protection during meetings and events. Unlike military or law enforcement settings, where security can often take precedence over other considerations, security must seamlessly integrate with the executive's business agenda in the corporate world. The objective is to ensure safety while allowing the executive to maintain productivity and uphold a positive public image.

Conducting Advance Work

Advance work is the cornerstone of effective executive protection and is crucial in balancing security needs with business requirements. It involves detailed planning and risk assessments for every location the executive will visit. This preparation is essential for identifying and mitigating potential threats before the executive arrives.

Advanced work includes several key elements:

➢ **Venue Assessment:** Every venue, whether a hotel, office, or conference center, must be thoroughly vetted. This involves checking for secure entry and exit points, evaluating the layout for potential vulnerabilities, and understanding the flow of people in and out of the location. Security teams often coordinate with venue management to ensure that the executive's movements can be controlled and monitored discreetly.

> **Coordination with Local Resources:** Collaborating with local law enforcement and private security providers is vital. These local entities have a deeper understanding of the area's security dynamics and can offer additional support if needed. Building these relationships beforehand allows for seamless coordination during the executive's visit and ensures a faster response in an emergency.

> **Logistics and Itinerary Planning:** Detailed planning of the executive's itinerary, including transportation routes and timing, is necessary to avoid potential security risks. This also helps minimize disruptions to the executive's schedule, as unexpected changes can increase security risks and cause delays affecting business engagements.

During a multi-site business tour, the executive I protected had a tightly packed schedule with back-to-back meetings in various cities. We had to ensure that security measures did not slow down their engagements or become a distraction. This required meticulous advance work, including arranging private, secure transportation, vetting hotel accommodations for secure access, and liaising with local law enforcement for each location.

The advance team was on-site at every venue well ahead of time, coordinating logistics and ensuring secure transitions from one location to the next. This proactive approach allowed the executive to focus on business without being hindered by security concerns.

Managing Secure Travel

Travel is often the most vulnerable aspect of an executive's itinerary. Whether it involves air travel, ground transportation, or navigating through crowded public spaces, security teams must be prepared to manage various risks. The goal is to ensure that travel is safe, efficient, and comfortable for the executive.

> **Secure Transportation:** Choosing the right mode of transportation is critical. Depending on the location and risk level, this may include using armored vehicles, private jets, or secure ground transportation with vetted drivers. The route must be planned with alternative options to avoid traffic delays, roadblocks, or other potential disruptions.

> **Airport and Hotel Security:** Airports and hotels are common points of vulnerability. Security teams must liaise with airport security to facilitate quick and secure passage through customs and checkpoints. Hotels should be pre-screened for security standards, and arrangements should be made for secure, private access

to rooms, with additional security personnel stationed discreetly on-site if necessary.

➢ **Communication and Monitoring:** Continuous monitoring of the executive's movements through GPS tracking and maintaining open lines of communication with all involved security personnel is crucial. Any changes in the environment or itinerary need to be communicated and managed to ensure safety without causing delays.

A well-documented instance of balancing secure travel with business needs involved former U.S. Secretary of State Hillary Clinton's trip to Libya in 2011. Amidst a volatile security environment, the protection team had to secure her travel through multiple high-risk zones while maintaining a discreet yet robust security presence.

Advance teams coordinated with local forces, secured travel routes and planned for rapid extraction in case of an emergency.

Despite the intense security measures, the focus was on allowing Clinton to engage in diplomatic discussions without the security presence overshadowing the purpose of her visit. This case underscores the importance of aligning security measures with the executive's mission and objectives.

Discreet Protection During Business Meetings and Events

Discreet protection is fundamental to corporate executive protection, especially during high-profile meetings and events. The security team must remain vigilant and prepared while blending into the environment to avoid drawing attention to the executive or making others uncomfortable.

> **Minimal Presence, Maximum Awareness:** The security team should maintain a low-profile presence, positioning themselves strategically to observe and react, if needed, without overshadowing the executive's interactions. This approach helps maintain the executive's public image and ensures that business discussions proceed without distractions.

> **Control of Access Points:** Discreetly managing access to the meeting area is crucial. Security personnel can be stationed at key entry points to screen attendees and manage the flow of people without appearing intrusive. This helps in preventing unauthorized access while maintaining a professional atmosphere.

> **Real-Time Risk Assessment:** Security personnel must continually assess the environment, watching for changes in body language, unexpected visitors, or anything unusual that could indicate a potential threat. Being

prepared to act swiftly and efficiently while maintaining a calm demeanor is essential in these situations.

Balancing security with business facilitation in executive protection is a complex but essential task. It requires thorough planning, secure yet efficient travel management, and discreet protection strategies that allow executives to operate without feeling constrained by security measures. By integrating these elements, security teams can provide robust protection that supports, rather than hinders, the executive's ability to conduct business effectively. The ultimate goal is to ensure that security is a seamless part of the executive's daily routine, enabling them to focus on their responsibilities confidently and with peace of mind.

Building Trust with Executive Clients

In executive protection, trust is the cornerstone of a successful relationship between the security professional and the executive. Executives need to feel secure in their physical safety and ability to conduct business without unnecessary intrusions. To achieve this, security professionals must not only provide effective protection but also respect the executive's personal and professional boundaries. This requires the protection team to be seen as trusted advisors on security matters rather than mere enforcers. Establishing this trust involves clear communication, understanding the executive's needs, and demonstrating flexibility in security strategies.

One of the most effective ways to build trust is through open communication. Security professionals must articulate the reasons behind security measures clearly and transparently. This involves explaining the potential risks, the rationale for certain precautions, and the benefits of the proposed security strategy. When executives understand why specific measures are in place, they are more likely to feel comfortable and confident in their security team's capabilities. Furthermore, being receptive to feedback and willing to adjust plans based on the executive's comfort level shows respect for their preferences and fosters a collaborative relationship.

Richard Branson's Approach to Security

A well-known case of balancing security with trust is the approach taken by Richard Branson, founder of the Virgin Group. Branson is known for his approachable and adventurous persona, which extends to his business style. He prefers a minimal, almost invisible security presence, allowing him to maintain a genuine connection with clients and the public.

His security team works diligently behind the scenes, using advanced surveillance and risk assessment tools to ensure his safety without interfering with his interactions or public appearances. This subtle yet effective approach has earned Branson's trust, as his security team is seen as enabling his business style rather than hindering it.

Becoming a Valued Advisor

To be seen as a valued advisor, security professionals must demonstrate their expertise in protecting the executive and their understanding of the business context in which the executive operates. This involves staying informed about the executive's schedule, business priorities, and the nature of their engagements.

For example, a security professional working with an executive attending a high-stakes business negotiation must know the importance of creating an environment conducive to trust and collaboration. This might mean opting for less visible security measures or using discreet technology to monitor the environment. In one instance, an executive I was tasked with protecting expressed concern about feeling "too monitored" during a high-profile business event.

They felt that the visible presence of the security team could potentially undermine their ability to connect with clients and partners. This feedback was crucial, highlighting the delicate balance between providing security and allowing the executive to maintain a sense of autonomy and openness. To address this, we decided to adjust our approach. We reduced the visible presence of security personnel, opting for a more covert strategy. We implemented remote monitoring systems and used real-time communication to keep track of the executive's surroundings without being overtly present. The result was a security setup that provided robust protection while allowing the executive to engage freely with attendees. This experience resolved the immediate concern and demonstrated to the executive that we were responsive and adaptable, significantly strengthening our relationship.

Maintaining Professional Boundaries

While building trust and being seen as an advisor is essential, maintaining professional boundaries is equally important. Security professionals must balance being approachable and respecting the executive's personal space and privacy. This can be challenging, as the role often requires proximity to the executive and, at times, their family. Knowing when to step back and allow the executive personal time is crucial in maintaining this balance.

For example, during private family events, it may be appropriate to scale back the visible security presence and rely more on perimeter controls and discreet surveillance. This shows respect for the executive's personal life and demonstrates that the security team is attentive to their needs beyond physical protection. In contrast, overstepping these boundaries, such as becoming too involved in personal matters or overly protective in low-risk situations, can erode trust and create friction.

Establishing Credibility Through Consistency

Consistency in both actions and communication is fundamental to building and maintaining trust. Executives must be able to rely on their security team to be consistent in their conduct, advice, and decision-making. This means that the security team should always follow through on commitments, maintain high professionalism, and be available to provide support and guidance as needed.

Consistency also applies to the way the security team handles information. Being discreet and maintaining confidentiality is vital. Executives must trust that sensitive information shared during protection will be dealt with with the utmost care and not be disclosed unnecessarily. Any breach of this trust, even inadvertently, can have severe repercussions on the relationship.

Building trust with executive clients is a dynamic process that requires a blend of security expertise, business acumen, and interpersonal skills. Security professionals can position themselves as valued advisors by being transparent, responsive, and respectful of the executive's boundaries.

This approach enhances the effectiveness of security measures and fosters a collaborative relationship crucial for navigating the complex and often high-stakes world of executive protection. Through careful balance and constant vigilance, security teams can provide a safe and supportive environment that enables executives to perform their roles confidently and without unnecessary constraints.

The Successful Executive Protection of Mark Zuckerberg

Executive protection programs are specialized security strategies designed to safeguard high-profile individuals, such as corporate executives, from potential threats. These programs encompass a range of measures, including comprehensive risk assessments, secure travel arrangements, residential security, and discreet protection during public appearances and business meetings. The goal is to maintain the safety and well-being of the executive while allowing them to perform their professional duties without disruption. Successful programs require strategic planning, advanced technology, and a well-trained security team capable of adapting to evolving risks and maintaining a balance between security and the executive's public image.

One of the most prominent examples of a well-executed executive protection program in the corporate world is the security strategy implemented by Mark Zuckerberg, the CEO of Meta Platforms (formerly Facebook). Given Zuckerberg's high public profile and the significant scrutiny faced by his company, his security detail provides a comprehensive look at best practices and lessons learned in executive protection.

Background

Mark Zuckerberg's executive protection is one of the world's most extensive and costly corporate security programs. Meta Platforms has consistently allocated significant resources to ensure the safety of its founder and CEO, spending over $27 million on his security in 2021 alone[14].

This investment reflects the high risk associated with his position and the commitment to a thorough and multifaceted security strategy. The need for such robust protection arises from various threats, including potential protests, targeted attacks, and cyber threats, given Zuckerberg's role in a company that impacts global communication and data privacy.

Comprehensive Security Measures

The security program designed for Zuckerberg is holistic, covering all aspects of his life. It includes physical security at his residences, secure transportation, and personal details that accompany him to all public and private events. This level of protection is necessary due to his visibility and the controversies surrounding Meta Platforms' influence on social and political issues.

Advance Planning and Risk Assessment

One of the critical components of Zuckerberg's security program is meticulous planning and risk assessment. Every location he visits is thoroughly vetted before his arrival. This

---

[14] https://www.livemint.com/news/world/meta-spent-43-million-on-mark-zuckerbergs-personal-security-in-3-years-report-11688867699127.html#:~:text=Reportedly%2C%20Meta%20earmarked%20around%20%2427,Meta%20Platforms%20Inc.

includes evaluating potential threats, identifying safe entry and exit routes, and planning for contingencies in emergencies. Advance teams are deployed to conduct on-site assessments and coordinate with local security forces, ensuring all bases are covered before Zuckerberg's arrival. For instance, security teams work closely with event organizers during public appearances or speaking engagements to secure venues, screen attendees, and monitor for any unusual activity. They also coordinate with local law enforcement to ensure additional security support. This proactive approach minimizes the risk of disruptions and allows Zuckerberg to focus on his engagements without concern for his safety.

Secure Travel Arrangements

Zuckerberg's security program also strongly emphasizes secure travel. His movements are carefully planned and monitored, whether by land or air. He often uses private armored vehicles driven by highly trained security professionals for land travel. When possible, air travel is conducted via private jets to ensure security and privacy. The security team conducts regular threat assessments along planned routes and has contingency plans for immediate evacuation.

Residential Security

Security at Zuckerberg's residences is another critical component of his protection program. His properties have state-of-the-art security systems, including surveillance cameras, alarms, and secure perimeters. Trained security personnel are stationed at his home around the clock, and strict protocols are in place for handling potential security breaches.

In 2019, it was reported that Zuckerberg had even purchased neighboring properties around his main residence to enhance privacy and security. This move secured his physical safety and reduced the risk of unwanted surveillance or disruptions from surrounding areas.

Adaptability and Discretion

One of the most challenging aspects of executive protection for high-profile figures like Zuckerberg is maintaining a balance between security and personal freedom.

Despite the comprehensive measures, Zuckerberg's security detail strives to remain as unobtrusive as possible, allowing him to engage with the public and participate in events without an overwhelming security presence.

This approach was evident during his testimony before the U.S. Congress in 2018. Despite the high-risk environment, the security team ensured the proceedings went smoothly without a heavy-handed security display. They managed security discreetly, allowing Zuckerberg to focus on his testimony without appearing overly guarded or isolated from the public.

Best Practices and Lessons Learned

The executive protection program for Mark Zuckerberg offers several key takeaways for managing high-level security in a corporate environment:

> ➤ **Comprehensive Risk Assessment and Planning:** A thorough understanding of potential risks is essential for developing effective protection strategies. Regular assessments and updates to the security plan ensure that the protection measures evolve with changing threat landscapes.

> ➤ **Coordination with Local Resources**: Building strong relationships with local law enforcement and security providers can significantly enhance the effectiveness of the protection plan. These partnerships provide additional support and local expertise crucial in high-risk situations.

> ➤ **Flexibility and Adaptability**: A successful executive protection strategy must adapt to changing circumstances. Security teams should be prepared to adjust their approach based on the executive's schedule, the environment, and the level of risk.

> ➤ **Maintaining a Low Profile**: High-profile individuals often need to maintain a public presence and engage with stakeholders. Ensuring their security without

drawing undue attention requires a low-profile, behind-the-scenes approach that still provides robust protection.

> **Investment in Technology and Resources:** Comprehensive security programs require significant investment in human and technological resources. Building a resilient security framework requires utilizing advanced surveillance systems, secure communication channels, and well-trained personnel.

The executive protection program for Mark Zuckerberg stands as a benchmark for effective corporate security, illustrating how a well-funded, strategically managed approach can safeguard even the most high-profile individuals.

By integrating meticulous planning, adaptability, and a balanced approach to visible and invisible security measures, the program demonstrates that successful executive protection is about more than just physical safety—enabling executives to perform their roles effectively and confidently in any environment. This case study underscores the importance of a comprehensive, proactive, and flexible approach to executive protection in the corporate world. In conclusion, the corporate world demands a sophisticated and adaptable approach to executive protection, where security measures must be seamlessly integrated into the executive's daily operations without compromising their effectiveness or reputation.

Successful executive protection programs prioritize trust, discretion, and proactive planning, ensuring that executives can navigate their roles with confidence and safety. By striking a balance between robust security and business facilitation, these programs enable leaders to focus on their strategic objectives, secure in the knowledge that their protection needs are being handled with the highest level of professionalism and care.

Chapter 17: Corporate Investigations

"Integrity is doing the right thing, even when no one is watching."
— **C.S. Lewis**

Corporate investigations are essential tools for maintaining organizational integrity, ensuring compliance with internal policies, and mitigating risks associated with fraud, theft, or workplace misconduct. Unlike law enforcement investigations, corporate investigations are internally focused, aiming to address issues that impact the company's operations, reputation, and financial stability.

However, the complexity of these investigations has grown with the increasing use of digital communication, the globalization of business operations, and the rise of sophisticated internal threats. Investigators must navigate a web of legal and ethical considerations, use advanced investigative techniques, and present findings effectively to ensure that their work supports the company's strategic objectives without compromising its ethical standards.

Comparing Law Enforcement and Corporate Investigations

Law enforcement and corporate investigations operate under distinct frameworks, driven by different authorities, resources, and objectives. While law enforcement agencies are vested with legal powers and responsibilities to investigate criminal activity and uphold public safety, corporate investigations are more internally focused, aiming to protect the company's interests, ensure compliance with internal policies, and maintain business integrity. Despite these differences, there are situations where corporate investigations uncover activities that necessitate the involvement of law enforcement, requiring a careful and strategic transition from an internal to a criminal investigation.

I have firsthand experience in corporate investigation in one of my previous jobs. During one investigation into financial misconduct at a company, it initially seemed like a straightforward internal issue that could be addressed through disciplinary actions. However, as I delved deeper, I began to uncover evidence that suggested a much larger problem involving potential criminal fraud. Realizing the gravity of the situation, I immediately consulted with senior leadership, legal counsel, and HR to evaluate the best course of action. After thorough discussions, we collectively decided that pursuing criminal charges was the appropriate response.

The transition was challenging, as it required us to hand over critical evidence to law enforcement while continuing to manage the situation internally. We had to ensure that this process did not disrupt the day-to-day operations of the business or damage the company's reputation. Throughout this experience, I learned the importance of recognizing when an issue extends beyond internal resolution and the need to escalate it to external authorities. Clear communication with all stakeholders was essential to maintaining trust and transparency during this sensitive transition.

Legal Authority and Jurisdiction

The most significant distinction between law enforcement and corporate investigations lies in their legal authority and jurisdiction. Law enforcement agencies, such as the police or federal investigators, have the legal power to enforce the law, conduct searches and seizures, issue subpoenas, and make arrests. They operate under strict legal frameworks that define their jurisdiction and the limits of their investigative powers. Their primary objective is to investigate crimes and bring perpetrators to justice, often culminating in criminal prosecutions.

In contrast, corporate investigators do not have legal authority outside of the company. Their jurisdiction is limited to the organization's internal affairs, and their investigative tools are restricted to methods such as interviews, reviewing internal documents, and analyzing digital records within the bounds of company policy and employment laws.

Their focus is on uncovering misconduct, fraud, or policy violations within the organization, and their findings typically lead to disciplinary actions, policy changes, or preventive measures rather than criminal charges. For example, in the case of an internal investigation into a data breach, a corporate investigator would have access to company systems and personnel to determine the source of the breach. However, if it were discovered that the breach involved a third-party hacker or a coordinated cyber-attack, the investigation would likely need to be escalated to law enforcement to pursue criminal charges against the perpetrators, as the corporate team lacks the authority to track and prosecute external actors.

Resources and Capabilities

Law enforcement agencies are equipped with extensive resources and specialized personnel to conduct comprehensive investigations. They have access to forensic laboratories, advanced surveillance technology, and a network of interagency collaborations. These resources enable them to tackle complex cases that involve cross-jurisdictional issues, organized crime, or large-scale fraud. Their investigative teams may include detectives, forensic analysts, cyber experts, and other specialized personnel who bring a broad spectrum of skills to the table.

On the other hand, corporate investigations are often limited by the resources available within the company. While larger organizations may have dedicated investigation teams with specialized skills in forensic accounting, cybersecurity, or legal compliance, smaller companies may rely on their internal audit or HR departments to conduct investigations. In such cases, the depth and scope of the investigation are constrained by the available resources, which can impact the effectiveness and thoroughness of the investigation. Despite these limitations, corporate investigators can leverage external resources, such as private investigation firms, forensic experts, or legal counsel, to augment their capabilities when dealing with complex cases. However, the use of such external resources must be carefully managed to maintain confidentiality and control costs.

Objectives and Outcomes

The objectives of law enforcement and corporate investigations also differ significantly. Law enforcement investigations are focused on identifying and prosecuting individuals who have violated the law. Their ultimate goal is to protect public safety, deter criminal activity, and ensure justice is served. The outcome of a successful law enforcement investigation is typically the apprehension and prosecution of the suspect, potentially leading to conviction and sentencing.

In contrast, corporate investigations aim to protect the organization from financial loss, reputational damage, and legal liability. The primary focus is on identifying the root cause of the issue, assessing its impact on the company, and implementing corrective measures to prevent future occurrences. The outcomes of corporate investigations often involve disciplinary actions, such as employee termination, policy changes, or enhanced controls. In cases where the investigation reveals criminal activity, the company may choose to report the matter to law enforcement, leading to potential criminal prosecution.

Navigating the Transition from Internal to Criminal Investigations

There are instances when a corporate investigation uncovers evidence of criminal activity that goes beyond the scope of internal resolution. In such cases, it is critical to manage the transition to law enforcement carefully to protect the company's interests and ensure that the investigation proceeds without jeopardizing the integrity of the evidence or the company's reputation.

The Case of Corporate Espionage

A notable example of the transition from a corporate to a criminal investigation occurred at Coca-Cola in 2007. An internal investigation revealed that an employee, along with two accomplices, had attempted to sell proprietary information and samples of a new product formula to a competitor, PepsiCo. Coca-Cola's internal security team conducted a thorough investigation, collecting evidence that included emails and recorded conversations. Recognizing the criminal nature of the conduct, Coca-Cola contacted the FBI.

The FBI then launched an undercover operation, culminating in the arrest of the individuals involved when they attempted to sell the stolen information for $1.5 million[15]. This case illustrates the importance of recognizing when an internal

---

[15] https://www.theguardian.com/media/2006/jul/07/marketingandpr.drink

investigation uncovers criminal behavior that warrants escalation to law enforcement. Coca-Cola's collaboration with the FBI not only protected the company's intellectual property but also demonstrated a commitment to ethical conduct and legal compliance.

The Importance of Collaboration and Communication

When transitioning from a corporate to a criminal investigation, effective collaboration and communication are essential. Corporate investigators must work closely with legal counsel, HR, and senior leadership to determine the appropriate course of action. Clear communication with law enforcement is also crucial to ensure that the handover of evidence and information is conducted legally and transparently.

Maintaining confidentiality during this process is vital to protect the company's reputation and avoid potential legal liabilities. A premature disclosure or mishandling of sensitive information could compromise both internal and criminal investigations, leading to negative publicity and financial repercussions for the company.

Corporate and law enforcement investigations serve different purposes and operate within distinct frameworks, but there are times when their paths intersect. Understanding the key differences in authority, resources, and objectives is essential for navigating these complex situations. When a corporate investigation reveals criminal activity, the ability to transition seamlessly to a law enforcement investigation while maintaining ethical standards and clear communication is critical. By recognizing the signs that an issue may go beyond internal resolution and knowing how to escalate appropriately, companies can protect their interests while ensuring that justice is served.

Common Types of Corporate Investigations

Corporate investigations typically aim to address and resolve internal issues such as fraud, theft, workplace misconduct, or violations of company policies. The goal is to mitigate risks, protect the company's assets, and maintain a healthy work environment. However, there are instances when the misconduct uncovered is so severe that it warrants criminal prosecution. This often occurs in cases involving large-scale fraud, embezzlement, or intellectual property theft. In these situations, the decision to escalate the matter from an internal investigation to criminal charges is a complex process that requires careful consideration and collaboration with senior leadership, legal teams, and HR departments.

Understanding the Threshold for Escalation

The decision to escalate an internal investigation to law enforcement is not taken lightly. It involves assessing the severity and impact of the misconduct, as well as the potential legal and reputational consequences for the company. Factors that may influence this decision include the scale of the financial loss, the involvement of external parties, and the potential risk to the company's reputation and stakeholders. For instance, in cases of minor fraud or theft, such as an employee misappropriating a small amount of company resources, the issue can often be resolved internally through disciplinary action or termination. However, when the fraud involves substantial amounts of money, impacts the company's financial statements, or involves external parties, the stakes are much higher. In such cases, resolving the matter internally may not be sufficient to address the seriousness of the offense or to deter future misconduct.

Collaboration with Stakeholders

When an internal investigation reveals criminal activity, involving all relevant stakeholders in the decision-making process is crucial. This includes senior leadership, legal teams, HR, and sometimes external experts such as forensic accountants or private investigators. Each of these parties brings a unique perspective and expertise to the table, helping to ensure that the decision to escalate is well-informed and that all potential risks and consequences have been considered. For example, the legal team plays a critical role in assessing the strength of the evidence and determining whether it meets the standard required for criminal prosecution. They will also consider the potential legal ramifications for the company, such as civil liability or regulatory scrutiny. HR may be involved in assessing the impact on employee relations and ensuring that any disciplinary actions taken are fair and consistent with company policies.

In my role as an investigator, I encountered a case where an initial investigation into financial misconduct appeared to be a relatively minor issue that could be addressed internally. However, as I dug deeper, it became clear that the misconduct was part of a larger scheme involving fraudulent transactions and potential embezzlement. At this point, I realized that the situation was beyond the scope of an internal resolution. I consulted with senior leadership, legal counsel, and HR to present my findings and recommend involving law enforcement. After a thorough review of the evidence and careful deliberation, we decided to escalate the case to criminal prosecution. The experience underscored the importance of knowing when to escalate an issue and the value of a collaborative approach in making that decision.

Managing the Transition to Criminal Prosecution

Once the decision to involve law enforcement is made, the transition must be managed carefully to protect the integrity of the investigation and the company's interests. This involves securing and preserving evidence, maintaining confidentiality, and ensuring that all legal and regulatory requirements are met.

The company must be prepared to cooperate fully with law enforcement, providing all relevant evidence and documentation. It is also important to communicate clearly with employees and other stakeholders to manage the potential impact on the organization. This may include addressing concerns about the investigation, reassuring employees about the company's commitment to ethical conduct, and protecting the company's reputation in the public eye.

The Enron Scandal

One of the most well-known case studies of a corporate investigation escalating to criminal prosecution is the Enron scandal. Initially, internal audits and whistleblower reports raised concerns about accounting irregularities and potential financial misconduct.

As the internal investigation progressed, it became evident that the scale of the fraud was massive, involving the manipulation of financial statements to conceal debt and inflate profits.

Recognizing the severity of the misconduct, Enron's internal audit team, along with external auditors and legal counsel, brought the matter to the attention of regulatory authorities and law enforcement[16].

---

[16] https://www.investopedia.com/updates/enron-scandal-summary/

The investigation ultimately led to criminal charges against several top executives and the collapse of the company. The Enron case highlights the importance of recognizing when internal resolution is not sufficient and the need for criminal prosecution to hold individuals accountable for their actions.

Lessons Learned and Best Practices

From both my personal experience and high-profile cases like Enron, several key lessons emerge for corporate investigators facing the decision to escalate an investigation:

- ➢ **Thorough Evidence Gathering**: Before deciding to escalate an issue, ensure that all evidence has been thoroughly gathered, documented, and preserved. Incomplete or mishandled evidence can jeopardize both the internal and criminal investigations.

- ➢ **Early Involvement of Legal Counsel:** Engage legal counsel early in the investigation to assess the strength of the evidence and the potential legal implications of escalating the matter.

- ➢ **Clear Communication with Stakeholders**: Keep senior leadership, HR and other relevant stakeholders informed throughout the investigation. This helps ensure that the decision to escalate is supported and that all potential risks have been considered.

➢ **Maintain Confidentiality**: Protecting the confidentiality of the investigation is crucial to avoid damaging the company's reputation and to prevent tipping off potential suspects before law enforcement is involved.

➢ **Cooperation with Law Enforcement**: Once the decision to escalate has been made, cooperate fully with law enforcement to ensure a smooth transition and to support the criminal investigation.

Deciding to escalate a corporate investigation to criminal prosecution is a complex and challenging decision that requires careful consideration and collaboration. While internal resolution is often preferred, there are cases where the severity of the misconduct warrants the involvement of law enforcement. By understanding the signs that an issue may require criminal prosecution and knowing how to manage the transition effectively, corporate investigators can protect the company's assets and reputation while ensuring that justice is served.

Legal and Ethical Considerations in Investigations

When a corporate investigation uncovers evidence of criminal activity, the decision to escalate the matter to law enforcement involves navigating a complex web of legal and ethical considerations. Companies must ensure that all evidence collected complies with local laws, including data protection and privacy regulations, while also safeguarding the rights of the employees involved. It is crucial to maintain the company's ethical standards throughout the process, treating all parties fairly and transparently. Collaboration with legal counsel, HR, and senior leadership is essential to making informed and responsible decisions about whether to escalate the investigation to criminal prosecution.

Ensuring Compliance with Legal Standards

One of the primary legal considerations in any internal investigation, particularly when it may lead to criminal charges, is compliance with data protection and privacy laws. In many jurisdictions, there are strict regulations governing how personal data can be collected, processed, and stored.

In the context of a corporate investigation, this means that investigators must be careful to obtain necessary consent and ensure that their data collection methods do not infringe on employees' privacy rights.

This is particularly challenging in cases where the investigation involves accessing private communications, such as emails or instant messages. Failure to comply with these regulations can not only undermine the investigation but also expose the company to significant legal liabilities, including fines and reputational damage. In a previous investigation I led, we faced a situation where an employee was suspected of embezzling funds. To build a strong case, we needed to access the employee's email records and transaction history. Before proceeding, I collaborated closely with our legal team to ensure that all data collection methods complied with relevant privacy laws. We made sure to document the legal basis for each step and obtained necessary consent where applicable. By meticulously following legal guidelines, we were able to gather the evidence needed without violating the employee's rights, ultimately allowing us to pursue the case ethically and legally.

Ethical Considerations in Employee Rights

Even when criminal activity is suspected, it is vital to ensure that the rights of the employee under investigation are respected. This includes maintaining confidentiality, providing the employee with the opportunity to respond to allegations, and avoiding actions that could be seen as prejudicial or unfair. The principle of "innocent until proven guilty" must be upheld to maintain the integrity of the investigation and the company's commitment to ethical behavior.

During an investigation, employees should be informed of their rights, including the right to representation and the right to privacy. If disciplinary actions are being considered, these should be based on clear evidence and conducted following company policies and employment laws. It is also important to ensure that the investigation does not create a hostile work environment or lead to unwarranted assumptions or rumors within the organization.

Collaborating with Legal and HR Teams

Collaboration with legal and HR teams is critical throughout the investigation process, especially when the potential for criminal charges arises. Legal counsel can provide guidance on the admissibility of evidence, the implications of data privacy laws, and the process for involving law enforcement. HR's role is to ensure that the investigation is conducted fairly and that any disciplinary actions taken are consistent with company policies and do not violate employment laws.

In another case, our team uncovered evidence of intellectual property theft involving an employee who was selling company secrets to a competitor. The situation was delicate, as it had significant legal and reputational implications for the company. I worked closely with our legal and HR teams to assess the evidence and determine the best course of action. We decided to confront the employee with the findings, allowing them to respond. Throughout the process, we made sure to document every interaction and decision meticulously, ensuring that the investigation was transparent and that the employee's rights were respected. Eventually, we handed the case over to law enforcement, but only after ensuring that all internal processes had been followed and that the company was fully protected from legal repercussions.

Managing the Transition to Criminal Prosecution

When the decision is made to escalate an investigation to law enforcement, the company must manage the transition carefully. This includes securing and preserving all evidence, maintaining strict confidentiality, and ensuring that any communication with law enforcement is coordinated and documented. The timing of this transition is also critical; premature involvement of law enforcement can disrupt the investigation and lead to unintended consequences, such as public disclosure of the allegations before the company is ready to manage the potential fallout.

Transparency with senior leadership and key stakeholders is essential during this phase. Regular updates should be provided, and any decisions to involve law enforcement should be made collectively, with a clear understanding of the potential risks and benefits. It is also important to consider the impact on the company's reputation and to have a communications strategy in place to manage any public disclosures that may arise.

The Siemens Bribery Scandal

The complexities involved in escalating an investigation to criminal prosecution in the Siemens bribery scandal are well known. In 2008, the German engineering giant was implicated in a global bribery scheme involving payments to government officials to secure business contracts[17]. Initially, Siemens conducted an internal investigation to understand the scope of the issue. As the investigation progressed, it became clear that the misconduct was widespread and involved senior executives.

Given the severity of the allegations, Siemens decided to cooperate fully with law enforcement authorities in Germany and the United States. The company shared evidence gathered during the internal investigation and worked closely with external legal counsel to navigate the complex legal and ethical issues. This cooperation ultimately led to Siemens agreeing to pay over $1.6 billion in fines, one of the largest settlements in corporate history. The case demonstrates the importance of managing the transition from an internal to a criminal investigation carefully and transparently, with full cooperation from all stakeholders.

Best Practices for Navigating Legal and Ethical Challenges

When conducting internal investigations that may lead to criminal charges, several best practices can help ensure that the process is handled ethically and legally:

> ➤ **Develop a Clear Investigation Framework**: Establish clear policies and procedures for conducting

---

[17] https://www.sec.gov/enforcement-litigation/litigation-releases/lr-20829

investigations, including guidelines for data collection, evidence handling, and employee rights.

➢ **Consult Legal and HR Teams Early**: Involve legal and HR teams from the outset to ensure the investigation complies with all relevant laws and company policies.

➢ **Maintain Transparency and Communication**: Keep senior leadership and key stakeholders informed throughout the investigation. Regular updates help manage expectations and ensure that all decisions are made collaboratively.

➢ **Document Every Step**: Thorough documentation of all actions taken during the investigation is essential. This includes collecting evidence, conducting interviews, and deciding about disciplinary actions or criminal prosecution.

➢ **Protect Employee Rights:** Ensure employees' rights are respected throughout the investigation. This includes maintaining confidentiality, avoiding prejudicial actions, and providing opportunities for employees to respond to allegations.

Navigating the legal and ethical complexities of internal investigations, especially when they may lead to criminal charges, requires a careful, well-coordinated approach.

Companies can manage these challenging situations effectively by collaborating closely with legal, HR, and senior leadership and adhering to a robust framework for evidence collection and decision-making. The key is to balance the need for accountability and justice with the company's ethical obligations to its employees and stakeholders.

Strategies for Conducting Effective and Discreet Investigations

Corporate investigations require a careful and methodical approach to uncover misconduct, fraud, or violations of company policy while maintaining confidentiality and minimizing disruption to the business. Effective investigations are discreet, thorough, and well-documented, ensuring that findings can withstand scrutiny and be presented clearly to management. This chapter will explore strategies for conducting effective and discreet investigations, focusing on digital forensics, interviewing techniques in corporate settings, and the best practices for presenting findings to management.

Digital Forensics in Corporate Investigations

Digital forensics has become essential in corporate investigations, particularly as more business activities are conducted electronically. Digital forensics involves identifying, preserving, extracting, and documenting digital evidence from electronic devices. This evidence can include emails, text messages, files, and internet browsing history, which may be crucial in proving or disproving misconduct allegations.

1. **Identifying and Preserving Evidence**: The first step in digital forensics is to identify the electronic devices and data sources that may hold relevant information. These could include computers, smartphones, servers, and cloud storage. It is crucial to act quickly to preserve this data to prevent tampering or deletion. Preservation involves creating a forensic image and a bit-by-bit copy of the data, ensuring the original information remains unaltered.

2. **Extracting and Analyzing Data:** Investigators must extract and analyze the data using specialized forensic tools once the data is preserved. This analysis often involves searching for specific keywords, analyzing metadata, and reconstructing deleted files or messages. Investigators must also be aware of encryption and data protection measures that may complicate access to the information.

3. **Ensuring Chain of Custody:** Maintaining a clear chain of custody is critical in digital forensics to ensure that the evidence remains admissible in legal proceedings. This involves meticulously documenting every step of the evidence collection, handling, and analysis process, including who has accessed the evidence and when.

Interviewing Techniques in Corporate Settings

Conducting interviews during a corporate investigation requires a nuanced approach. Unlike law enforcement interviews, corporate investigations often involve colleagues, subordinates, or superiors, making the process more delicate. The goal is to gather accurate information without creating a hostile environment or tipping off the subject of the investigation.

1. **Preparation**: Thorough preparation is essential before conducting interviews. Investigators should review all available evidence and background information on the interviewee to formulate relevant questions. They should also be aware of the interviewee's role within the company and potential involvement in the issue being investigated.

2. **Establishing a Comfortable Setting**: Creating a comfortable environment helps put the interviewee at ease and encourages open communication. The interview should be conducted privately, free from interruptions, where the interviewee feels they can speak candidly without fear of retribution.

3. **Building Rapport and Gaining Trust**: Building rapport is crucial in corporate settings, where the relationship between the investigator and interviewee can significantly impact the quality of the information

gathered. Starting the interview with non-confrontational, open-ended questions helps establish a positive tone. Demonstrating empathy and active listening can also encourage the interviewee to be more forthcoming.

4. **Documenting the Interview**: Accurate documentation of the interview is critical. It is advisable to take detailed notes and, if permissible, record the interview with the interviewee's consent. This ensures that the information gathered can be referenced accurately in the final report and helps protect against allegations of misrepresentation.

Presenting Findings to Management

The final step in a corporate investigation is presenting the findings to management. This presentation must be clear, concise, and supported by well-documented evidence. It is essential to communicate the investigation's results in a way that allows management to understand the facts and make informed decisions.

1. **Structuring the Report:** The investigation report should be well-structured, beginning with an executive summary that outlines the key findings and recommendations. The body of the report should detail the evidence collected, the methodology used, and the conclusions drawn. Supporting documents, such as

emails, financial records, or interview transcripts, should be included in appendices.

2. **Maintaining Objectivity**: The report should be objective and fact-based, avoiding speculation or subjective judgments. It is important to present both corroborating and conflicting evidence to provide a balanced view of the situation.

3. **Recommending Actions:** Based on the findings, the report should include recommendations for management action. This could range from disciplinary measures and policy changes to suggesting further investigation or escalation to law enforcement. The recommendations should be practical and aligned with the company's policies and legal obligations.

4. **Managing Confidentiality**: The presentation of the findings should be conducted in a confidential setting, involving only those who need to be informed. Sensitive information should be handled carefully to protect those involved's privacy and prevent unnecessary reputational harm to the company.

Conducting effective and discreet corporate investigations requires a combination of technical expertise, interpersonal skills, and strategic communication. Whether using digital forensics to uncover evidence, conducting interviews with tact and professionalism, or presenting findings to management with clarity and objectivity, each step must be carefully executed to ensure a successful outcome. By following these strategies, investigators can protect the company's interests while upholding the highest standards of integrity and confidentiality.

Effective corporate investigations require technical expertise, strategic planning, and ethical integrity. Investigators must be adept at employing digital forensics, conducting sensitive interviews, and presenting findings to facilitate informed decision-making.

By maintaining a high standard of confidentiality and objectivity throughout the investigative process, companies can address internal issues proactively, protect their assets, and uphold their reputations. As business environments continue to evolve, the role of corporate investigations in safeguarding organizational integrity will only become more critical, necessitating ongoing adaptation and refinement of investigative methodologies.

In conclusion, effective corporate investigations require a blend of technical expertise, strategic planning, and ethical integrity. Investigators must be adept at employing digital forensics, conducting sensitive interviews, and presenting findings to facilitate informed decision-making. By maintaining a high standard of confidentiality and objectivity throughout the investigative process, companies can address internal issues proactively, protect their assets, and uphold their reputations. As business environments continue to evolve, the role of corporate investigations in safeguarding organizational integrity will only become more critical, necessitating ongoing adaptation and refinement of investigative methodologies.

Chapter 18: Budgeting and Resource Management

As Peter Drucker, a pioneer in modern management, once said,

"What gets measured gets managed."

Budgeting and resource management are crucial pillars in corporate security planning. These processes ensure that security initiatives are appropriately funded and aligned with overall business goals, allowing organizations to protect assets without unnecessary financial strain.

Effective security budgeting involves allocating resources to current and future threats while integrating the company's risk management strategies.

The aim is to balance cost-effectiveness and robust security measures, ensuring that every dollar spent contributes to safeguarding the organization and its operations. Businesses can maintain financial discipline and a strong security posture by carefully planning budgets, managing security resources, and ensuring efficient vendor management. This chapter delves into these intricacies, providing practical strategies and insights to optimize security spending.

Strategic Corporate Budgeting Integrating Security with Business Objectives

In corporate environments, budgeting is a critical process that aligns a company's financial resources with its business objectives and operational needs. Security budgets, while often seen as a subset of the broader corporate financial plan, are increasingly recognized as essential for safeguarding assets, maintaining compliance, and ensuring business continuity. Integrating security spending into the overall budgeting process requires a strategic approach that aligns security initiatives with the company's core objectives while demonstrating return on investment (ROI) to stakeholders.

The Basics of Corporate Budgeting Processes

Corporate budgeting involves allocating financial resources to different departments, initiatives, and projects based on projected revenues, operational costs, and strategic priorities. This process typically involves several stages:

- ➢ **Forecasting and Goal Setting**: Companies begin by projecting future revenues and setting business objectives, including expanding operations, launching new products, or improving efficiency.

- ➢ **Cost Estimation**: Once objectives are defined, departments and business units estimate the costs associated with achieving them. This includes salaries, overheads, operational costs, and any new investments needed.

> **Budget Negotiation and Approval**: Departmental budgets are reviewed and negotiated with corporate leadership. This stage often involves compromises to align spending with broader corporate goals and to manage available financial resources.

> **Monitoring and Adjustments**: Once approved, the budget is monitored over the fiscal year. Adjustments may be made based on performance, changing business conditions, or unforeseen challenges.

Security Budgets in Corporate Financial Planning

Security budgets are vital to corporate financial planning, especially as businesses face increasing threats from cyberattacks, physical breaches, and regulatory non-compliance. A well-structured security budget ensures the company can protect its assets, comply with regulations, and minimize financial and reputational risks.

Traditionally, security spending was often viewed as a cost center—a necessary but non-revenue-generating expense. However, the rise in high-profile security breaches and the increasing complexity of regulatory frameworks have shifted this perception. Companies now understand that inadequate security spending can lead to significant financial losses, legal liabilities, and reputational damage. For example, a study conducted by **IBM Security** revealed that the average cost of a data breach in 2023 was approximately **\$4.45 million**[18], a significant increase from previous years. These figures underscore the need for robust security investments, as failure to adequately fund security programs can expose a company to catastrophic losses that far outweigh the cost of proactive prevention.

Aligning Security Spending with Business Objectives

Aligning security initiatives with overall business objectives is key to successfully integrating security budgets into corporate financial planning. Security investments should support business growth, regulatory compliance, and operational efficiency.

➢ **Risk Management:** Security spending should be risk-based, focusing on protecting the company's most critical assets. For instance, businesses handling sensitive customer data may prioritize investments in cybersecurity tools like encryption, firewalls, and multi-factor authentication to protect against data breaches. A company's physical security budget may include advanced surveillance systems, secure access control, and personnel training to protect physical infrastructure.

➢ **Compliance and Regulatory Requirements**: Compliance with regulations like the General Data Protection

---

[18] https://www.upguard.com/blog/cost-of-data-breach#:~:text=A%20Complete%20Guide%20to%20Data%20Breaches&text=In%202023%2C%20the%20average%20cost,(US%24%204.35%20milion).

Regulation (GDPR) and the California Consumer Privacy Act (CCPA) often requires significant security investments. These regulations impose strict data privacy and protection standards, and failure to comply can result in severe financial penalties. For example, companies found in violation of GDPR can be fined up to €20 million or 4% of annual global turnover, whichever is higher[19]. Therefore, aligning security spending with regulatory requirements ensures legal compliance and the avoidance of costly penalties.

➢ **Demonstrating ROI**: It's crucial to demonstrate their ROI to corporate leadership to justify security investments. This can be done by highlighting how security spending reduces risk, avoids financial losses from breaches, and improves business continuity. For example, after Target's 2013 data breach, which resulted in over $18.5 million in settlements and fines, the company drastically increased its cybersecurity budget[20]. The return on this investment was seen in preventing future breaches and protecting the brand's reputation.

In some cases, security investments may also contribute to revenue generation. For example, customers may be likelier to do business with companies with strong security and data protection measures. This is particularly important in industries

---

[19] https://gdpr-info.eu/issues/fines-penalties/#:~:text=For%20especially%20severe%20violations%2C%20listed,fiscal%20year%2C%20whichever%20is%20higher.
[20]https://redriver.com/security/target-data-breach:~:text=Target%20was%20required%20to%20pay,which%20are%20still%20valid%20today.

like finance, healthcare, and e-commerce, where customers expect high levels of security for their personal information.

Justifying Security Expenditures to Executives

Justifying security expenditures to executives is critical for security professionals, particularly as security investments can often be seen as cost centers with little visible return on investment (ROI). To bridge this gap, security leaders must communicate the tangible and intangible benefits of security measures, emphasizing these investments' preventative value and long-term cost savings. This requires aligning security expenditures with business goals and quantifying their potential impacts in a way that resonates with executives' financial priorities.

Strategies for Demonstrating ROI on Security

Risk Assessment and Quantifying Potential Losses

One of the most effective ways to justify security spending is by presenting a risk assessment that quantifies potential losses if security measures are not implemented. This involves evaluating risks—such as data breaches, physical theft, intellectual property loss, or operational disruptions—and calculating the potential financial impact. Security leaders can then compare these potential losses to the cost of implementing preventative measures, demonstrating the ROI through cost avoidance. Another example comes from the 2020 Ponemon Institute's Cost of Insider Threats Report, which found that insider threats cost organizations an average of $11.45 million annually[21]. Insider threats include data leaks, sabotage, and fraud by employees, contractors, or other internal actors. By investing in advanced monitoring systems, access control technologies, and employee training programs, organizations can significantly mitigate these risks and reduce their exposure to financial and reputational damage.

Aligning Security with Business Objectives

Another critical strategy is to align security initiatives with the company's broader business objectives. For executives focused on revenue generation, market expansion, or cost control, security spending should be framed as an enabler rather than an obstacle. This might involve linking security to customer trust, compliance with regulatory standards, or protecting key intellectual property—all factors directly impacting the company's ability to operate efficiently and grow.

For instance, in industries like healthcare or finance, where regulatory compliance is essential, security investments that ensure compliance with regulations such as HIPAA (Health Insurance Portability and Accountability Act) or PCI DSS (Payment Card Industry Data Security Standard) can help avoid

---

[21] https://securityintelligence.com/posts/gaining-insight-into-the-ponemon-institutes-2020-cost-of-insider-threats-report/

costly fines and maintain the ability to operate in certain markets. In this context, security spending ensures continued business operations and competitive standing, thus aligning directly with executive priorities.

Techniques for Quantifying Preventative Security Measures

Cost of Downtime and Operational Disruptions

Downtime can be incredibly costly for businesses, particularly manufacturing, e-commerce, or logistics. By showing how security measures can prevent operational disruptions, security leaders can quantify the value of those investments in terms of minimized losses. For example, according to Gartner, the average cost of IT downtime is estimated to be around $5,600 per minute[22].

By illustrating how specific security investments—like network security, physical barriers, or surveillance—reduce the risk of downtime due to breaches or incidents, executives can see how the initial expenditure prevents significant financial harm. In 2017, the NotPetya ransomware attack caused Maersk, a global shipping company, to lose $300 million due to its impact

---

[22] https://www.atlassian.com/incident-management/kpis/cost-of-downtime#:~:text=The%20average%20cost%20of%20downtime%20is%20%245%2C600%20per%20minute%2C%20according,company%20size%20and%20industry%20vertical.

on operations[23]. If security measures had been in place to prevent the attack, such as stronger network segmentation or quicker incident response, the company might have saved millions in operational costs and avoided the significant hit to its reputation.

Insurance Premium Reductions

Another effective technique for demonstrating ROI is showing how security investments can lower insurance premiums. Many insurance providers offer lower premiums to companies implementing strong security measures, particularly for cybersecurity or physical security threats. By implementing higher levels of protection, businesses can often reduce their liability coverage costs, providing direct savings that can be quantified and presented to executives.

For instance, companies that invest in advanced fire suppression systems, CCTV, and on-site security personnel may be able to reduce their property and liability insurance costs.

Similarly, businesses with robust cybersecurity measures, including data encryption, multi-factor authentication, and endpoint detection, may receive lower cyber insurance premiums. Highlighting these long-term savings adds a financial incentive for security investments, making the case for spending

---

[23] https://www.digitalguardian.com/blog/cost-malware-infection-maersk-300-million

more palatable to decision-makers. By using risk assessments, aligning security investments with business goals, and quantifying the ROI of preventative security measures, security professionals can present a strong case for expenditures that might otherwise be viewed as discretionary.

Maximizing Resource Efficiency in Security Operations

One of the most prominent examples of maximizing resource efficiency in security operations is the case of London's Metropolitan Police Service during the 2012 Olympics. With millions of visitors, high-profile athletes, and dignitaries, security was paramount, yet resources were limited. The police faced the challenge of balancing tight security while being cost-effective and optimizing their personnel deployment.

The solution involved an intelligent blend of technology and strategic personnel allocation. Advanced CCTV systems, facial recognition software, and other surveillance technologies allowed for efficient monitoring of large crowds without the need for overwhelming numbers of officers.

Additionally, security personnel were strategically deployed to high-risk areas while other locations were monitored remotely, ensuring that resources were used where they were most needed. This strategy kept the event secure and saved significant operational costs, showing how leveraging technology and optimizing resources can lead to effective, large-scale security solutions.

Techniques for Maximizing Resource Efficiency

Leveraging Technology

Technology plays a crucial role in maximizing security efficiency. By adopting technologies such as AI-driven surveillance, automated access controls, and cybersecurity systems, companies can reduce the need for constant human oversight. For instance, automated alarm systems and sensors can detect unauthorized access, allowing security personnel to respond swiftly without having to monitor every point of entry manually.

Furthermore, integrating cloud-based solutions can streamline communication and coordination among different security teams, especially for large organizations across multiple locations. This technology reduces the need for excessive manpower and allows for a more dynamic and flexible approach to incident response.

Optimizing Personnel Deployment

Another effective way to maximize resource efficiency is by strategically deploying security personnel. In the 2012 Olympics case, the Metropolitan Police utilized a layered approach, assigning officers based on threat levels and risk assessments. This technique can be applied to corporate security settings as well. By conducting thorough risk assessments, security teams can determine which areas need a physical presence and which can be monitored using technology, ensuring that human resources are allocated to the highest priority areas. Additionally, cross-training personnel to handle multiple tasks can further optimize efficiency. For example, security personnel can be trained to manage physical security tasks (like patrolling) and digital security threats (such as monitoring network systems), reducing the need for separate teams and expanding the workforce's skill set.

Implementing Cost-Effective Security Solutions

To manage budgets effectively, businesses should look for cost-effective security measures that don't compromise on quality. Open-source cybersecurity tools, for instance, provide high levels of protection without the hefty price tag of commercial alternatives. Similarly, security technologies that offer scalability allow businesses to invest in systems that grow with their needs, reducing the need for frequent, costly upgrades.

For example, cloud-based surveillance systems not only reduce the cost of physical storage but also enable remote monitoring, reducing the need for an on-site control room. Many companies have adopted this approach to cut costs while maintaining high levels of security through a combination of physical measures and technology. Hence, maximizing resource efficiency in security operations can be achieved by leveraging technology, optimizing personnel deployment, and implementing cost-effective solutions. These strategies ensure that security remains robust without overwhelming costs, a balance crucial for large events and everyday corporate operations.

Effective Vendor Management and Outsourcing in Security Operations

Vendor management and outsourcing are critical components in modern security operations, especially as companies increasingly rely on third-party providers to meet security needs. Organizations can reduce costs, improve efficiency, and focus on core business objectives by outsourcing certain security functions. However, selecting the right security service providers, managing contracts effectively, and ensuring quality control in outsourced security operations are essential to maintaining a high-security standard.

Selecting Security Service Providers

The first step in successful outsourcing is selecting the right vendor. The security provider must meet the organization's needs, culture, and industry standards. Several key factors should be considered when choosing a security vendor:

> **Reputation and Experience**: Assessing a vendor's track record, industry expertise, and reputation in the field is crucial. This can be done by reviewing case studies, client testimonials, and industry certifications.

Companies should look for vendors with a history of managing similar security requirements and challenges.

➤ **Compliance and Certifications**: The security provider should comply with local, national, and international regulations, particularly concerning sensitive data or critical infrastructure. Look for vendors with certifications such as ISO 27001 (Information Security Management) or compliance with the General Data Protection Regulation (GDPR) for data handling.

➤ **Technological Capabilities**: Technology plays a significant role in security operations today. Evaluate whether the vendor uses advanced security technologies such as AI-driven monitoring systems, cybersecurity tools, and other automated systems that can enhance security effectiveness.

➤ **Scalability and Flexibility**: Security needs can fluctuate, especially in industries subject to seasonal demand or unexpected challenges. It's important to choose a vendor that can scale operations up or down depending on business requirements. Contract flexibility can also allow organizations to adapt services as needs change without incurring excessive costs.

For instance, companies like Securitas or G4S provide both global reach and advanced technological capabilities, making them leading choices for large-scale businesses. Securitas, which offers services in over 50 countries, incorporates technology into its operations with surveillance, remote monitoring, and access control. Their flexibility and technological integration help companies maintain cost-effective, high-quality security solutions.

Managing Contracts

After selecting the right vendor, managing the contract is essential for ensuring that both parties meet expectations. Poor contract management can lead to cost overruns, reduced service quality, and legal disputes. Here are some best practices:

➢ **Clear Scope and Expectations:** The contract should clearly define the scope of services, including specific security responsibilities, hours of operation, staff numbers, and service-level agreements (SLAs). This ensures that the vendor understands what is required and can plan accordingly.

➢ **Performance Metrics and KPIs:** Organizations should establish clear performance metrics and key performance indicators (KPIs) to measure the vendor's effectiveness. The contract should include metrics such as response times, incident resolution rates, and compliance with SLAs. Regular performance reviews will help ensure the vendor remains accountable for delivering the expected outcomes.

➢ **Penalties and Incentives:** Contracts should include penalties for non-compliance or underperformance, such as reduced payments or termination clauses. On the other hand, vendors can be incentivized to exceed expectations, perhaps through bonuses for achieving or surpassing security goals.

➢ **Legal and Financial Considerations:** Organizations must ensure the contract meets all legal requirements and does not expose them to undue risks. Vendors should provide proof of liability insurance to cover any damages that might occur during the execution of their duties. Additionally, the contract should address payment terms, including contingency costs for unplanned services or incidents.

➢ **Termination Clauses:** Every security contract should include a clear and fair termination process. This process should define the conditions under which either party can terminate the contract, including failure to meet performance standards, changes in business needs, or breaches of trust.

In 2020, a multinational company faced significant challenges with an outsourced cybersecurity firm failing to meet its service level agreements (SLAs). The case involved issues such as poor incident response times, which ultimately put the company's data and systems at risk during a critical period when remote work increased cyber threats globally. Outsourcing key security operations can expose businesses to substantial risks if the external provider fails to deliver timely or adequate services, as highlighted in a 2019 Deloitte survey, where 44% of C-level executives reported outsourcing security operations, yet ensuring compliance with SLAs remains an ongoing challenge[24].

Ensuring Quality Control

Even after selecting a vendor and signing a contract, organizations must continuously monitor and ensure the quality of outsourced security services. Outsourcing does not mean relinquishing control over security operations. Instead, it requires close supervision and ongoing collaboration with the vendor.

> ➤ **Regular Audits and Reviews:** Schedule regular audits to review the vendor's performance. This can be done through scheduled and surprise audits to ensure the vendor maintains high standards and compliance with the contract. Analyzing incident logs, response times, and client feedback are essential components of the review process.

> ➤ **Real-Time Monitoring and Reporting:** Use technology to ensure vendor performance is up to par.

---

[24] https://www.infosecinstitute.com/resources/general-security/outsourcing-cybersecurity-what-services-to-outsource-what-to-keep-in-house/

Remote surveillance systems or automated reporting tools can help monitor the security vendor's activities. Ensure you have access to these systems to verify whether the vendor meets agreed-upon standards.

➢ **Open Lines of Communication:** Maintain open and constant communication with the security vendor. Regular meetings to discuss performance, address concerns, and share updates can help foster a collaborative relationship. This approach also makes it easier to address problems before they escalate into bigger issues.

➢ **Feedback Loop:** Establish a feedback loop with employees and clients interacting with the outsourced security service. Their input can provide valuable insights into areas where service quality can be improved.

Outsourcing security operations can lead to significant cost savings and efficiency gains, but only if managed effectively. By selecting the right vendors, establishing clear contracts, and maintaining rigorous quality control, companies can ensure they receive top-notch security services that align with their business needs.

In conclusion, efficient budgeting and resource management are essential for maintaining robust security systems and critical for driving value and sustainability within an organization. By aligning security investments with business objectives, leveraging technology, and optimizing personnel deployment, companies can protect their assets without overextending financial resources. Moreover, maintaining vigilant oversight through vendor management and regular audits ensures that security providers deliver high-quality service, ultimately allowing organizations to stay ahead of potential threats. These strategies in an increasingly complex security landscape allow companies to remain financially sound and well-protected.

Chapter 19: Career Progression in Corporate Security

Corporate security offers a diverse and evolving career path, with opportunities ranging from entry-level positions like security officers to executive roles such as Chief Security Officer (CSO).

As organizations increasingly prioritize security, professionals in this field are tasked with safeguarding assets, ensuring regulatory compliance, and mitigating risks. Career progression in corporate security requires technical expertise, leadership, business acumen, and strategic thinking. Whether moving up within a company or transitioning across industries, understanding how to advance through various stages is crucial for long-term success and influence in the security landscape.

"Success is where preparation and opportunity meet."
– Bobby Unser

Career Paths in Corporate Security

Corporate security offers a range of career opportunities, with roles spanning from entry-level positions to executive leadership, such as the Chief Security Officer (CSO). Understanding the typical career paths within this field is essential for professionals looking to build a successful career in security. In this overview, we'll explore the different levels within corporate security, the skills and experience required for each, and how one can advance from foundational roles to senior leadership.

Entry-Level Positions in Corporate Security

Security Officer/Guard

A typical entry point into corporate security is the role of a security officer or guard. These professionals are responsible for maintaining a safe environment by monitoring premises, performing security checks, and responding to security breaches or alarms. Security officers may also control basic access, ensuring only authorized personnel can enter certain areas. This position is ideal for individuals starting their careers in security or transitioning from related fields like law enforcement or the military.

Required Skills and Experience: Entry-level security roles often require basic qualifications, such as a high school diploma or equivalent, and in some regions, certification or licensing. Key skills include situational awareness, attention to detail, communication, and a calm demeanor in high-pressure situations. Physical fitness is also important, as the job may require long hours standing or patrolling. With experience, security officers can advance to supervisory roles or specialized security positions.

Potential Career Path:

Security Officer → Security Supervisor → Security Manager

Mid-Level Security Roles

Security Supervisor/Team Lead

As professionals gain experience, they may progress to supervisory or team lead positions. In this role, individuals manage a team of security officers, coordinate shifts, and ensure that security protocols are followed. Security supervisors act as the primary point of contact between frontline security staff and upper management, reporting incidents and suggesting improvements to security operations.

Required Skills and Experience: Security supervisors typically have several years of experience in entry-level roles and possess strong leadership and communication skills. They must also have a deep understanding of security policies and procedures and the ability to manage and motivate a team. Knowledge of basic incident reporting and investigation techniques is often necessary.

Potential Career Path:

Security Supervisor → Security Manager → Director of Security

Security Analyst

A more specialized mid-level role is that of a security analyst who focuses on cybersecurity or physical security analytics. Security analysts are responsible for identifying vulnerabilities, assessing risks, and implementing systems to protect the organization from threats. This role requires technical expertise in security software, risk management, and compliance with security regulations.

Required Skills and Experience: Security analysts often need a bachelor's degree in cybersecurity, information technology, or a related field. Additionally, certifications like Certified Information Systems Security Professional (CISSP) or Certified Ethical Hacker (CEH) are highly valuable. Strong analytical skills, attention to detail, and problem-solving capabilities are critical for success in this role.

Potential Career Path:

Security Analyst → Senior Analyst → Security Manager

Senior-Level Roles

Security Manager

As security managers, professionals oversee the organization's daily security operations. They ensure that the security staff is adequately trained, develop and implement security policies, and work closely with other departments to integrate security measures across the business. Security managers also handle budget management and vendor relationships and may lead investigations into security incidents.

Required Skills and Experience: Security managers typically have several years of experience in supervisory roles and a deep understanding of physical and cyber security principles. A bachelor's degree in business administration, criminal justice, or a related field can be advantageous, and certifications like Certified Protection Professional (CPP) from ASIS International enhance credibility. Strong leadership, communication, and decision-making skills are essential for success.

Potential Career Path:

Security Manager → Director of Security → Chief Security Officer

Director of Security

Directors of security oversee security across multiple sites or divisions of a company. Their responsibilities include long-term strategic planning, risk management, policy development, and managing large security teams. Directors report to senior executives and may sit on the executive management team. This role requires collaboration with various stakeholders, including HR, IT, and legal departments, to ensure comprehensive security coverage.

Required Skills and Experience: Security directors often possess a combination of technical expertise, managerial experience, and a deep understanding of industry regulations. Many directors have a background in law enforcement or military service and a bachelor's or master's degree in business, criminal justice, or security management. Certifications such as the CPP or Physical Security Professional (PSP) are highly recommended. Directors need exceptional leadership, risk management, and strategic planning skills.

Potential Career Path:
Director of Security → Chief Security Officer (CSO)

Executive Roles

Chief Security Officer (CSO)

The Chief Security Officer (CSO) is the highest level of corporate security leadership. The CSO is responsible for the overall security strategy of the organization, encompassing physical security, cybersecurity, and information security. As an executive leadership team member, the CSO works closely with the Chief Executive Officer (CEO) and other C-suite executives to align security initiatives with the company's broader business objectives. The role involves overseeing the entire security function, from risk assessment and crisis management to regulatory compliance and global security operations.

Required Skills and Experience: CSOs typically have over a decade of experience in security leadership roles and are recognized experts in their field. A master's degree in business administration, security management, or a related field is common, along with advanced certifications. Strong leadership, strategic vision, and the ability to communicate complex security concepts to non-technical executives are crucial for this role.

Career Path Overview:

➤ **Entry-Level:** Security Officer

➤ **Mid-Level:** Security Supervisor, Security Analyst

➤ **Senior-Level:** Security Manager, Director of Security

➤ **Executive:** Chief Security Officer (CSO)

The corporate security career path offers a structured progression from operational roles to strategic leadership, with each step requiring hands-on experience, leadership abilities, and specialized knowledge in security and risk management.

Strategies for Continuous Professional Development in Corporate Security

Continuous professional development is essential for staying competitive and effective in the ever-evolving field of corporate security. As security threats and technologies rapidly evolve, professionals must continuously grow, adapt, and stay ahead of new trends. Corporate security professionals can ensure they remain dynamic and forward-thinking by focusing on mentorship, industry involvement, and staying current with emerging technologies.

Here's how these strategies foster ongoing development and success in the field of security:

Mentorship and Networking

Engaging in mentorship and building a strong professional network are cornerstones of long-term professional growth in corporate security. Security professionals at any career stage benefit from both mentorship and mentoring others.

➤ **Engage with Experienced Mentors**: Mentors who have navigated the complexities of corporate security provide invaluable insights and guidance. Their real-world experience helps mentees understand how to handle complex security challenges, develop leadership skills, and stay abreast of industry changes. Long-term relationships with experienced mentors allow for ongoing learning and feedback, enabling mentees to continuously refine their security management approaches.

➤ **Mentoring Others:** Taking on the role of a mentor reinforces knowledge and builds leadership skills. As I've seen in my career, helping develop the next generation of security professionals strengthens the organization's security culture. It creates a feedback loop where both mentor and mentee learn from each other, fostering a culture of continuous improvement.

> ➤ **Building a Professional Network:** Active participation in security-related organizations, such as ASIS International or the International Security Management Association (ISMA), is another avenue for continuous learning. By networking with industry peers, security professionals stay connected with the latest security practices and trends. Networking at conferences or through professional associations facilitates knowledge sharing, collaboration, and problem-solving on industry-wide challenges.

One security manager I knew found immense value in joining ASIS International, gaining access to a vast network of senior leaders who had navigated similar security challenges. The manager connected with key mentors through conference participation and regular meetings, enabling him to better manage his international security operations and extend his professional reach through speaking engagements and networking.

Industry Involvement and Certifications

Involvement in industry associations and obtaining certifications are key strategies for remaining current in the ever-changing security landscape.

- ➢ **Engage with Industry Associations**: Industry involvement provides security professionals opportunities to stay connected with thought leaders and industry innovations. Attending events like NRF Protect, ISC West, or the Global Security Exchange (GSX) keeps professionals updated on new technologies, regulatory changes, and emerging threats. Such events allow for exposure to cutting-edge security tools and solutions, ensuring that security professionals remain competitive.

- ➢ **Pursue Certifications**: Security certifications such as Certified Protection Professional (CPP), Certified Information Systems Security Professional (CISSP), and Physical Security Professional (PSP) validate expertise and ensure security leaders are up-to-date on the latest security protocols. These certifications enhance a professional's reputation in the industry, opening doors for career advancement and providing a competitive edge.

- ➢ **Speaking at Conferences**: Sharing expertise by speaking at industry events or conferences positions security professionals as thought leaders and deepens their understanding of the field. Leading panels and presenting case studies encourage active learning and position speakers to engage with the latest trends and challenges.

By leading a panel on integrating physical and digital security at an industry conference, a security leader I worked with expanded his professional network and built relationships with potential collaborators. This opportunity helped him stay engaged with the latest security trends and enhanced his visibility as a leader in the security community.

Staying Current with Emerging Trends and Technologies

Rapid technological advancement means security professionals must continuously update their knowledge to stay ahead of potential threats.

➢ **Regularly Engage with Industry Publications:** Reading industry-specific publications such as Security Management and Cybersecurity Insiders is vital for staying informed about new security trends. These sources offer analysis of emerging threats, regulatory changes, and the latest innovations in security technology, keeping professionals informed and prepared to address new challenges.

➢ **Leverage Online Learning Platforms:** Platforms like Coursera, LinkedIn Learning, and edX offer courses on cybersecurity, AI, machine learning, and other cutting-edge technologies shaping the future of security. Engaging with these learning platforms allows security professionals to continually upskill without formal, time-consuming classroom training.

Explore New Security Technologies: Researching and adopting innovative security technologies, such as AI-driven surveillance systems, drone patrols, and machine learning-based threat detection, ensures security professionals stay competitive. The recognition of AI's potential has led 76% of enterprises to prioritize AI and machine learning in their IT budgets, driven by the immense volume of data that necessitates analysis to identify and combat security threats effectively[25].

Cross-Disciplinary Learning and Collaboration

Engaging with other departments and cross-disciplinary teams broadens security professionals' perspectives and helps integrate security solutions across the business.

> ➤ Collaborate Across Departments: Regular collaboration with IT, legal, and operations departments ensures that security leaders understand the broader business implications of security decisions. This approach helps integrate security holistically into the company's overall strategy, resulting in more effective risk management.

---

[25] https://www.techmagic.co/blog/ai-in-cybersecurity/

➤ **Understand Business Operations:** Security professionals who understand business operations and financial management can more effectively align their security strategies with corporate objectives. They should regularly participate in cross-functional training, such as cybersecurity awareness workshops or business continuity planning, to ensure a comprehensive understanding of the broader business landscape.

➤ **Continuous Learning Through Real-World Experience**: Embracing challenging security assignments, such as managing high-profile events or implementing new security technologies, offers valuable real-world learning opportunities. Post-incident reviews and after-action reports also provide important lessons, allowing security leaders to reflect on performance and continuously improve their strategies.

Security professionals can foster continuous growth and adaptability by investing in mentorship, industry involvement, emerging technologies, and cross-disciplinary collaboration. This approach ensures that security leaders remain at the forefront of the field, capable of implementing innovative solutions and responding to ever-changing threats in the corporate security landscape.

Positioning for Senior Leadership in Corporate Security

Positioning oneself for senior leadership roles in corporate security requires a strategic approach that extends beyond technical expertise. Success in senior roles demands the development of business acumen, a deep understanding of corporate strategy, and a proven track record of adding value beyond traditional security functions. Here's how these essential elements combine to help security professionals advance into senior leadership roles.

Developing Business Acumen

> **Learning the Language of Business**: In senior leadership, it is critical to understand how security initiatives intersect with the broader financial and operational goals of the company. Business acumen involves knowing key metrics like Return on Investment (ROI), profit margins, and cost-benefit analysis. Security professionals must learn to frame security spending and initiatives regarding these financial outcomes.

> **Participating in Leadership Development Programs**: To build business acumen, leadership development programs play a pivotal role. Programs such as the Wharton Executive Leadership course help security leaders understand the intricacies of financial management, corporate governance, and how to create

value through security initiatives.

➢ **Collaboration with Other Departments**: Building relationships with other departments, such as finance, legal, IT, and HR, fosters an understanding of how their operations impact security. Collaborating across departments allows security leaders to present security not as a cost center but as a business enabler. A security director at a multinational bank, for example, collaborated with the legal department to ensure that data protection measures met regulatory standards, reducing potential fines and litigation risks, which saved the company millions of dollars.

Broadening Understanding of Corporate Strategy

➢ **Aligning Security with Corporate Objectives**: In senior leadership, aligning security with overarching corporate goals is essential. For example, if the company is focused on innovation and expansion, security professionals should demonstrate how robust security frameworks can enable business growth by protecting intellectual property and customer data. According to a report by Accenture, companies that prioritized cybersecurity as part of their business growth strategy reduced data breaches by 30%26.

➤ **Engaging in Strategic Discussions**: Participating in high-level strategic discussions allows security professionals to understand long-term business goals and contribute proactively. These discussions shift from merely preventing threats to positioning security as a tool for business continuity and operational efficiency. For instance, by recommending cybersecurity solutions that reduce downtime, security leaders can demonstrate the role of security in ensuring productivity.

➤ **Driving Cross-Functional Projects**: Leading cross-functional projects, such as integrating cybersecurity with physical security, showcases a security leader's ability to collaborate with different departments and align security with corporate strategy. In one case, a CSO at a technology company led a project to streamline security across 20 global offices, coordinating with IT and operations to create a unified security protocol that enhanced compliance and efficiency.

---

[26] https://newsroom.accenture.com/news/2023/aligning-cybersecurity-to-business-objectives-helps-drive-revenue-growth-and-lower-costs-of-breaches-accenture-report-finds

Demonstrating Value Beyond Traditional Security Functions

➤ **Showcasing Security as a Value-Add:** In today's business environment, security must go beyond asset protection to demonstrate value in areas like operational efficiency and regulatory compliance. According to a survey by Deloitte, 73% of consumers would lose trust in a company if their data was compromised[27]. In senior leadership, showcasing how security can protect the brand's reputation and reduce financial risks helps elevate security's role within the organization.

➤ **Proposing Innovations in Security Operations:** Adopting new technologies such as artificial intelligence (AI) and data analytics enables security leaders to address emerging threats proactively while improving operational effectiveness.

➤ **Risk Management and Business Continuity:** Positioning security as a crucial component of risk management is another way to demonstrate value beyond traditional roles. Companies integrating security into their risk management frameworks are better equipped to handle crises. For example, rising production costs (37%) and talent acquisition and retention (31%) rounded out health industries' top five most serious business risks. In January 2022, the PwC Pulse Survey found health industry executives already grappling with

---

[27] https://www2.deloitte.com/content/dam/Deloitte/uk/Documents/risk/deloitte-uk-responding-to-a-cyber-data-incident.pdf

staffing shortages and the risks COVID-19 variants pose to growth[28].

Building Leadership Skills

> **Developing Emotional Intelligence and Communication Skills:** Strong communication and emotional intelligence are vital for building relationships with peers and gaining the trust of senior leadership. Articulating the business value of security initiatives is essential when advocating for investments.

> **Mentoring and Developing Others:** Leadership in corporate security also involves developing the next generation of security professionals. Senior leaders create a culture of growth and continuous learning by mentoring and nurturing talent within the team. This not only enhances the effectiveness of the security team but also demonstrates the leader's commitment to fostering long-term value for the organization.

> **Leading by Example in Crisis Management:** Crises are a true test of leadership. Taking charge during high-stakes incidents, such as data breaches or large-scale security threats, showcases a leader's ability to remain calm, make quick decisions, and effectively guide teams

---

[28] https://www.pwc.com/us/en/library/pulse-survey/managing-business-risks.html

through challenging circumstances. Leaders who excel in crisis management are often recognized for their ability to handle pressure, a key trait for senior roles.

Taking Ownership of Large-Scale Projects

➢ **Leading Major Security Initiatives:** Senior leadership often requires overseeing significant, cross-functional security initiatives. For instance, leading the security planning for a new corporate headquarters or managing the rollout of a global cybersecurity policy requires technical expertise, strong project management, and leadership skills.

➢ **Managing Global and Regional Security:** For global companies, senior security leaders must be adept at managing regional security challenges, understanding different regulatory environments, and tailoring security solutions to local needs. Managing global security programs, including physical security across multiple locations or cybersecurity in various regulatory contexts, demonstrates a leader's ability to operate at a high strategic level.

By developing business acumen, understanding corporate strategy, and taking ownership of significant security projects, security professionals can position themselves effectively for senior leadership roles. In doing so, they demonstrate the value of security beyond traditional functions and become integral to the organization's success.

Navigating Career Transitions in Corporate Security

Career transitions in corporate security are becoming increasingly common as professionals seek to expand their expertise, move between industries, or explore broader risk management and consulting roles. While some security professionals may choose to specialize further within their current domain, others may find that transitioning to new sectors or positions provides opportunities for growth, broader influence, and greater job satisfaction. Understanding when and how to make these transitions is crucial for long-term career success.

Recognizing When It's Time for a Career Transition

The first step in any career transition is recognizing when it's the right time to make a move. Several indicators can signal that it's time to explore new opportunities:

- ➢ **Lack of Growth Opportunities:** If you feel your growth has plateaued—whether in terms of promotions, skill development, or leadership opportunities—it may be time to consider a career shift. For instance, some professionals may realize that their organization does not provide pathways to senior leadership or strategic roles.

➤ **Desire for Broader Impact:** Security professionals with extensive experience in a particular area, such as cybersecurity, may seek roles with a broader scope. This might include transitioning to broader risk management roles where they can influence business strategy, compliance, and operational risks beyond security.

➤ **Industry Evolution:** Industries change, and new challenges and opportunities come with these changes. For example, in the wake of the COVID-19 pandemic, many industries have emphasized remote work security and supply chain resilience. Professionals who feel their industry is not evolving as rapidly as their skills might look to sectors where their expertise can be more impactful.

➤ **Seeking a New Challenge:** Security professionals who have managed high-stakes projects, led large teams or implemented enterprise-wide security programs may seek new challenges, such as consulting, where they can help multiple organizations solve complex security issues.

Transitioning Between Industries

One common career transition for corporate security professionals is moving between industries. While the core principles of security remain consistent, different industries have unique challenges, regulatory requirements, and risk profiles. Professionals considering such a transition must be ready to adapt their skills and learn about the new industry's specific needs.

Healthcare and Finance

Healthcare and finance are two industries where security is paramount, but the challenges differ significantly. In healthcare, security professionals often focus on protecting patient data and ensuring compliance with regulations like HIPAA. In finance, the focus might shift to protecting financial transactions, mitigating fraud, and complying with regulations such as PCI DSS (Payment Card Industry Data Security Standard).

Professionals moving from one of these industries to the other would need to adapt their knowledge to new regulatory frameworks and threat landscapes. For example, a security professional moving from finance to healthcare would need to prioritize data protection and patient confidentiality while familiarizing themselves with healthcare-specific compliance requirements.

One notable example is **Anthem**, a major health insurer. After suffering a data breach in 2015 that exposed the personal information of 78.8 million individuals, Anthem hired cybersecurity experts with experience in other industries, including finance and retail, to strengthen its defenses[29]. The company recognized the need to diversify its security leadership by incorporating industry expertise with strong data protection practices.

Shifting to Consulting Roles

Consulting is an attractive option for experienced security professionals who want to leverage their expertise across multiple organizations. Consultants are brought in to solve specific problems, implement security solutions, or help companies navigate compliance and risk management challenges. This type of role offers the chance to work on varied and complex security issues and often provides more flexibility and autonomy. To successfully transition to consulting, professionals need to develop strong communication and business development skills. Consultants must be able to identify security gaps and recommend solutions, as well as adept at building client relationships and demonstrating ROI.

---

[29] https://www.insurance.ca.gov/0400-news/0100-press-releases/anthemcyberattack.cfm

Deloitte's Cybersecurity Consulting Practice

Consultants in firms like **Deloitte** work with clients across industries, providing insights on cybersecurity, risk management, and regulatory compliance. Deloitte's cybersecurity consulting team helps organizations develop comprehensive security strategies, implement advanced technologies, and build resilience against cyber threats. Many of the consultants in this practice transitioned from senior in-house roles in finance, healthcare, and retail, bringing industry-specific insights and leadership experience. This highlights how professionals can pivot into consulting by leveraging their prior expertise and adapting it to broader contexts.

Transitioning to Broader Risk Management Roles

Another viable career transition for security professionals is moving into broader risk management roles. As companies face increasingly complex risks—from cyber threats and regulatory changes to supply chain disruptions and global pandemics—there is growing demand for professionals who can manage these risks holistically.

Risk management roles require an understanding of not only security but also other areas, such as compliance, insurance, business continuity, and operational risk. Security professionals who can expand their expertise into these domains can position themselves for roles such as Chief Risk Officer (CRO) or Vice President of Risk Management. Security professionals should focus on building cross-functional knowledge to transition into risk management. This might involve working closely with legal, compliance, and finance teams, pursuing certifications such as the **Certified Risk Manager (CRM)** designation, or leading enterprise-wide initiatives that touch on broader aspects of risk.

JPMorgan Chase's Risk Management

JPMorgan Chase, one of the world's largest financial institutions, has a robust risk management framework integrating cybersecurity with operational and financial risk management.

Many of its senior risk management professionals have backgrounds in security, and the bank prioritizes cross-disciplinary experience. This demonstrates the growing convergence of security and broader risk management functions in complex organizations.

Making career transitions in corporate security requires careful consideration of one's long-term goals, skillsets, and industry trends.

Whether moving between industries, shifting into consulting, or transitioning to broader risk management roles, security professionals who remain adaptable and open to learning will be well-positioned for success in an ever-evolving landscape.

In conclusion, career progression in corporate security is a journey that requires continuous development, strategic thinking, and a willingness to adapt to changing threats and industries. Whether advancing through traditional corporate security roles or transitioning to consulting or risk management, professionals who invest in building their skills and broadening their knowledge are well-positioned for leadership roles. By aligning security initiatives with business goals, leading cross-functional teams, and remaining adaptable, security professionals can ensure their career growth and success in this evolving field.

Chapter 20: The Future of Corporate Security

"The only way to predict the future is to have the power to shape it."
— Eric Hoffer

The future of corporate security is shaped by evolving threats and rapidly advancing technology. As organizations expand into digital spaces, the security landscape now involves addressing cybersecurity, physical security, and emerging risks like geopolitical instability. With remote work becoming more prevalent, companies are balancing convenience and security while technologies like AI and machine learning are transforming how threats are identified and managed. To stay ahead, security professionals must be adaptable and integrate technical innovations and strategic foresight into their security operations.

Emerging Trends in the Corporate Security Landscape

Emerging trends in the corporate security landscape are reshaping how organizations protect their assets, employees, and data. With rapid technological advancements and evolving threats, the need for innovation in security practices has become crucial. Some key trends include the integration of artificial intelligence (AI) in security operations, the increasing focus on data protection, and new strategies to manage insider threats.

The Impact of Artificial Intelligence on Security

Artificial intelligence (AI) has transformed corporate security by enhancing threat detection, improving incident response times, and optimizing security operations. AI-powered systems can analyze large volumes of data, allowing security teams to detect anomalies and potential security threats much more quickly than traditional methods. This not only improves efficiency but also reduces the risk of missed incidents.

According to a 2024 report by EY, companies that have integrated AI into their cybersecurity operations have significantly enhanced their threat detection and response capabilities. Specifically, organizations using AI-powered security systems reported a 36% reduction in the time spent detecting and responding to security threats[30]. This underscores the critical role of AI in streamlining security processes, improving efficiency, and reducing operational costs. Moreover, AI's predictive analytics capabilities enable security teams to anticipate potential threats by analyzing past data and patterns. This helps in proactive security planning, allowing organizations to be better prepared for emerging risks. As AI technology advances, its role in corporate security will likely expand, offering even more sophisticated tools for safeguarding assets and information.

---

[30] https://www.ey.com/en_gl/insights/consulting/transform-cybersecurity-to-accelerate-value-from-ai

Growing Importance of Data Protection

In today's digital age, data protection has become one of the most critical aspects of corporate security. With an increasing reliance on digital infrastructure and cloud storage, companies are more vulnerable to data breaches, hacking, and ransomware attacks. The rise in remote work due to the COVID-19 pandemic has also exposed organizations to new cybersecurity risks, making data protection a top priority for corporate security teams.

According to a 2023 IBM report, the average cost of a data breach globally is $4.45 million[31].

This staggering figure underscores the importance of robust data protection measures. Organizations invest heavily in encryption, multi-factor authentication, and endpoint security solutions to safeguard sensitive information.

As the volume of data grows, so does the need for stronger protection protocols. This includes securing data across multiple endpoints, cloud environments, and third-party vendors. Data protection is no longer just a cybersecurity issue but a critical business risk, requiring a comprehensive strategy that aligns with broader corporate governance and compliance goals.

---

[31] https://therecord.media/ibm-breach-report-cost-rise-to-5-million#:~:text=What%20stood%20out%20most%20to,the%20cost%20was%20was%20%20%244.45%20million.

The Evolution of Insider Threat Management

While external threats such as hacking and phishing are widely recognized, insider threats remain one of the most challenging security issues for organizations. Insider threats involve employees, contractors, or other trusted individuals who misuse their access to company resources to cause harm, whether intentionally or accidentally.

Managing insider threats requires a delicate balance of monitoring and trust-building. On one hand, organizations must implement systems to detect and mitigate risks, such as user activity monitoring, access controls, and behavior analytics. On the other hand, companies must ensure that these measures do not infringe on employees' privacy or create a culture of mistrust. As of 2020, the average global cost of insider threats was USD 11.45 million, and the frequency has risen by 47% since 2018[32].

This cost includes not only the immediate losses but also the long-term consequences, such as reputational damage and regulatory fines. To mitigate insider threats, organizations are turning to advanced tools that use machine learning to detect unusual behavior and flag potential risks before they escalate.

Additionally, insider threat management programs are evolving to focus more on employee education and awareness. By providing employees with clear guidelines on data usage and

---

[32] https://www.sciencedirect.com/science/article/abs/pii/S0167404820303394

security protocols, companies can reduce the likelihood of accidental breaches while maintaining a secure environment.

How Military and Law Enforcement Experience Shapes Corporate Security

A military or law enforcement background provides a powerful foundation for success in corporate security. Professionals from these fields possess a unique set of skills—adaptability, strategic thinking, and crisis management—that are essential for navigating the complexities of modern security environments. As corporate security evolves to meet the challenges of digitalization, insider threats, and globalized operations, those with military or law enforcement experience are well-positioned to drive innovation and safeguard organizations from various risks.

Adaptability: Thriving in an Ever-Changing Landscape

Adaptability is crucial in military and law enforcement roles, where evolving threats and shifting objectives require professionals to make quick decisions in uncertain environments. This skill translates seamlessly to corporate security, where adaptability is necessary to avoid emerging risks and integrate new technologies.

The corporate security landscape is continuously changing, particularly with new technologies like artificial intelligence (AI), machine learning, and Internet of Things (IoT)-driven systems.

Security professionals from military or law enforcement backgrounds are accustomed to learning new tools and systems quickly, often in high-pressure situations. In a corporate setting, this adaptability can make all the difference when integrating AI-powered surveillance systems or adopting advanced cybersecurity technologies to detect and prevent threats.

For example, the ability to respond to cyber threats with agility is now essential. Security breaches are increasingly sophisticated and dynamic, requiring real-time decision-making. Former military personnel, trained to adjust strategies on the battlefield, can bring this same approach to corporate security. Creating security protocols that evolve with new risks ensures the company's protection remains effective in the face of changing technologies and threat landscapes.

Strategic Thinking: Security as a Core Business Enabler

Military and law enforcement professionals are trained to think strategically, balancing immediate operational needs with long-term objectives. This strategic thinking is invaluable in corporate security, where aligning security efforts with broader business goals is key to gaining executive support and securing the necessary resources.

In the military, strategic decisions involve assessing risk, prioritizing objectives, and planning for multiple outcomes. Similarly, in corporate security, strategic thinking means understanding how different risks—whether physical, digital, or reputational—interconnect and how security can mitigate those risks to enable business success. Corporate security is no longer just about protecting assets but also about ensuring business continuity, regulatory compliance, and reputation management.

By aligning security with business objectives, professionals from military or law enforcement backgrounds can demonstrate the value of security beyond mere protection. For instance, companies focused on global expansion will need to ensure their operations are secure in new, possibly high-risk markets. A strategic security leader will anticipate these risks and implement proactive measures to support growth, allowing the company to move forward confidently. Strategic thinking also applies to crisis prevention and response. Those with military or law enforcement experience are adept at creating comprehensive security strategies, including robust risk assessments, long-term planning, and detailed incident response frameworks. This type of forward-thinking security planning helps organizations avoid potential threats and react swiftly when issues arise.

Crisis Management: Leadership in High-Stakes Situations

One of the most valuable contributions that military and law enforcement professionals make to corporate security is their expertise in crisis management. Whether responding to natural disasters, cyberattacks, or internal security breaches, these professionals know how to stay calm, assess risks, and take decisive action to protect people and assets in high-pressure situations.

In corporate environments, data breaches or physical intrusions can devastate business operations. Leaders with experience in military or law enforcement are trained to lead during these critical moments, making quick, well-informed decisions that minimize damage and restore order. Their ability to remain calm under pressure and provide clear direction ensures that crises are handled efficiently, preventing further escalation.

For example, in 2014, Sony Pictures Entertainment was hit by a major cyberattack believed to be linked to North Korea, resulting in the theft of sensitive data and causing over $15 million in immediate IT repairs and security costs[33]. The attack crippled their internal network and leaked confidential information, including unreleased films and employee data.

A security leader with a military background, familiar with crisis management protocols, would have immediately assessed the situation, rallied cross-functional teams, and executed a coordinated response plan. This type of crisis leadership ensures that recovery efforts are swift and the damage to the company's reputation and operations is minimized.

---

[33] https://blog.gigas.com/en/famous-cyber-attacks-sony-pictures-2014

Beyond immediate crisis response, professionals from these backgrounds are also skilled at building long-term crisis management frameworks. They understand that preparation is key and invest time in training, simulations, and after-action reviews to ensure their teams are ready for any eventuality. This emphasis on continuous improvement ensures that organizations survive crises and become more resilient over time.

Driving Innovation in Corporate Security

Military and law enforcement backgrounds foster a mindset of resilience, leadership, and innovation—qualities essential for shaping corporate security's future. As technology continues to evolve, so too must security strategies. Professionals from these fields are uniquely equipped to lead this transformation, ensuring that corporate security remains dynamic and adaptable to known and emerging threats.

For instance, AI-driven surveillance and threat detection systems are integral to modern security operations. Professionals from military backgrounds who are used to leveraging cutting-edge technology in high-stakes environments can bring this same forward-thinking approach to corporate security, implementing innovative solutions that enhance operational efficiency and threat detection capabilities. Moreover, the rise of insider threats—where employees or trusted individuals compromise security from within—presents a growing challenge. Law enforcement professionals trained in human behavior and investigative techniques are well-positioned to develop insider threat management programs that go beyond technology and incorporate human intelligence, psychological analysis, and behavioral monitoring. Hence, the adaptability, strategic thinking, and crisis management skills honed in military and law enforcement careers are directly transferable to corporate security. These professionals are not only equipped to protect organizations from current threats. They are also poised to drive innovation, ensuring that corporate security remains robust and forward-looking in an increasingly complex and interconnected world.

Challenges and Opportunities Shaping the Future of Corporate Security

Corporate security is at a pivotal moment, facing new challenges and opportunities driven by the rise of remote work, physical and cyber security convergence, and global crises like climate change and geopolitical instability. As businesses increasingly operate in decentralized environments, security teams must adapt to protect data, assets, and people across a distributed workforce. The integration of physical and cybersecurity is essential to handle multifaceted threats. Moreover, corporate security must now address larger global concerns, from climate impacts to international political instability, ensuring organizational resilience and safety.

Zoom and the Security Challenges of Remote Work

The COVID-19 pandemic dramatically changed how businesses operate, with a significant shift to remote work. This transition brought unique security challenges, particularly as millions of employees relied on video conferencing tools such as Zoom to conduct daily business activities.

While Zoom had been a widely used platform before the pandemic, the sudden and unprecedented surge in its user base from 10 million to over 300 million daily meeting participants revealed numerous security vulnerabilities, leading to widespread scrutiny[34].

The Rise of Remote Work and Zoom's Security Struggles

At the start of the pandemic, Zoom became the go-to solution for remote meetings, both for corporate environments and social interactions. However, its rapid growth exposed significant flaws in the platform's security infrastructure. One of the most publicized issues was "Zoombombing," where uninvited users gained access to meetings, sometimes disrupting them with inappropriate content or, more seriously, accessing sensitive business information.

For instance, schools and businesses reported incidents where strangers infiltrated online classrooms and corporate board meetings, compromising privacy and operational integrity.

---

[34] https://www.tomsguide.com/news/zoom-security-privacy-woes

This highlighted Zoom's lack of end-to-end encryption and weak default security settings, such as publicly shared meeting links, a lack of meeting password requirements, and ineffective waiting rooms for participants. These flaws underscored how quickly an organization must adapt its security protocols in response to sudden changes in user demand and risk exposure.

Zoom's Response and the Evolution of Its Security

As the security breaches mounted, Zoom responded with a series of updates to strengthen its platform's security infrastructure. Zoom's CEO, Eric Yuan, acknowledged the company's shortcomings, and in response, the company enacted a 90-day feature freeze to focus solely on addressing security concerns. One of the first steps Zoom took was to implement end-to-end encryption, ensuring that only meeting participants had access to the content of their communications.

Zoom also introduced several new security features, including:

➤ **Mandatory Passwords** for all meetings, webinars, and recordings.

➤ **Waiting Rooms** allowed hosts to screen participants before allowing them into the meeting.

➤ **Restricting Screen Sharing** to hosts by default.

➢ **Zoom 5.0 Encryption Update** introduced stronger encryption standards (AES 256-bit GCM encryption) for enhanced data protection and meeting confidentiality.

➢ **Enhancing Reporting Functions** to allow users to report participants engaging in disruptive or malicious activities more effectively.

These updates aimed to address immediate security concerns and reassure the corporate world that Zoom could be a secure platform for business meetings and sensitive communications.

The Broader Implications of Remote Work Security

The rise of remote work brought broader security implications that organizations had to consider. With a distributed workforce, the attack surface for cyber threats increased significantly.

Employees were no longer protected by the robust security infrastructure of their office environments. Instead, they accessed corporate data from home networks, often using personal devices with inadequate security measures.

For businesses, this shift demanded rapid investment in cybersecurity tools to secure remote endpoints. VPNs (Virtual Private Networks) and multi-factor authentication became essential for ensuring secure access to corporate systems. Additionally, companies needed to invest in training employees on secure practices for remote work, such as identifying phishing attempts, which surged during the pandemic, and ensuring data was transmitted securely during virtual meetings.

With society leaning more heavily on digital interactions during the pandemic, companies embraced remote work and the cloud as they shifted to accommodate this increasingly online world. The IBM report found that these factors significantly impacted data breach response. Nearly 20% of organizations studied reported that remote work was a factor in the data breach, and these breaches ended up costing companies $4.96 million (nearly 15% more than the average breach)[35].

Lessons Learned and Future Security Strategies

Zoom's response to its early security challenges offers valuable lessons for other organizations managing remote security risks. One key takeaway is the importance of being proactive in addressing security vulnerabilities. A reactive approach exacerbated Zoom's initial missteps, but the subsequent improvements demonstrated that companies can quickly regain user trust by placing security at the forefront.

---

[35] https://newsroom.ibm.com/2021-07-28-IBM-Report-Cost-of-a-Data-Breach-Hits-Record-High-During-Pandemic

Another lesson involves balancing convenience and security. Zoom initially focused on ease of use, prioritizing quick and seamless connections, contributing to its early success. However, this approach left it vulnerable to cyberattacks. In the corporate security landscape, convenience should never trump security. Businesses must evaluate their tools and platforms carefully, ensuring they provide robust security features while maintaining usability.

Lastly, the integration of physical and cybersecurity is becoming increasingly critical. As seen in the Zoom case, digital platforms that become essential to daily operations can present significant vulnerabilities if not secured. Organizations must invest in technologies that protect their physical assets and digital operations. This convergence of physical and cybersecurity strategies will likely define the future of corporate security.

Looking Ahead

The pandemic may have accelerated the transition to remote work, but its influence on the corporate world is here to stay.

Companies will continue to rely on virtual communication platforms like Zoom for day-to-day operations, making building security into these tools from the ground up essential. As remote work becomes normalized, businesses must view security as a long-term investment rather than a short-term fix.

The lessons learned from Zoom's challenges illustrate the need for organizations to be agile, adaptable, and proactive in securing their operations. Companies can mitigate the risks associated with an increasingly digital and remote workforce by investing in robust cybersecurity measures, training employees, and continuously updating security protocols.

Leading the Future of Corporate Security

As we conclude this chapter, it's important to recognize your pivotal role in shaping corporate security's future. The industry is evolving rapidly, and leaders who can adapt, innovate, and inspire will be the driving force behind positive change. Here are key ways you can lead this transformation:

> **Leverage Your Unique Background:** Whether your experience is in law enforcement, the military, or a corporate environment, use the skills and knowledge you've acquired to introduce fresh perspectives to security challenges. Your ability to bring adaptability, crisis management, and strategic thinking into corporate security can set you apart as a thought leader.

> **Drive Thought Leadership:** Contributing to the conversation on emerging security threats and trends can position you as a leader. Engage in speaking at industry events, writing for publications, or leading discussions on security innovation. By sharing your

expertise, you showcase your knowledge and influence how security evolves in your field.

> **Promote a Proactive Security Culture**: Security needs to be seen as a business enabler, not just a cost. Foster a culture where security is integrated into every aspect of the organization—from IT and HR to legal and operations. By aligning security initiatives with business objectives, you make the case that security can drive operational efficiency, brand protection, and business growth.

> **Adapt to Global Challenges:** Global risks, such as climate change, geopolitical instability, and supply chain vulnerabilities, demand security leaders who can think beyond the traditional boundaries of corporate security. Advocate for a holistic approach integrating physical and cyber security strategies to respond to these interconnected challenges. Your ability to anticipate and respond to these threats can secure your organization's future.

> **Champion Continuous Learning:** The security landscape is always changing, so continuous professional development is essential. Pursue certifications, attend industry events, and encourage your team to do the same. Leaders prioritizing learning and development

ensure they can handle the latest security threats and technologies.

> **Foster Innovation:** The future of corporate security will be driven by those open to new technologies and methodologies. Embrace AI-driven security solutions, machine learning, and IoT innovations that enhance the capabilities of your security framework. Leaders willing to experiment with new systems will create more efficient and effective security operations.

> **Promote Ethical Leadership**: As a security leader, your decisions impact your organization and the broader community. Ethical leadership means being transparent, maintaining integrity, and making decisions that prioritize the safety and well-being of everyone involved. Lead by example, ensuring that your approach to security reflects the highest ethical standards.

By leveraging your experience, fostering a culture of innovation, and prioritizing ethical leadership, you can help shape the future of corporate security. The industry needs leaders willing to challenge traditional approaches, integrate cutting-edge technologies, and continuously adapt to an ever-changing landscape. Your actions today will protect your organization and inspire the next generation of security professionals to continue evolving the field.

The future of corporate security demands forward-thinking leaders who are ready to embrace new technologies, navigate global risks, and anticipate evolving threats. By leveraging innovations like AI and data analytics while remaining vigilant about cyber and physical security, companies can strengthen their resilience in uncertainty. The convergence of diverse security needs presents both challenges and opportunities, but with a proactive and adaptive approach, security professionals can not only protect organizations but also drive innovation and long-term success in an increasingly interconnected world.

As we look toward the future, one thing is certain: the security landscape will keep evolving. Whether it's physical security, technological advancements, or the expanding cybersecurity domain, our challenges will constantly change— and so will we. Thriving as security professionals means adopting a mindset of lifelong learning. Staying informed on the latest technologies, strategies, and best practices isn't just an option; it's necessary. The ability to adapt, learn, and grow will determine our success in protecting the people, assets, and data we are entrusted with.

Alongside technological knowledge, understanding the legal frameworks governing our operations is crucial. Whether your work spans one state, multiple regions, or the global stage, your security program must reflect a solid understanding of local, state, and federal laws. This ensures that our protective efforts are effective and compliant with regulations shaping the business landscape. This understanding is more critical than ever in today's environment, where legal requirements can vary widely from region to region. The future of security is bright and brimming with opportunities for innovation and leadership. As you continue your professional journey, remember that leadership in this field goes beyond risk management. It's about being forward-thinking, proactive, and adaptable in anticipating future threats and needs. The same skills, determination, and resilience that have brought you to where you are today will continue to serve you well as you navigate the challenges of tomorrow. Stay curious, flexible, and, most importantly, committed to your growth. The world around us will keep changing, but with the right mindset and knowledge, you'll always be ready to face what's next.

Thank you for taking this journey with me. It's been an honor to share these insights, and I hope they serve you well as you continue to lead, protect, and inspire. Here's to a future filled with success and innovation. Together, we can shape the future of corporate security.

Semper FI,

William Burgess

****